Tahiti
& French Polynesia
a travel survival kit

Robert F Kay

Tahiti & French Polynesia – a travel survival kit
   3rd edition

Published by
   Lonely Planet Publications
   Head Office: PO Box 617, Hawthorn, Vic 3122, Australia
   Branches: 155 Filbert St, Suite 251, Oakland, CA 94607, USA
                   10 Barley Mow Passage, Chiswick, London W4 4PH, UK
                   71 bis rue du Cardinal Lemoine, 75005 Paris, France

Printed by
   Colorcraft Ltd, Hong Kong

Photographs by
   Compagnie Polynésienne de Transport Maritime (CPTM)
   Giles Hucault (GH)
   Rob Kay (RK)
   Tahiti Tourism Board (TTB)

   Front cover: H. Cao, courtesy of Tahiti Tourism Board

First Published
   October 1985

This Edition
   May 1992

Although the authors and publisher have tried to make the information as accurate as possible, they accept no responsibility for any loss, injury or inconvenience sustained by any person using this book.

National Library of Australia Cataloguing in Publication Data

Kay, Robert F., 1953-
   Tahiti & French Polynesia, a travel survival kit.

   3rd ed.
   Includes index
   ISBN 0 86442 143 5.

   1. French Polynesia – Guidebooks. 2. Tahiti - Guidebooks.
   I. Title. II. Title: Travel survival kit.

919.6204

Rob Kay

After graduating from a liberal arts college in the Pacific Northwest and travelling around Europe in the mid-70s, Rob Kay, a San Francisco, California native, settled into journalism as the news director for a small radio station in the Sierra Nevada foothills. When he tired of inventing ways to make small-town news exciting, Rob caught the tradewinds for Tahiti where, between stints as a bartender, he covered French Polynesia for *Pacific News Service*, NBC radio, *New Pacific*, *Pacific Islands Monthly* and the *San Francisco Chronicle*.

Wishing to see more of the Pacific, he signed on as a tour guide for French Polynesia, Fiji, Tonga, American Samoa and Western Samoa. He liked Fiji so much, he returned for a year's stay, once again freelancing for a number of publications. The idea for his guides to French Polynesia and Fiji came about as he saw the need for comprehensive, in-depth coverage of travel and culture in these countries. Rob continues to travel frequently in the Pacific and has contributed feature articles to *Newsday*, *Los Angeles Times*, *San Jose Mercury*, *Arizona Republic*, *Philadelphia Inquirer*, *San Diego Tribune*, *San Francisco Magazine*, *Islands* and other publications. Between trips he spends his spare time restoring a Victorian home in San Francisco's Haight-Ashbury district.

From the Author

My first interest in French Polynesia resulted from a six-month stay in 1977. During that period I had the opportunity to travel throughout the beautiful islands of French Polynesia and meet a variety of people. In a few instances, some of these acquaintances became friends for life. I have returned to the islands on subsequent occasions and most recently to update this book.

For their aid and assistance I particularly wish to thank Bengt and Marie-Therese Danielsson, who were unfailingly kind to someone they knew only as a vagabond; and I will always be in awe of and grateful for their pioneering work in Tahiti. Thanks to

Marie Ateni and Tiare Sanford of the Tahiti Tourist Board, and Al Prince of *Tahiti Beach Press*, for assistance in preparing this third edition. Thanks to Mr Gilles Hucault for his photographs of the Marquesas and the Tuamotus.

I'd also like to thank my colleague, Tom Huhti, for his comments and research, particularly on the islands of Raiatea, Huahine, Tahaa, Rangiroa and the Marquesas Islands.

To be quite accurate the title of this book need only be *French Polynesia – a travel survival kit*. But who knows where that is? It's Tahiti which is the name with the magic, so that's the name that goes on the cover. Tahiti is just one of the many islands – with evocative names like Bora Bora, Huahine, Rangiroa or Fatu Hiva – which are representative of the five main island groups of French Polynesia.

From the Publisher

This edition of *Tahiti & French Polynesia – a travel survival kit* was edited at the Lonely Planet office in Melbourne, Australia, by Kay Waters. Map corrections, layout, illustrations and cover design were done by Ann Jeffree. Thanks to Tom Smallman for supervision and final proofing.

Thanks must go to the travellers who used the second edition of this book and wrote to Lonely Planet with information, comments and suggestions:

Brad Alberts (USA), Alfie Anderson (USA), Philippe Beck (Aus), Lisa Bedson (Aus), Mike Bidgood (UK), Mel Bloom, Simon Bourke (UK), Neil R Boyd (UK), Steve Boyle (Aus), Elliot Brown (USA), Louisa Bungey (UK), Christine Carter (Can), Carolyn Caton (UK), S Cauty, B L Chamberlain (F), Will & Cynthia de Prado (USA), Walt Deas (Aus), L Deptuch (Can), Steve Emery (Can), Kent Fenton (Can), Peter Fiske (Aus), John Flatt, Scott Funk, David Gaughan (Ire), Brett Gordon, Susan Grinsdell (NZ), Neil & Nora Hagen (Can), Ursula Haink (USA), Jack Hamm (Aus), F Harris (UK), Ian Hawkins (Aus), Colleen Henry (Aus), Laura Heraty (USA), Winona Hubbard (USA), R Hunt (Aus), Steve Hutson (Aus), Karen Jacobsen (USA), Mark Javorski (USA), Susan & Greg Johnson (USA), Jay & Margie Johnson, Craig Jung (USA), Gary Kanaby (USA), Ruth Kaufman (USA), David Kitching (UK), Edward Kosower (Isr), Rajend Kumar, Lucy Kunkel (USA), Lucy Kunkel (USA), Sue Lolohem (USA), Carrie Loranger, Ejvind Marteusen (Dk), Neil McCrindle (UK), Lisa Mead (Aus), Frederico Medici (It), William Methven (USA), John Minson (NZ), David Nash (USA), Markus Nussli (Sw), Marcus Oliver (USA), Manfred Ossendorf (G), Laurie Price (USA), Jan Price (NZ), Reila & Per (Dk), Julia Richardson, Catherine Roberts (UK), Rod Russell (Aus), Bruce Rutherford (Aus), Brian Rutherford (Aus), Bruce Samuels (USA), Glen Schlueter (Aus), Don Schuler (USA), M Slater (UK), Steve Hansen Smythe (Can), John Spurway (Aus), C Stevens (USA), John Surinchak (USA), James Trujillo (USA), Tomas Valentine, Neal Watts (UK), Linda Weil (USA), J D Williams (Can), Marge Williams, Elizabeth Woolnough (Can).

Aus – Australia, Can – Canada, F – France, G – Germany, Dk – Denmark, Ire – Ireland, Isr – Israel, It – Italy, NZ – New Zealand, Sw – Sweden, Tah – Tahiti, UK – UK, USA – USA.

Warning & Request

Things change – prices go up, schedules change, good places go bad and bad places go bankrupt – nothing stays the same. So if you find things better or worse, recently opened or long since closed, please write and tell us, so we can make the next edition better!

All information is greatly appreciated and the best letters will receive a free copy of the next edition, or any other Lonely Planet book of your choice.

Your letters will be used to help update future editions and, where possible, important changes will also be included as a Stop Press section in reprints.

Contents

Map Legend

BOUNDARIES

— · — · — · —	........International Boundary
— · · — · · — · ·	...............Internal Boundary
++++++++++	....National Park or Reserve
- - - - - - - -	.......................The Equator
· · · · · · · · · · · · · · ·	.........................The Tropics

SYMBOLS

◉ NEW DELHI	......................National Capital
● BOMBAY	.........Provincial or State Capital
● Pune	.................................Major Town
● Barsi	.................................Minor Town
■	............................Places to Stay
▼	.............................Places to Eat
♛	..................................Post Office
✈	....Airport
i	....................Tourist Information
⊖	.............Bus Station or Terminal
66	............Highway Route Number
☪ † ‡	......Mosque, Church, Cathedral
∴	.........................Temple or Ruin
✚	....Hospital
※	....Lookout
⚊	.............................Camping Area
⊓	..................................Picnic Area
⌂	................................Hut or Chalet
/⋀	.........................Mountain or Hill
┼──	.........................Railway Station
═	..............................Road Bridge
═	...........................Railway Bridge
⊐ ⊏	..................................Road Tunnel
→ ←	...............................Railway Tunnel
⌇⌇	....................Escarpment or Cliff
⌣	....Pass
⌇⌇⌇	............Ancient or Historic Wall

ROUTES

────────	.......Major Road or Highway
- - - - - - - -	.........Unsealed Major Road
────────	.......................Sealed Road
- - - - - - - -	.....Unsealed Road or Track
════════	...........................City Street
++++++++	.................................Railway
━━●━━	................................Subway
· · · · · · · · · · · ·	......................Walking Track
- - - - - - - -	..........................Ferry Route
┼┼┼┼┼┼┼┼	........Cable Car or Chair Lift

HYDROGRAPHIC FEATURES

	......................River or Creek
	..............Intermittent Stream
	........Lake, Intermittent Lake
	...........................Coast Line
	....................................Spring
	............................Waterfall
	.................................Swamp
	................Salt Lake or Reef
	..................................Glacier

OTHER FEATURES

	Park, Garden or National Park
	........................Built Up Area
	... Market or Pedestrian Mall
	.........Plaza or Town Square
	...........................Cemetery

Note: not all symbols displayed above appear in this book

Introduction

Right now it rains. My hand sticks to this paper. Everything here is drenched – with sweat, with sensuality, with growing things, with sky, water, solitude. It is so fertile, so slow, so hot, so heavy, you sigh and let go and then, when the wonder of the place passes over you, the 'paradise' myth, the 'dream zone', fade – and guess what? It is only more of the world, as it is. And it is both wonderful and sad.
Larry Levinger, US writer on Tahiti, 1991

To this day, Tahiti, the best known of French Polynesia's 130 islands, is synonymous with the modern world's romantic vision of the South Seas. This vision is a blend of fact and fiction born from glowing reports of its earliest visitors. On his arrival in 1768, the French explorer Louis de Bougainville thought he had been transported into the Garden of Eden. He promptly named the island New Cytheria, after the birthplace of Aphrodite, the Greek goddess of love. The inhabitants' kindness was summed up in the first report of the London Missionary Society:

Their manners are affable and engaging; their step easy and firm, and graceful; their behaviour free and unguarded; always boundless in generosity towards each other, and to strangers; their tempers mild, gentle and unaffected; slow to take offence, easily pacified, and seldom retaining resentment or revenge, whatever the provocation they may have received.

Captain Samuel Wallis, the English navigator who in 1767 was the first European to set foot on Tahiti, noted that 'the women in general are very handsome, some really great beauties...' They were also very accessible, and tales of a newly found Garden of Eden filtered back to Europe.

The myth of Tahiti as an unspoiled paradise was further fuelled by the 18th-century philosophy of Jean-Jacques Rousseau. The reports of a nonviolent Tahitian society bound by free love coincided neatly with Rousseau's social theory that natural humans were innately good animals whose problems had originated with the introduction of private property, agriculture and industry.

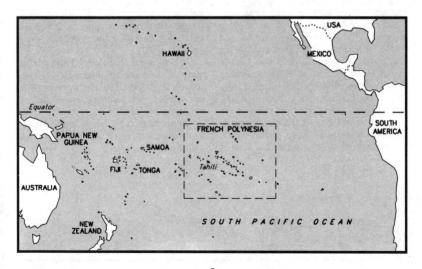

Rousseau's adherents were elated to hear that the noble savage was alive and well in Tahiti, which proved what they had been saying all along.

Unfortunately, the tales of paradise that followed Tahiti's discovery did not match the subsequent realities of influenza, tuberculosis, venereal disease and other maladies which decimated the vulnerable population, and the accompanying breakdown of the fabric of native society that marked the initial stages of the island's colonisation. This was evident to the famous painter Paul Gauguin, who arrived in Tahiti in 1891 and was sorely disappointed by what he saw. Little was left of Tahitian culture; Tahiti had been replaced by a narrow-minded provincial French colony. Despite these changes, Gauguin immortalised the languid grace and unquenchable spirit of the Tahitian people, qualities they still possess today.

Both the advent of jet travel accompanied by tourism and the bureaucracy created by nuclear testing have accelerated change in the islands. New buildings have gone up, new jobs have been created and the cost of living has soared.

Like all South Pacific island nations, French Polynesia will continue to experience the impact of 20th-century values and technology on traditional ways of life. Among the islands, Tahiti is the one most influenced by the West because it is a centre of tourism and trade. Meanwhile, the outer islands evolve more slowly. In Papeete, French Polynesia's capital city, residents suffer from traffic congestion and young men and women dance to the disco beat, while dwellers on some of the outer islands still kindle lanterns at night to keep ghosts away. Although tourism has changed the face of Tahiti, many of the outer islands remain relatively untouched by large-scale commercialism, and the inhabitants continue to enjoy the novelty of entertaining visitors.

Although Tahiti has gained fame as the 'island of love' (a dubious reputation at best) it is also known as one of the more expensive destinations on the planet. While it may not be *the* most expensive place to visit in the South Pacific (Papua New Guinea in some cases might even be more expensive), Tahiti is certainly not cheap.

Given this set of economic circumstances, some of my readers fault me for not listing the inexpensive places to stay and, worse, accuse me of being a bourgeoisie running dog who no longer writes for *real* travellers. Please keep in mind that I do look for the out-of-the-way bargains in Tahiti that have made Lonely Planet guides famous. Sad to say, however, in Tahiti these places are few and very far between. As the pop song goes, what you see is what you get.

Bargain hunters will never confuse Tahiti with Indonesia or the Philippines. To be explicit, if you are the kind of traveller who is expecting to stay at a pension or a road house for a few Canadian or Australian dollars a night you will be sadly disappointed. You can get by in French Polynesia on the inexpensive but not on the cheap. Expect to spend some money or don't bother to come at all.

On the positive side, French Polynesia has some of the most breathtakingly beautiful scenery in the South Pacific, a great cuisine and some of the most attractive inhabitants on earth. Travellers who come to French Polynesia with openness and understanding about the economic situation will find their visit well worth it.

Facts about the Country

HISTORY

The most widely accepted theory of the origin of the Polynesian race is that it is a blend of peoples originating in various parts of Asia. Indications are that this amalgamation took place in the area extending from the Malay Peninsula through the islands of Indonesia. After an indeterminable length of time in this region the people made their way across the Pacific, possibly between 3000 and 1000 BC.

Perhaps the most famous alternative theory, expounded by the adventurer Thor Heyerdahl, is that Polynesians may also have migrated from South America. His theory was given at least some credence by the successful crossing of his *Kon-Tiki* expedition from Peru to French Polynesia in 1947.

Archaeologists tell us that the ancient history of Tahiti and its neighbouring islands goes back about 2000 years to when the Marquesas Islands were first settled by migrating Polynesians from the Samoa and Tonga regions. From this point of dispersal, Hawaii, New Zealand, Easter Island and the Society Islands (of which Tahiti is part) were settled by ancient Polynesian mariners who arrived in huge double-hulled canoes.

The Polynesians were among the finest sailors in the world. They used the sun, stars, currents, wave motion and flight patterns of birds to navigate the vast reaches of the Pacific. When for some reason, whether tribal warfare or overpopulation, Polynesians had to settle elsewhere, they put their families, worldly goods, plant cuttings, animals and several months' supplies of food into their canoes and set sail to find new homes.

Through radiocarbon dating techniques and comparative studies of artefacts, scientists pinpoint the settlement of Tahiti and its neighbouring islands at around 850 AD. The most intensive research in this area is being undertaken by Dr Y H Sinoto of the Bishop Museum in Honolulu. In 1973 Sinoto began excavation of the Vaito'otia/Fa'ahia site (on the grounds of the Bali Hai Hotel) on Huahine and found it to be the oldest settlement yet discovered in the Society Islands. Implements excavated closely match those found in the Marquesas Islands, strengthening the theory that the islands were settled by Polynesians migrating from the Marquesas.

The most visible (but certainly not the earliest) traces of pre-European Tahitian culture are the stone remains of open-air temples called *marae*. Marae are found on all the Society Islands but are most abundant on Huahine. The most important marae (a national monument) is Taputaputea on Raiatea, which was the most prominent political and religious centre in the Society Islands.

First European Contact

In 1767 Captain Samuel Wallis, commander of the HMS *Dolphin*, became the first European to set foot on Tahiti and claimed it in the name of King George III. It was pure chance that no Europeans had arrived in Tahiti before Wallis. Close to 250 years had passed since Magellan sailed to the East Indies, and about 20 explorers had sailed the Pacific since then. But islands were few and far between on this vast ocean and navigational aids were often inaccurate, leaving explorers with no idea where they were. Thus even if they discovered a new island, it might be difficult to ever find it again.

The initial contact between the crew of the HMS *Dolphin* and the Tahitians was of a mixed nature. The crew bartered beads, looking glasses and knives for food and eventually for sex. Nails quickly became the most sought-after item by the Tahitians, who used them to make fish-hooks. To the horror of those responsible for the seaworthiness of the vessel, nails rapidly disappeared from the *Dolphin* and became the chief medium of exchange for sexual encounters. However, not all the meetings were amicable. On one

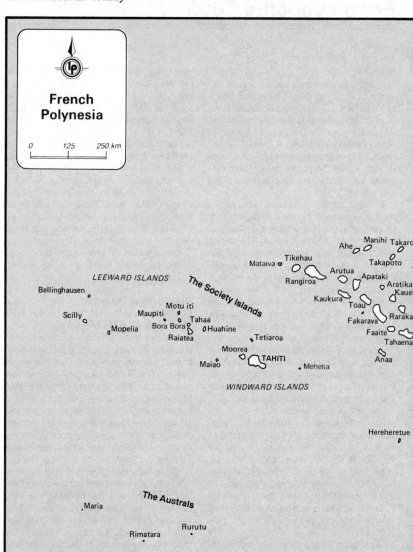

French
Polynesia

0   125   250 km

Manihi Takaro
Ahe
Mataiva Tikehau   Arutua Takapoto
LEEWARD ISLANDS   The Society Islands   Rangiroa Apataki Aratika
Bellinghausen   Kauè
Kaukura Toau
Scilly   Motu iti   Fakarava Raraka
Maupiti   Tahaa
Mopelia Bora Bora   Huahine   Faaite
Raiatea   Tahaena
Moorea   Tetiaroa   Anaa
Maiao   TAHITI   Mehetia

WINDWARD ISLANDS

Hereheretue

The Australs

Maria

Rururu
Rimatara   Rururutu

Tropic   of   Capricorn   Tubuai

Raivavae

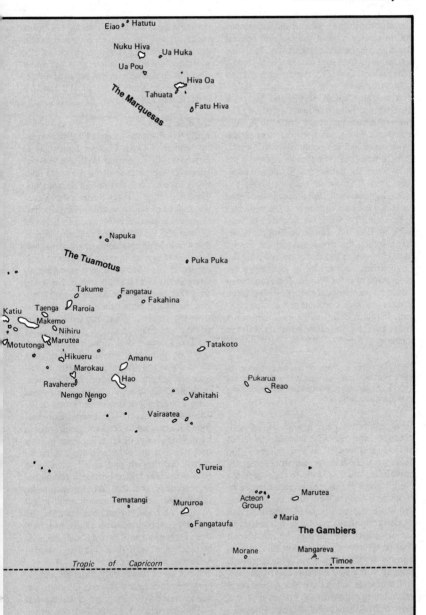

occasion the English were pelted with stones and in savage reprisal the *Dolphin* opened fire with cannon and muskets. The Tahitians set about making amends by giving lavish gifts, which included the favours of the women.

Although Captain Wallis and his crew 'discovered' Tahiti, the first English explorers really learned very little about the Tahitians. Wallis, who was ill most of the time, never had the opportunity to investigate the new land as he should. Although the crew found the natives hospitable and carefree, they discovered nothing about the island's government, religion or laws. These remained for later explorers to understand.

In April 1768, while Wallis was on his way back to England, Louis de Bougainville, commanding the *Boudeuse* and the *Etoile*, found his way to Tahiti and, not realising the English had beaten him to the task, took possession of it for France. The Frenchman was met by a flotilla of canoes bearing green boughs, bananas, coconuts and fowl as presents. In return Bougainville gave them nails and earrings. Bougainville described the scene:

They pressed us to choose a woman and come on shore with her; and their gestures, which were not ambiguous, denoted in what manner we should form an acquaintance with her.

Once ashore the French were treated with kindness and quickly learned the most obvious qualities about their guests – the Tahitians were friendly, generous, sexually uninhibited and they stole. To their credit the French were philosophical about the latter characteristic, realising that the islanders simply did not have the same sense of private property that Europeans did. In contrast to the experience with the English, the French visit produced only one report of violence, which was fairly easily mitigated. Bougainville's stay was cut short by anchorage problems among the dangerous coral heads but in retrospect the French visit was more fruitful than the English one. Bougainville, unlike his English counterpart, was a

distinguished scholar and perhaps a better observer, and because of his good health during the visit had the opportunity to mix more freely with the Tahitians. In just a few days the French captain had acquired a skeletal working knowledge of the island's government and customs.

Captain Cook

In 1769 perhaps the greatest English navigator who ever lived, Captain James Cook, arrived in Tahiti on the HMS *Endeavour*. However, the purpose of his visit had relatively little to do with Tahiti or its residents. Cook had come to study the transit of Venus across the sun, which would enable scientists to measure precisely the distance between the sun and the earth. The determination of this would be an invaluable navigational aid. For the voyage, an impressive group of scientists, scholars and artists was assembled to study Tahiti as well as the transit. However, their 18th-century instruments weren't accurate enough to gather the needed data, and from the aspect of observing the transit the voyage was a failure.

Cook's three-month Tahitian sojourn did, however, provide a wealth of information about the island and its people. His experience was generally a good one but there were problems. Cook was a tolerant man but simply could not deal with one aspect of the Tahitian character – thievery. Tahitians found it amusing to confound their visitors by devising ways of relieving them of their property. For the natives it was a game to outwit the English and usually they gave back what was taken. For Cook the matter was deadly serious. At one point he impounded Tahitian canoes in order to get equipment back. In another instance, he unfairly imprisoned five chiefs and held them for ransom until two of his sailors, who had deserted with their Tahitian 'wives', were returned to his custody.

Cook cared desperately about his and his crew's behaviour towards the Tahitians and was bothered by a shooting incident that left a Tahitian dead. He was also concerned about the spread of venereal disease (which the English later blamed on the French), and about the internment of the chiefs. Two days before the *Endeavour* lifted anchor he wrote, 'We are likely to leave these people in disgust at our behaviour'. Perhaps Cook was too sensitive. One of the Tahitians' greatest qualities is their forgiving nature and when Cook left the Tahitians genuinely wept. He was to return to Tahiti two more times before his death in Hawaii.

Bligh & the Bounty

The year 1788 marked the arrival of the HMS *Bounty*, a name that will forever be associated with legendary Tahiti. It also marked the end of the era of exploration and the beginning of exploitation.

The *Bounty's* mission was to retrieve breadfruit plants needed as a cheap source of food for the numerous slaves working in West Indies plantations. The voyage was led by Captain William Bligh, a former sailing master who had accompanied Cook on a previous visit to Tahiti. Bligh, who may have been unfairly maligned in the annals of history because of his reputation as a ruthless taskmaster, spent six months in Tahiti supervising his crew's transplanting of the valuable plants onto a makeshift greenhouse aboard the ship. The crew made the most of their time, befriending the very fun-loving Tahitians and living like sultans, so that some of the crew did not really wish to depart. Three weeks after leaving Tahiti, a mutinous band of men led by Fletcher Christian coldly turned Bligh and 18 other crew members adrift in a 23-foot cutter with minimal provisions.

Bligh and his followers faced what seemed like certain death through uncharted waters, tempestuous weather and islands teeming with savage cannibals but, miraculously, they survived 41 days in an open craft, travelling 5822 km to the Dutch-held island of Timor in Indonesia.

Meanwhile, under orders from Christian, who wished to avoid returning to Tahiti, the *Bounty* sailed for the island of Tubuai in the Austral Group, where the mutineers briefly attempted to settle. Finding the natives unfriendly, Christian later sailed to Tahiti to pick up pigs for food and female consorts for companionship on Tubuai. Not all wished to return with him to this forlorn island so Christian allowed seven loyalists and nine mutineers to remain behind on Tahiti.

The attempt to establish a community on Tubuai failed because of the hostility of the locals. The *Bounty's* final destination was lonely Pitcairn Island, where Fletcher Christian and his men soon quarrelled with their erstwhile Tahitian comrades. Only one survived the butchering that ensued during the following months. The mutinous crew's descendants still live on Pitcairn Island today and are quite proud of their English/Polynesian roots.

Bligh returned to Tahiti for his breadfruit – this time with a contingent of 19 marines aboard. He was not one to take chances on another uprising. In the interim, the survivors of the crew that Christian had left behind on Tahiti had been rounded up by another British ship, the *Pandora*, put in shackles and taken back to England to stand trial before Bligh returned.

Still a matter of debate is the cause of the celebrated mutiny. Historians write that the real cause of the uprising may have been the sailors' longing to return to their Tahitian girlfriends rather than Captain Bligh's cruelty. Still, subsequent novels and films (the exception being the 1983 production *Return of the Bounty* by De Laurentiis) have portrayed Bligh as a monster, when in fact the real villain may have been the unstable and perhaps emotionally disturbed Fletcher Christian. In his book *Pitcairn: Children of Mutiny*, Australian journalist Ian M Ball tells us that if anything, Bligh, a former officer under the legendary Captain Cook, was a tolerant man who treated his men better than did the average English captain of his day. After the *Bounty* affair Bligh was promoted to admiral and eventually became governor of New South Wales in Australia.

Another book worth consulting on this subject is *Mutiny and Romance in the South Seas: A Companion to the Bounty Adventure* by a California-based writer, Sven Wahlroos.

Wahlroos is less than sanguine about Ball's work, and offers a different perspective on the *Bounty* saga.

The Missionaries

As always, in the wake of explorers came the men of the cloth. In 1797, 30 members of the London Missionary Society came to Tahiti. Although previous visitors had been appalled by customs such as human sacrifice, the Society seemed more distraught at the overt sexual proclivities of Tahitians. They attempted to dissuade the population from this 'immoral' behaviour by converting the king to Christianity. Anthropologist Bengt Danielsson writes that they also persuaded the natives to drink tea, eat with a knife and fork, wear bonnets and coats, sleep in beds, sit on chairs and live in stone houses – in short, to emulate the English lower/middle-class manner of Society members. Within a few years, the missionaries succeeded in converting the entire population and managed to rid them of customs such as infanticide and human sacrifice. However, they never quite convinced the natives to give up their 'hedonistic' ways. As an example of this, even after his conversion to Christianity, Tahitian King Pomare II continued his relationship with two sisters (only one of whom he was married to) and died from the effects of alcoholism.

The French

In 1836 a French naval vessel under Admiral du Petit-Thours arrived in Papeete and demanded indemnity for a previous expulsion of Catholic missionaries from Tahiti. Queen Pomare, the current ruler, paid the money under threat of naval bombardment and later was forced to sign an agreement that would allow French missionaries to spread Catholicism. Admiral du Petit-Thours returned to Polynesia in 1842 and annexed the Marquesas Islands with the idea of turning them into a penal colony. In the process of procuring land, he decided to annexe Tahiti as well. This move outraged the London Missionary Society and almost whipped up enough anti-French sentiment in England to send the two nations to war. The French returned to Tahiti with three ships in 1843 to take formal possession of the island. This marked the beginning of European colonisation in the South Pacific.

After the Tahitians realised the French were there to stay, they took up arms (bush knives and a few muzzle-loaders) and waged a three-year guerrilla war on French garrisons, settlements and missionary stations. In the end, the Tahitians were crushed and Queen Pomare came out of hiding to become a rubber-stamp monarch. Likewise, the Missionary Society, seeing the futility of resisting French influence, ceded their holdings to a French Protestant group and headed for greener pastures.

The Islands in the 20th Century

French Polynesia remained a backwater colony until the 1960s, when three events triggered drastic changes in the islands. These were the building of an international airport in Tahiti, the beginning of nuclear weapons testing in the nearby Tuamotu Islands and the making of the MGM film *Mutiny on the Bounty* starring Marlon Brando and Trevor Howard. As tourists – lured no doubt by Hollywood's version of the islands – and military personnel flooded Tahiti in increasing numbers, the character of the once sleepy island changed dramatically. Money was pumped into the economy, new businesses sprang up to accommodate the influx of arrivals, and thousands of Polynesians left their far-flung island homes to look for work in Papeete. Suddenly, Tahiti was very much in the 20th century. The topics of the day were dissent over nuclear testing, brawls between soldiers and Tahitians, inflation and a shift from a subsistence economy to one based completely on money.

The increased French presence was not without its positive effects, such as new roads, schools, hospitals, agriculture and aquaculture projects, many new airstrips and eventually the highest standard of living in the South Pacific. Accompanying economic growth was a greater political awareness and a demand by Polynesians for more voice in the government, which was controlled more or less by France. In 1977 French Polynesia was finally granted a much greater degree of autonomy under the auspices of a new constitution. The new arrangement provided Polynesians with a larger voice in internal affairs, which included managing their own budget.

In 1984, a statute passed by the French parliament in Paris created yet another incarnation of the French Polynesian constitution, giving Tahiti even greater self-government. For the first time the legislative body was allowed to elect the Territorial government's own president. Prior to this, the highest position a Tahitian could hold was Vice-President of the Territorial Government Council. Thus, instead of sharing power with the Paris-appointed High Commissioner, which the Vice-President had to do, the President is able to run the Council of Ministers alone.

The 1984 statute has not created complete autonomy for Tahiti's local government but it has increased its self-governing role tremendously. In areas that remain apart from local government control, such as defence or foreign affairs, Tahitian government has been granted the right to participate in far more negotiations regarding matters that may have a bearing on French Polynesia's future.

GEOGRAPHY

French Polynesia lies in the South Pacific, halfway between Australia and California, and approximately halfway between Tokyo and Santiago. Although French Polynesia is spread over an expanse of water the size of Western Europe, the total land mass of its 130 islands adds up to only 4000 sq km. The islands are divided into five archipelagos, all culturally, ethnically and climatically distinct. They include the Marquesas, the Tuamotus, the Society Islands, the Australs and the Gambiers.

Geologically, the islands are divided into two categories: atolls (or low islands) and high islands. An atoll is what Daniel Defoe had in mind when he wrote *Robinson Crusoe* – a flat island with little more than scrub growth and coconut palms. An atoll is actually a ring of coral that once surrounded a volcano. The sinking of the volcano leaves only the coral, which then surrounds a lagoon. The colours of an atoll are so brilliant they assault the eye: the ocean laps at a blindingly white coral shore, the sun shines with dazzling intensity on a lagoon made up of many primitive blues and greens – lapis lazuli, cobalt and turquoise.

High islands can be either volcanic in origin or the result of an upheaval from the ocean floor, as is the phosphate island of Makatea. Their terrain can be smooth, rocky and barren, or incredibly precipitous and covered with lush rainforest. Unlike atolls, where drinking water must be collected in cisterns and a limited range of crops can be grown, high islands often have an abundance of water and have the soil to support a variety of fruits and vegetables.

CLIMATE

French Polynesia has a climate ranging from subtropical in the southern archipelagos near the Tropic of Capricorn (Gambier and Austral Islands) to steamy and equatorial in the Marquesas Islands to the north. The Society and Tuamotu groups have a mild tropical climate that ranges between the two extremes. There are basically two seasons: the warm and humid period between November and April when rains can fall intermittently, and the dry season between May and October. The average annual temperature in the Society Islands is 25°C, with variations from 21 to 34°C. As a result of vegetation and wind factors, high islands are generally more humid than atolls, where you can enjoy the cooling influence of the trade winds.

Forces of Nature

Although many of French Polynesia's high islands are volcanic in origin, strong earthquakes are quite rare. Cyclones are also infrequent, but when they strike the results can be devastating. Until 1983 the Society

Islands had been spared this type of natural disaster for 76 years. As a result of the warming caused by the now infamous El Nino, Tahiti and neighbouring islands were battered by five consecutive cyclones in 1983 which cost one life and destroyed millions of dollars worth of property.

If you're interested in reading about the destruction wrought by cyclones and hurricanes, find a copy of *Islands of Desire* by Robert Dean Frisbie. The author describes in nearly unbelievable terms how, during a storm that inundated his tiny island home, he saved his family by tying them to trees.

FLORA & FAUNA

When the original settlers of French Polynesia, the Polynesians, arrived in the 7th or 8th century, the variety of vegetation was limited to the seeds and spores borne by wind, sea and birds that happened to find their way to the islands. To provide food and materials for shelter the Polynesians brought taro, yams, coconuts, bananas and breadfruit. To the bafflement of scientists they also cultivated the South American sweet potato – a plant that does not exist in Asia. Later, the missionaries introduced corn, cotton, sugar cane, citrus fruits, tamarinds, pineapples, guavas, figs, coffee and other vegetables. Tahiti also owes quite a bit to Edouard Raoul, a pharmacist-botanist who in 1887 brought a cargo of 1500 varieties of plants to the islands, and experimented with the cultivation of hundreds of types of fruit trees. Other tree species included kauri (from New Zealand), red cedar, eucalyptus, rubber, gum and jack. A decade after his arrival Raoul's gardens were donating about 150 species of plants to farmers to improve their stock.

In 1919 Harrison Smith, a US university professor turned botanist, purchased 340 acres in Papaeri and settled down to cultivate hundreds of plant varieties he had imported from tropical regions throughout the world. Like Raoul, he helped local farmers by giving them seeds and cuttings to better their crops. (For more information on Smith see Botanical Gardens in the Around the Island section of the Tahiti chapter.)

Tahitians take pride in their gardens, which are richly ornamented with flowers and shrubs, including frangipani and a variety of camellias. Fruits are usually abundant on every home site; during the harvest season they provide an important staple. They include a species of huge avocado, mangoes, papayas, custard apples, bananas, *pamplemousse* (a kind of grapefruit), oranges and pineapples.

Like the flora, most of the fauna found in Tahiti was introduced by humans. Pigs, dogs, chickens, lizards and even rats were brought by the Polynesians. Later, Captain Cook imported cattle and cats. The only 'wild' animals are pigs, the descendants of those that escaped domestication and now live in the bush.

GOVERNMENT

French Polynesia is governed by a 34-member Territorial Assembly elected by popular vote every five years. The members

Breadfruit

select 10 among them to form a Council of Ministers *(Conseil de Ministres)*, the most powerful ruling body. The assembly also elects the President.

French Polynesia's official status is 'Overseas Territory of France', which roughly means it is a semiautonomous colony, much like the US territories of Puerto Rico and Guam. However, unlike people in those territories, French Polynesians are permitted to vote in national elections and to elect representatives (two deputies and a senator) to the metropolitan French National Assembly and Senate in Paris.

The metropolitan French government runs French Polynesia's foreign affairs, defence, police, justice system and secondary education. In addition to local rule, a French High Commissioner is charged with administrative duties, especially regarding the observance of French law.

The first French Polynesian President, Gaston Flosse, was elected in 1984. In 1986 Flosse became Under Minister for South Pacific Affairs *(Secretaire d'État Charge du Pacifique Sur)* a subministerial position with the metropolitan French government, while retaining his presidency of French Polynesia. He was forced to resign the presidency in 1987 at the request of Jacky Teuira, a political adversary.

Jacky Teuira, of Flosse's conservative (Gaullist) Tahoeraa Huiraatira Party, was subsequently elected president by the Territorial Assembly.

Teuira's presidency was short-lived. On 7 December 1987 (nine months after Teuira's election as president) he resigned when it became obvious that his former Minister of Economics, Alexander Leontieff, had formed a majority coalition which ultimately would have unseated him. On 9 December 1987 Leontieff was installed by the new majority coalition as Tahiti's third territorial president.

The catalyst for Tahiti's political upheaval came on 'Black Friday', 23 October or, as one local newspaper perhaps over-dramatically called it, 'The Night of Living Hell in Paradise'. On this evening French security forces were sent to Papeete's docks to break up a picket line set up by local longshoremen. The result was pandemonium. US journalist Al Prince described it this way:

...strikers, curious onlookers, juvenile delinquents and just plain ordinary citizens suddenly turned into a human wave of destruction that descended on downtown Papeete as night fell. It took French security forces and local firemen three hours to bring everything under control after the worst violence and social unrest the city of more than 23,000 had ever witnessed.

More than 100 stores and businesses were damaged or destroyed by the rioting, looting, burning and general mayhem. Damage was estimated at around US$70 million. The riot made people acutely aware of the social and economic problems that had too long been buried under the rug. In November 1987 the then minister Leontieff released a sensational report on the state of the economy in French Polynesia. It spelled out in no uncertain terms that Tahiti faced dire economic problems and needed a forceful recovery programme. President Teuira proposed an austere provisional budget for 1988, which was criticised by both party stalwarts and opposition leaders. Meanwhile, on 1 December 1988, Leontieff and two other ministers resigned from the Teuira government. By the end of the month Leontieff was the new president.

Leontieff's fortunes changed in 1991. Gaston Flosse, the old political warrior, managed to mould a coalition from various parties that won a strong victory in April. Backed by business interests and a populace that was looking for change in a government wracked by scandal, Flosse was firmly in power once again.

ECONOMY

Although French Polynesians cling to traditional values, the face of Tahiti has changed drastically in the past 30 years. The influx of money from both tourism and the large military presence has transformed the region's economy from an agriculturally based subsistence level to a modern consumer society.

Money, not essential to an islander years ago, is now necessary for buying outboard motors, stereos, colour televisions, video decks, cars, motorcycles, gasoline and – when one can afford them – the latest fashions. The younger generation has become enamoured with the things money can buy and their ability to consume is tempered only by the high price of imported goods.

The main source of hard currency for French Polynesia is the tourism industry and moneys generated by bureaucracies of the metropolitan French government. The bulk of French Polynesians make their living working at jobs associated with tourism, retail business or government.

Agriculture, the second main source of revenue, plays an important role in supporting the rural population. The leading product is copra (dried coconut), produced by drying coconut meat in the sun, after which it is processed into oil for copra cakes (cattle feed), soap, cosmetics, margarine and other items. Processed coconut oil known as *monoi* is scented with flower blossoms and used locally for skin care. It makes a fine, inexpensive souvenir. Copra is a vital source of income to families on the outer islands who have difficulty eking out a living on remote islands because of poor resources and/or poor accessibility of distant markets. The government buys the dried coconut at higher prices to subsidise French Polynesians caught in this situation. Other

aquacultural and agricultural products include cultured black pearls, pearl shell, vanilla, coffee, fruit, fish, shrimp and oysters.

Lured by the promise of a better life, French Polynesians from the outer islands have moved to Tahiti in ever greater numbers. Life in Papeete, however, is often not easy for those who have left their distant homes. In the capital the cost of living is high, and assimilation for the new inhabitants is fraught with basic problems such as finding housing and employment. In Papeete it is simply not possible to fish for an evening meal or gather fruits and vegetables from the land. Thus for those who have migrated, traditional life has been exchanged for an urban existence and all its woes. To counter this trend, the Tahitian government promotes economic development of the outer islands. Through aquaculture, tourism and commercial pearl ventures, the authorities hope to encourage the rural population to stay put.

Why Is It So Bloody Expensive Here?

There are several reasons. Perhaps the pivotal one is the high tariffs the government tacks on to almost everything that is imported. Only certain foodstuffs such as sugar and flour are exempt from import duties. (This explains why bread is so inexpensive in the stores compared with other goods.) When you combine very high tariffs, the price of transport to get the goods to Tahiti and add the profit (often a large margin) that merchants tack on, it's simple to comprehend why prices are so high.

You might also wonder how Tahitians pay for these goods and services that seemingly well-heeled visitors find so expensive. The answer is that many people are well paid. Government bureaucrats are more than compensated for their efforts, as are those in private industry. The minimum wage for unskilled labour is almost US$7 per hour and an experienced school teacher may earn as much as US$50,000 per year.

Despite high tariffs, the revenue raised by these duties covers only 70% or so of the

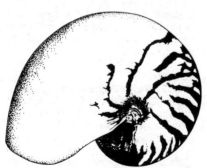

government's operating budget. The government still needs a yearly infusion of capital from France in order to pay the roughly 30% deficit. France's largess probably encourages a 'French-will-take-care-of-it' attitude which in turn hardly fosters budgetary restraint or a Puritan ethic.

To complicate things even more, the tremendous outflow of capital overseas to pay for exports goes against every sane economic tenet. After all, the classic definition of a solvent economy is one that exports more than it imports – not the other way around. However, if a government depends almost totally on import duties for its revenue, it will have difficulty surviving without encouraging spending on imported goods. And spending money on imported goods is something Tahitians do a lot of.

Papeete is a wonderland of tropical materialism. Walking through the capital it's almost impossible not to notice that many of the people drive late model cars, sport flashy diving watches, drip with jewellery by Cartier and wear the latest Paris fashions. Often even the most humble Tahitian shack will have a good stereo, a VCR and a television – all costing double what one would pay in a developed country.

Even those high in government acknowledge that there are serious problems for a nation that spends an awful lot on imports and produces nothing except beautiful brown babies. There is little, however, that can be done to alleviate Tahiti's economic woes and high prices. Though French Polynesia is beginning to export fruit juice, pineapples, black pearls and some fish, the islands have practically no export crops or minerals to provide substantial amounts of hard currency. No one in Tahiti knows what the future will bring given these circumstances. No one in Tahiti really likes to think about it.

Black Pearl Industry

The black pearl industry remains one of the few bright spots in the Tahitian economy. Prior to the commercial exploitation of pearl shell in French Polynesia early in the 19th century, locals had used it for religious and decorative ornamentation as well as for implements such as fish-hooks and lures. Harvesting oysters for pearls gained importance in the Tuamotu Islands during the 1850s but it wasn't until the early 1960s that scientists began cultivation experiments with the indigenous black pearl oyster *Pinctada margaritifera*. Today the pearls are cultivated in the Gambier and Tuamotu islands.

Over the past several years pearl cultivation has become an increasingly important source of income for French Polynesia, particularly as consumers become more aware of the black pearl in the international marketplace. The Tahiti Pearl Centre & Museum in Papeete was opened in May 1984 by a Tahitian entrepreneur with precisely this 'PR' factor in mind – to educate the public about the black pearl. Although the 'museum' is privately owned and is more a shop-cum-exhibition, it does a remarkably thorough job – through placards, display cases and videotapes – of illustrating the history of the pearl in civilisation, with particular emphasis on the black pearl.

The process of 'making pearls' is briefly as follows: three to five-year-old oysters are collected by divers and selected for pearl cultivation. A nucleus, or tiny mother-of-pearl sphere fashioned from the shell of a Mississippi River mussel, is then attached to a graft of tissue from the oyster and placed inside the animal's gonad (sex organ). If all goes well the tiny graft grows around the nucleus and acts as an irritant which causes the slow formation of layer upon layer of black pearl. After a donor nucleus has been added to each oyster, they are placed inside cages to protect them from predators. Under ideal growing conditions they are left to recuperate from the operation for 18 months to three years before harvesting. Meanwhile the shells are repeatedly inspected and hauled to the surface for cleaning. Water conditions are scrupulously checked for salinity, temperature and possible pollutants.

Only 20% of the oysters implanted with a nucleus ever bear saleable pearls, and only 5% of the crop harvested bear 'perfect' pearls

– specimens that meet the exacting industry standards. Value is determined by size, lustre, sheen, colour and lack of defects such as bumps, dents or scratches. The price for a perfect pearl is about 100,000 CFP (US$1000) but prices may range from 5000 to 250,000 CFP (US$50 to US$2500) for an individual pearl. The museum is open Monday to Friday from 8 am to noon and 2 to 5 pm, and Saturday from 8 am to noon.

POPULATION

The population of French Polynesia is an amalgam of Polynesians (75%), Chinese (10%) and Europeans (15%). Among these racial categories exists every conceivable mixture. It would not be unusual for a Tahitian named Pierre Jamison to have Chinese, American, Polynesian and French ancestors. Racial intermarriage, which is not frowned upon, accounts for the physical beauty of the inhabitants.

The current population of French Polynesia numbers around 200,000, half of whom are under 20 years of age. Approximately 75% of the population live on the island of Tahiti.

Tahitian Society

The social structure of French Polynesia is a complicated study in politics, economics and intermarriage. Economically, the Chinese are the most powerful group, while 'demis' (half-castes) control the political sphere. Demis of Polynesian and Caucasian blood make up a class of 'Europeanised' Tahitians. The demi population maintains an interesting mixture of Tahitian and European values. While some have adopted French culture and eschew speaking Tahitian, others identify with both cultures and find no shame in their Tahitian heritage. The majority of the population – those whose ancestry is mostly Polynesian – are known as *kaina* (rhymes with myna) and are at the lowest rung of the socioeconomic ladder.

The Chinese first came to Tahiti as plantation workers at the time of the US Civil War. They were the labour force in a scheme hatched by two Scottish businessmen to produce cotton, then unavailable in northern USA. When the Civil War ended, the venture went bankrupt and the Chinese indentured workers remained. Through the years, Chinese have continued to migrate to Tahiti, while keeping their culture, and many have married Polynesians or Europeans. Because of their wealth, they are sometimes the object of resentment and jealousy from Polynesians, but without the Chinese to run the shops and businesses, the French Polynesian economy would be in serious trouble.

EDUCATION

Formal education is mandatory in Tahiti for every child to the age of 14. Primary education begins at age five, and continues to the age of 12, when children begin secondary education.

There are several technical and vocational schools in Tahiti, as well as a large adult education programme. Vocational training includes hotel, restaurant, nursing and teaching programmes.

ART & CULTURE

Upper-class Tahitians have adopted Western pop culture to a 'T'. French Polynesians wear the 'chicest' fashions, the tightest jeans, listen to the latest pop music and, if they can afford it, drive the newest US cars and Japanese motorcycles. Yet they still have their own language and customs despite 200 years of foreign influence.

As in all cultures, modern Tahitian music and dance owe quite a bit to outside influences. The music is an admixture of popular US songs, French *chansons* and hymns borrowed from the missionaries. Tahitian bands equipped with the most modern Fender guitars and Yamaha amplifiers crank out endless songs about love, romance and betrayal just like any other band in the world. Traditional percussionists, who always accompany dance troupes, are one of the purest expressions of Polynesian music and are as much a part of the music scene today as electric guitarists. To hear the thunder of their drumming for the first time is a stirring experience.

Perhaps the most popularised aspect of Tahitian culture is expressed in dance, in particular the hip-shaking and often very erotic *tamure*, a step that every Tahitian is taught at an early age. The tamure resembles the Hawaiian hula from the waist down, but is more forceful, suggestive and sometimes more violent than the Hawaiian dance. Tahitian dancers have amazingly flexible and controlled hip movements – an art that has to be seen to be appreciated. The modern tamure is descended from traditional dance forms presented by troupes acting out a legend or event depicting warriors, kings, fisherfolk, heroes, priests and the like – a far cry from today's slick, often showbiz-style productions.

Cultural Renaissance

As with other Third-World peoples, Tahitians experienced a cultural blossoming and reawakening in the 1970s, manifested through the 'Maohi' or 'Neo-Polynesian' artistic movement. Artists explored traditional Polynesian motifs, while writers and playwrights went digging into their own mythology for themes. According to the late Bobby Holcomb, a respected Hawaiian-US artist who lived in Tahiti until his death in 1991, Neo-Polynesian painters like himself use the Polynesian colour scale (earthy browns, reds, yellows) as well as traditional Polynesian historical and mythical themes. Neo-Polynesian art is often more abstract than traditional Pacific art and may exhibit heightened eroticism, sensuality, local flora and fauna, and classic Polynesian geometric patterns as displayed in tattoos and tapa cloth. Politically, the movement produced nationalist stirrings, calling for greater autonomy or even independence from France.

Today the maelstrom has died down but the 'back to the roots' sentiment has taken hold over a greater portion of society. Teaching the Tahitian language in schools, once against the law, is now part of the curriculum. Politicians of every stripe espouse traditional Tahitian culture, and painters and artists enjoy the support of the state instead of fighting against it. In the last several years the French Polynesian government has nurtured the talents of young artists by displaying their works in exhibitions and providing cash prizes. Displays of Tahitian art and re-enactments of ancient ceremonies – such as the crowning of a king – can be readily seen during *Tiurai*, the Bastille Day celebrations.

On the popular front, singers and musicians (whose profession is Tahiti's national pastime) continue to compose music for the masses on subjects they have always written about – love and the sea – while enriching their songs with reggae and Latin rhythms. Throughout the country, women's groups are reviving dying art forms such as hat making, mat weaving, quilting and the fashioning of floral crowns.

One of the most novel groups to appear on the cultural scene is Pupu Arioi, a small but dedicated organisation that specialises in teaching children about their Polynesian heritage. Named after an ancient Polynesian society that allowed members to criticise their leaders and rise in an otherwise rigid world, Pupu Arioi began its existence in 1977 as a theatre troupe. Later, the group's emphasis shifted from theatre to education. Members now go from school to school, teaching teachers and pupils relaxation techniques, which calm sometimes unruly children and put them into a more receptive state, before introducing them to theatre, dance, music and costume. Children are not pushed, but nudged into thinking about their culture and traditions. Pupu Arioi members may also discuss Polynesian mythology and philosophy with the idea of educating children in the oral traditions which were once the backbone of Tahitian culture. Perhaps they will be successful in reinfusing values into a society that for many reasons has lost its old traditions.

Flowers in Their Hair

You will never see a race of people so enamoured with putting flowers in their hair as the French Polynesians. Fresh *tiare* or hibiscus blossoms are always worn behind the ear or braided with palm fronds and other greenery into floral crowns. Tradition has it that if a woman or man tucks the flower behind the left ear she or he is taken; a flower placed behind the right ear means the person is available. Tahitians joke that if someone waves a flower behind their head it means 'follow me'. I have never witnessed this but will report the outcome of such an invitation if fortunate enough to experience it.

Sex & the Tahitian Myth

A visitor who is romantically inclined should be handsome and have money, preferably lots of money.
John W McDermott, travel writer

When discussing Tahiti, it is only a matter of time before the subject of sex arises. Since the time of Wallis and Cook, the myth of Tahiti as the 'Isle of Love' has flourished and is still used as a major selling point by the travel industry. As a result of books such as *The Marriage of Loti* and movies such as *Mutiny on the Bounty*, countless people have travelled to Tahiti's shores in search of its beguilements.

According to early accounts, Tahitian women genuinely relished lovemaking, and sailors

arriving in the islands were greeted by boatloads of willing maidens. For Tahitians the arrival of a ship was like a circus visiting a small town. Days and nights were filled with wild abandon, rum drinking and the comic sight of pale white men in strange costume. Amorous flings had the benefit of material rewards as well, usually a trinket of some sort. In Cook's day, nails were often given as gifts. This sometimes reached a hazardous stage as eager sailors began to wrench nails from the very ships themselves.

Today things are quite different. Tahitians have by no means lost their gay abandon, but male visitors are very mistaken if they think Tahitian women share their amorous notions. Overseas tourists are advised not to adopt the attitude that they are God's gift to Tahitians. More often than not, they will feel that they are on the outside, looking into a totally different world.

And what a different world it is. But those who think Tahitians are promiscuous should remember that Tahitian customs and traditions, which are foreign to the Judeo-Christian ethic, existed long before white visitors appeared on the scene. However, it is equally wrong to assume that Tahitians are totally uninhibited and free from neuroses. As with people everywhere, they have their share of hang-ups and sexual problems.

A final word on this subject: for those of us lucky in love, Tahiti will be just like anywhere else, only warmer.

Tahiti's Third Sex

Homosexuality has been a culturally accepted lifestyle in Polynesia for centuries. When the Europeans came they were shocked and puzzled at the behaviour of male transvestites who did striptease acts for the crews and unabashedly had sexual relations with other men. Commenting on this behaviour, Captain Bligh said:

It is strange that in so prolific a country as this men should be led into such sensual and beastly acts of gratification, but perhaps no place in the world are they so common or extraordinary as in this island.

In the years that followed, the brethren from the London Missionary Society did their best to convert the Tahitians into upright Protestants, but with little success. The cultural heritage of the *mahu* (transvestite) lives on and they continue to play an important role in Polynesian culture. According to anthropologist Bengt Danielsson, the mahu is 'a popular and honoured member of every village throughout the Society Islands'.

Anthropologist Robert I Levy writes that one becomes a mahu by choice, by being coaxed into the role, or both, at an early age. The boy associates primarily with females and learns to perform the traditionally feminine household tasks. After puberty, the mahu may assume a woman's role by cooking, cleaning, looking after children and wearing feminine clothing. He may dance what are normally the women's parts during festivals, often with greater skill than the women around him. In the villages he may work as a maid, and in Papeete can often find employment as a waiter, professional dancer or bartender.

Although Tahitians may poke fun at mahus there is none of the deep-seated hostility that exists towards homosexuals in the West. Young adolescents may seek out mahus for sexual favours, but generally only if there are no girls available. If a young man does have sex with a mahu, there is little stigma attached to the act. Mahus are accepted as human beings, not aberrations. In Papeete there are several nightclubs which feature male striptease acts and cater to a varied sexual spectrum.

Danielsson fears that the mahu tradition is in danger of disappearing because of what he calls the 'brutal modernisation process'. He has already noticed the trend of mahus turning to Western-style homosexual prostitution as a way of making a living in a modern society incompatible with the traditional mahu way of life.

RELIGION & THE SUPERNATURAL

Most French Polynesians (about 55%) are Protestants, followed by Roman Catholics (30%), Mormons (6%), Seventh-Day Adventists (2%) and a number of Buddhists and Confucianists among the Chinese colony (2%). The church is an important institution throughout the Pacific island nations and French Polynesia is no exception. On the outer islands the local priest or minister often wields a powerful hand in community affairs. In most areas church attendance is high.

Although Christianity has spread throughout the islands, there is still a strong belief in vestiges of the pre-Christian religion. In the outlying areas especially, myths of gods, giants and supernatural creatures are spoken of as fact and it is not unusual for a person to have had encounters with *tupa'pau* (ghosts).

One man in Maupiti matter-of-factly described to me the occasion on which he had seen a dozen ghosts floating down a moonlit road outside his village. These ghosts, he said, were the spirits of passengers who had perished in a shipwreck several weeks earlier. The spirits were those of native Maupitans, returning home as the dead always do.

Accepting the locals' belief that the supernatural is a normal part of life often makes Westerners question their own beliefs. In the Tuamotus, I met a young Frenchman by the name of Patrick who had spent several years living on the atoll of Ahe. He said that one evening he and an old villager were fishing in a skiff inside the atoll's lagoon. The Frenchman spotted an object resembling a ball of fire which rose from a spit of land on the lagoon's far edge and floated in the direction of the village. Awe-struck by the sight, he pointed it out to the old man who sat contentedly fishing. The Tahitian glanced at the luminous ball and nonchalantly remarked that it was only the spirits returning to the village and really nothing to get excited about.

LANGUAGE

The official languages of French Polynesia are Tahitian and French but other tongues spoken are Paumotu (the language of the Tuamotu Islands), Mangarevan (spoken in the Gambiers) and Marquesan (the language of the Marquesas Islands). These languages belong to the great Austronesian or Malayo-European language family. This widely scattered family includes the languages of Micronesia and Melanesia as well as Bahasa Malay (the language of Malaysia and Indonesia), Malagasy (the language of Madagascar) and the original languages of Taiwan. Thus the origins of Tahitian date back 5000 years to the ancient languages of Indonesia, which later spread to Fiji and then to Samoa and Tonga.

The first explorers to set foot on Tahiti thought the Tahitian language childishly simple. Cook recorded 157 words and Bougainville estimated the entire vocabulary to be only about 500 words. Tahiti was chosen as a fertile ground for evangelical groups such as the London Missionary Society partly because Tahitian seemed a simple language to learn. As the missionaries were to discover, however, their assumption was certainly wrong. As each day passed they encountered baffling subtleties, foreign idioms and confusing sounds. The slightest change in pronunciation, barely discernible to the untrained ear, could give a very different meaning. Although there were no words to express Western ideas about the arts, sciences or business there were words describing the natural environment such as the weather, the ocean, the stars, animal behaviour and the like that the Europeans could not even begin to understand, because their powers of observation were not attuned to see what Tahitians took for granted.

At least one of the reasons Tahitian was so difficult for early visitors to grasp was that it was a language of oral record. People were expected to know their genealogies and could recite them seemingly forever back into time. Thus they knew intimately the details of their forebears' lives and sometimes the origins of property claims. When no written language existed, memory alone was relied upon.

Once exclusively the language of Tahiti and its neighbours, Tahitian is now spoken on about 100 islands of French Polynesia. The language gained prominence because Tahiti was the most populous island and the chief one chosen for missionary work. As the written word and Christianity were spread by native pastors, the printed Tahitian word more or less superseded other local dialects and languages.

Like all languages, Tahitian was influenced by foreigners, mostly early missionaries and seafarers who mingled with the local population. Many languages, including Hebrew, Greek, Latin, English and French, contributed words that have become part of modern-day Tahitian. The translation of the Bible into Tahitian necessarily introduced words such as *Sabati* (Sabbath); but the English connection provided many loan words such as baby, butter, money, tea, pineapple and frying pan, which became *pepe, pata, moni, ti, painapo* and *faraipani* in Tahitian.

Useful Concepts

Those who have spent any time in the Islands are sure to run into catch phrases containing important concepts in trying to understand the Tahitian character.

Fiu This expression encompasses varying shades of boredom, despair, hopelessness and frustration. Put yourself in the place of a person who has spent his or her life on a small island, perhaps only a bit of coral in the the midst of a blue expanse of ocean. The only stimuli are the ceaseless trade winds, the sound of the waves crashing on the reef, the sight of the sun bleaching the coral white and the sweltering heat. You can always go fishing or turn on Radio Tahiti, but this can get boring after a while. Life can be an endless monotone, and when someone mutters, 'I'm *fiu*' with husband or with job, very little explanation is necessary. The essence of 'fiu' is in the languorous tropical air.

Aita P'ape'a Another often-used expression, *aita p'ape'a'* translates literally as 'no problem'. It means take things the way they are and don't worry about them. It is basically the Tahitian equivalent of 'manana'. At best it implies a fatalistic and easy-going acceptance of the here and now. At worst, it is a kind of intellectual lethargy and lack of concern.

Pronunciation

There are five vowels in Tahitian:

a   as in 'but'
e   as in 'day'
i   as in 'machine'
o   as in 'gold'
u   as in 'flute'

There are eight consonant sounds in Tahitian:

f   as in 'fried'
h   as in 'house'; pronounced 'sh' as in 'shark' when preceded by 'i' and followed by 'o', as in *iho* (only, just)
m   as in 'man'
n   as in 'noted'
p   as in 'spark' – shorter than the 'p' of 'pan'
r   as in 'run' – sometimes trilled like a Scottish 'r'
t   as in 'stark' – softer than the 't' of 'tar'
v   as in 'victory'

Aside from the eight consonants a glottal stop is used in many words. For example, the word for 'pig' is *pua'a*; 'person' is *ta'ata*; 'beer' is *pia* and 'coconut' is *ha'ari*. A US English equivalent, as D T Tryon points out in his excellent Tahitian primer *Say it in Tahitian*, is 'co'n' for 'cotton'.

Although English is spoken by many shopkeepers, hotel personnel and students, it would help to have some command of French. If you really want to talk with the people and acquire knowledge of the culture, learn Tahitian.

Place Names

Papeete (Pa-pee-ay-tay)
Raiatea (Rye-ah-tay-ah)
Tahaa (Tah-ha-ah)
Maupiti (Mau-pee-tee)
Rangiroa (Rang-ghee-row-ah)

Manihi (Mahn-nee-hee)
Ahe (Ah-hay)
Mangareva (Mahng-ah-rave-ah)
Tubuai (Toop-oo-eye)
Nuku Hiva (New-kew-hee-vah)
Faaa (Fah-ah-ah)
Tuamotu (Too-ah-mow-too)
Huahine (Who-ah-hee-nay)
Gambier (Tahm-bee-aye)

Some Useful Words & Phrases

good morning; good day
    ia ora na
    your-rah-nah
goodbye
    nana
    nah-nah
thank you
    maruru
    mah-rhu-rhu
good
    maita'i
    my-tye
very good
    maita'i roa
    my-tye-row-ah
no
    aita
    eye-tah
no good
    aita maita'i
    eye-tah-my-tye
no problem; don't worry
    aita pe'ape'a
    eye-tah-pay-ah-pay-ah
woman
    vahine
    vah-hee-nay
man
    tane
    tah-nay
friend
    e hoa
    ay-oh-ah
American
    marite
    mah-ree-tay
finish, finished
    oti
    woh-tee

Cheers! Down the hatch.
manuia!
mahn-wee-ah
I'm bored; disgusted
fiu
phew
ancient temple
marae
mah-rye
traditional dance
tamure
tah-mu-ray

house
fare
fah-ray
crazy
taravana
tar-ah-vah-nah
pretty, beautiful
nehenehe
nay-he-nay-he

Facts for the Visitor

VISAS & CONSULATES

Visitors need passports and onward tickets, but visas are not required for citizens of EC countries for stays of three months or less. Citizens of the USA, Canada and Japan can stay for up to 30 days without a visa. Naturally, it's a good idea to bring your passport. Thus for these three countries it is *not* necessary to visit the French consulate beforehand to obtain a visa. Australian and New Zealand citizens must have a visa before going to French Polynesia or they might not be granted permission to enter. This is what happened to one Australian who arrived in Papeete in December 1987:

I arrived in Papeete...and was told that it was now necessary for Australian citizens to have a visa before entering French Polynesia. I was forced to sign a document in French stating that I had arrived in Papeete without a visa...I was denied entry, told that it was useless trying to contact the Australian Consulate on a Sunday and then escorted back to the plane to Sydney.

Visitors from Sweden, Norway, Finland and a host of other nations from South America, Africa and Asia are obligated to apply for their visa before entering French Polynesia, but do not need the approval of the local French High Commissioner. Visitors from Eastern Europe and the remaining nations need the approval of the French High Commissioner before visiting the country.

In most cases visitors will be automatically granted visas of up to three months without the High Commissioner's approval. Upon expiration, tourist visas may be extended for another three months, with a possibility of renewal for an additional six months. No foreigner can stay for more than a year with a tourist visa.

For visitors who wish to extend their stays in French Polynesia beyond the normal 30-day limit and wish to apply for a visa, the best bet is to go back to the airport immigration office and organise things there, instead of going to the government offices in town. (The immigration people in Papeete will eventually send you to the airport anyway.) After filling out the necessary forms, the airport people will then send you to the post office to purchase a 3000 CFP stamp. To avoid the hassle and spending the 3000 CFP, if you know before leaving for Tahiti that you will stay for more than 30 days, it's better to arrange things with the nearest French consulate.

Work Permits

To live and work in Tahiti is not easy for nonresidents. A work permit is necessarily tied with a residence permit and is issued two months following the request for a work contract. The permit is issued care of the employer, who is responsible for the employee's return to his or her homeland. A local is always given first priority in filling a job, so the person seeking work in Tahiti has to be able to provide a special skill not found on the island. To sum it up, landing a job in Tahiti is extremely difficult. US citizens skilled in the hotel/restaurant business may have the best chance, as some of the hotels in Tahiti are owned or operated by Americans.

Entry Formalities for Yachts

Captain and crew must have valid passports and previously secured tourist visas. A five-day transit visa is also desirable. If coming from a country that does not have a French consulate, the visitor must after five days secure a valid visa from the Immigration Service – good for three months for all of French Polynesia, counting the first day of arrival.

Along with the visa each crew member must have a deposit in a special account at a local bank or at the Trésorerie Générale equal to the fare from Tahiti back to the country of origin. During the yacht's stay in French Polynesia the crew list must correspond with the list of passengers made at the time of arrival. Any changes must be accounted for with the Chief of Immigration. Crew changes can only be made in harbours or anchorages where there are gendarmes. Disembarkation of crew members can only be authorised if the person in question has an airline ticket with a confirmed reservation. Yachts may not stay longer than one year. There is a branch of the Immigration Office near the Fare Manihini (Visitors' Bureau) directly on the waterfront.

Foreign Consulates in Tahiti

Austria
> BP 4560, Papeete; Honorary Consul Paul Maetz (☎ 43-91-14 office, 43-21-22 home)

Belgium
> BP 1602, Papeete; Honorary Consul Pierre Soufflet (☎ 42-53-89 office, 53-27-20 home)

Chile
> BP 952, Papeete, Immeuble Norman Hall, Rue du General de Gaulle; Honorary Consul Roger Divin (☎ 43-89-19 office, 43-25-67 home)

Finland
> BP 2870, Papeete; Honorary Consul Janine Laguesse (☎ 42-97-39 home)

Germany
> BP 452, Papeete, Rue Le Bihan-Fautaua; Honorary Consul Claude Eliane Weinmann (☎ 42-99-94 office, 42-56-30 home)

Italy
> BP 420, Papeete, c/o Tikichimic, Fare Ute, Papeete; Honorary Consul Augusto Confalonieri (☎ 58-20-29 office, 43-91-70 home)

Korea
> BP 2061, Papeete; Honorary Consul Bernard Baudry (☎ 43-04-47 office, 42-58-96 home)

Monaco
> BP 33 Papeete; Honorary Consul Paul Emile Victor (☎ 42-53-29)

Norway
> BP 306, Papeete, c/o Services Mobil, Fare Ute Papeete; Honorary Consul Victor Siu (☎ 42-97-21 office, 42-05-62 home)

Netherlands
> BP 2804, Papeete, c/o Immeuble Wong Liao, Building d'Alsace, Papeete; Honorary Consul Jan Den Freejen Engelbertus (☎ 42-49-37 office, 43-58-74 home)

Sweden
> BP 2, Papeete, c/o Ets Soari, Passage Cardella; Honorary Consul Michel Solari (☎ 42-53-59 office, 42-47-60 home)

MONEY

The currency used in French Polynesia is the Central Pacific Franc or CFP. Notes come in denominations of 500, 1000, 5000 and 10,000, and coins in denominations of 1, 2, 5, 10, 20, 50 and 100. Visa credit cards are accepted (banks will give you a cash advance), as are American Express and, in some places, Master Charge. Travellers' cheques are easily cashed.

Exchange Rates

The current value of the CFP (at the time of writing) in relation to selected major international currencies is:

US$1	=	97 CFP
A$1	=	71 CFP
UK£1	=	174 CFP
C$1	=	84 CFP
NZ$1	=	53 CFP
DM1	=	61 CFP

Banking Hours

Regular banking hours vary slightly. The Bank of Tahiti opens for business at 7.45 am and closes for lunch from 11.45 am to 2.00 pm. It reopens at 2.00 pm and closes at 4.00 pm. The Bank of Polynesia has the same hours except that it opens at 7.30 am. The Bank of Indochina is open from 7.30 am to 3.30 pm. Some banks (eg the Bank of Tahiti) are open from 7.45 to 11.30 am on Saturday mornings. If you need to get to a bank on Saturday your hotel can tell you which is the nearest one open. Note that banks charge a standard 350 CFP commission on every travellers' cheque transaction.

Tipping

Tipping is discouraged by the tourism office but Tahitians have been introduced to this practice and are not averse to it.

WHAT TO BRING

Dress in Tahiti is almost always casual and, because of the warm climate, it is easy to subscribe to the adage 'travel light'. Unless you are planning to travel to the outer fringes of French Polynesia, say the Austral Islands, you can be certain it will always be warm, even at night. Therefore, clothing should be light. Bathing suit and shorts (for both men and women) are always practical and fashionable. Cotton shirts and dresses are also necessary, as are sandals, a light plastic raincoat or a windbreaker for the odd tropical downpour, a light sweater, a hat to shield you from the intense rays of the sun, sunscreen, insect repellent, first-aid kit and perhaps some small souvenirs or toys for Tahitian children.

TOURIST OFFICES

The main information office (OPATTI) is on the quay nearly opposite the Vaima Shopping Centre, in a cluster of brown buildings constructed to resemble traditional Tahitian dwellings (fares). It is known as the Fare Manihini, which translates as 'guest house'. Inside you will likely find several demi Tahitian women who will be more than happy to give you information, in perfect English. The address of the Tahiti office is Fare Manihini (☎ 42-96-26), Boulevard Pomare, BP 65, Papeete, Tahiti, French Polynesia.

Overseas Reps

Overseas addresses of the Tahiti Tourist Board are:

Chile
    Delegacion General de Tahiti, Santiago Centro Edificio, Suite 709, Box 14002 STG 021 Santiago (☎ (562) 696-10-08, (005) 262-76-10-08)
France
    Office du Tourisme de Tahiti et ses Îles, 28, Boulevard Saint Germain, 75005 Paris (☎ (46) 34-50-59)
Hong Kong
    Tahiti Tourist Promotion Board, c/o Pacific Leisure Group, Tung Ming Building, 10th floor, 40, Des Voeux Rd, Central Hong Kong (☎ (5) 241-361)
Japan
    Tahiti Tourist Promotion Board, Sankyo Building (No 20), Room 802, 3-11-5 Iidabashi, Chiyoda-Ku, Tokyo (☎ (03) 265-0468)

New Caledonia
    Office de Tourisme de Tahiti, BP 443, 12em etage, Immeuble Indosuez, Rue Marechal Foch, Noumea, New Caledonia (☎ 27-81-03)
New Zealand
    Tahiti Tourist Promotion Board, No 4 Ophir St, Newton, Auckland, New Zealand (☎ (649) 732-649)
USA
    Tahiti Tourist Promotion Board, 9841 Airport Blvd, Suite 1108, Los Angeles, California 90045 (☎ (310) 649-2884). For free information on Tahiti call UTA airlines.

BUSINESS HOURS & HOLIDAYS
Business Hours

Most businesses open their doors between 8 and 10 am and close at 5 pm. Some larger stores stay open until 7 pm; smaller family corner stores may not close until 10 pm. There is usually a very long lunch hour (noon to 2 pm), but banks are open during this time. Shops close at 11 am on Saturdays. Banking hours are 7.45 am to 3.30 pm Monday to Friday, and some banks (eg the Bank of Tahiti) are open on Saturday from 7.45 to 11.30 am. Exchange counters are available at Faaa International Airport.

Holidays & Festivals
New Year's Day
    Celebrated on 1 January, friends and families gather for merrymaking.
Chinese New Year
    Celebrated during January/February with dances and fireworks.
Miss Bora Bora Contest
    Held in April.
Maire Day
    Fern exhibition held in May in Papeete followed by a ball.
Miss Moorea Contest
    Held in June
Miss Tahiti & Miss Tiurai Contest
    Miss Tahiti is chosen in July to represent the country in international beauty pageants. Miss Tiurai reigns over the Bastille Day celebrations.
Bastille Day
    France's Independence Day and the biggest holiday of the year is celebrated on 14 July and is known as *La Fête* by the French and Tiurai by the Polynesians, the carnival actually begins on 29 June and lasts about three weeks.
Night of the Guitar & Ute
    In August local musicians compete in performing *ute*, satirical improvisational songs.

Te Vahine e te Tiare (The Woman & the Flower)
Tahitian women dress up for floral theme ball in September.

All Saints Day
On 1 November families visit cemeteries and illuminate graves with candles.

Thousand Flowers Contest & Pareu Day
In November there are exhibitions of flowers followed by (you guessed it) another ball. Attendees wear *pareu*, or wraparound dresses.

Tiare Tahiti (National Flower Day)
In December flowers are distributed throughout Papeete – on the streets, in hotels and on departing planes. Yet another ball.

CULTURAL EVENTS
Bastille Day (Tiurai)

The Bastille Day celebration, or Tiurai as it is called in French Polynesia, is a month-long orgy of dance, food and drink. It is the islands' most important holiday, a combination of Mardi Gras, 4th of July and Walpurgis Night rolled into one. During this period, which lasts from the end of June until the third week of July, business grinds to a halt and is replaced by serious partying. Many island communities put on their own *fête* consisting of traditional dance competitions, rock'n'roll bands, foot and canoe races, javelin throwing, spearfishing and other sports activities. The largest celebration occurs in Papeete, which assumes a carnival air. There the waterfront is turned into a fairground crowded with hastily constructed booths, makeshift bars and restaurants, a ferris wheel and a grandstand for viewing the dance competition.

The event opens with a parade featuring beauty contestants, sports association members, folkloric and tamure (dance) groups, and flower-studded floats. On the first day of the celebrations there is usually a historic re-enactment at Marae Arahurahu. In times past this has been the 'crowning of the king' ceremony. On Bastille Day (14 July) there is a military parade which begins with a salvo of canons, followed by a sea of uniforms, brass bands playing military marches, and baton twirling troupes of majorettes. The grand finale in the evening is the 'Ball' held at the mayor's residence.

The three weeks are crowded with numerous activities such as horse races, speedboat races, bicycle races, parachuting displays, motorcycle competition, an international golf tournament and water-skiing. There is even room for the more traditional Polynesian sports of fruit-carrying races and archery contests, as well as displays of tattooing, basket weaving, tapa cloth manufacture, copra cutting, and displays of Polynesian arts and crafts.

During this period French Polynesians from throughout the islands and tourists from all over the world converge on Tahiti to watch the dancing and partake in the good times. It is not unusual for Tahitians to stay up all night and frolic, sleep through the day, start chug-a-lugging Hinano beer and begin the cycle again. When it comes to dissipation, Tahitians are indefatigable; their capacity to enjoy themselves is superhuman. Tiurai is above all a time to socialise, forget your troubles, spend a good deal of money on liquor and perhaps mend fences with a neighbour.

One criticism that long-time residents of Papeete have about Tiurai in their town is that it has become too commercialised. During the holiday, prices shoot up and merchants make windfall profits. Commercialised or not, Tiurai in Papeete is packed with shoulder-to-shoulder throngs of people shoving their way along the carnival row. In one section, a crowd gathers in front of madly gesticulating Chinese shills, who spin the wheels of fortune in their gambling booths and attempt to outbark each other on bullhorns. Meanwhile, locals try their luck at the shooting galleries, vendors hawk kewpie dolls and cowboy hats, and young children tug their parents' arms in the direction of the merry-go-round. The temporary outdoor cafes selling beer, barbecued chicken and steak swell with inebriated tourists and Tahitians.

Outside the grandstand entrance, the scene is a mob of performers and gawkers. Troupes of tasselled, straw-skirted dancers mill around on the grass awaiting their turn to go on stage. They are the crème de la crème of all French Polynesian dancers. The troupe directors hype up the youngsters like football coaches before a big game. The air is thick with nervous energy and the scent of Tiare Tahiti blossoms. Nearly everyone has a crown of flowers on their head, or a single blossom behind the ear.

Tiurai offers more than a carnival atmosphere. For local entrepreneurs of the smaller island communities, the festival is economically important. Not only is it a big affair for the established merchants, but ordinary families can cash in on the holiday spirit by setting up small concessions selling food and liquor. The Tiurai festivities are in part subsidised by the French Polynesian government and the individual communities, which share the cost of maintenance and cash prizes for the various sports and competitions. The celebration also performs an important educational function. It provides French Polynesian youth with an outlet for traditional cultural expression, which is in increasing danger of being lost with the encroaching influence of Western culture.

POST & TELECOMMUNICATIONS
Post
The French Polynesian postal system is generally efficient. Due to the numerous flights in and out of Papeete, delivery time from the islands to the USA, Australia and Europe is usually no longer than a week. The main post office in Papeete is a gleaming 20th-century wonder. Stamps from Polynesie Française are gorgeous and sought after by collectors. Sets are available in special philatelic windows.

Foreigners wishing to receive mail may do so by asking at the poste restante (general delivery) window. Holders of American Express cards and/or travellers' cheques may receive mail at the American Express office at Tahiti Tours, Rue Jeanne d'Arc. Telegrams, telexes and a 'fax' service are also available from the post office. Hours are 7.30 am to 5.00 pm on weekdays and 7.30 to 11.30 am on Saturdays.

Most postal addresses given in this book include a BP (boîte postale), or post office box number.

Telephone
The phone service in Tahiti is quite good. There are a few public phones scattered here and there but more often than not in an emergency you may have to ask a shopkeeper's permission to make a call. A local phone call costs 50 to 100 CFP. Long-distance or overseas calls can be made at post offices and from hotels.

TIME
French Polynesia is 10 hours behind GMT, two hours behind US Pacific Standard time and 21 hours behind Australian Eastern Standard time. Thus, when it is noon Sunday in Tahiti, it is 2 pm Sunday in Los Angeles and 9 am Monday in Sydney. Once in French Polynesia you will realise that locals have their own standard of time, usually one to two hours behind what you had planned.

ELECTRICITY
The current is 220 volts AC in the more modern hotels and 110 volts in the older facilities. Don't plug in a thing until you check with the hotel. If in doubt check the voltage on the light. Many hotels also have converters for your appliances.

BOOKS
A formidable number of books have been written about French Polynesia, some of them only readily available in the islands themselves. There are also several good bookshops in French Polynesia.

Bookshops
Hachette Pacifique on Avenue Bruat is the largest book distributor in French Polynesia and has several bookshops (known as librairies) in Papeete. They stock a limited number of English titles as well as US magazines. There are stores at the Latin Quarter branch, Rue Gauguin and Vaima Shopping Centre (upstairs branch).

Other bookshops include Libraire Klima, Place Notre Dame; Ping Pong, next to the Moana Iti restaurant on Boulevard Pomare (sell and trade books); Le Kioske, in the Vaima Shopping Centre (street level); and

Bookstore, across the side street from the main post office in Papeete.

Exploration & History

The classic edition of Cook's logbooks is *The Voyages of the Endeavour, 1768-1771* (1955) by Captain James Cook, edited by J C Beaglehole, four volumes.

Tahiti: a Paradise Lost (1984) by David Howarth is the best book I've encountered on the experience of the early explorers of French Polynesia – Wallis, Cook, Bougainville and company. It's fascinating and reads almost like a novel. A must for South Pacific addicts.

The Fatal Impact by Alan Moorehead is, along with Howarth's book, the best available historical account of early Tahiti. It centres mainly around the three voyages of Captain Cook, portraying him as a humane commander but with the premise that contact with white civilisation in general was to have horrible repercussions. Moorehead points out that within 80 years of Cook's visit to Tahiti the population decreased from 40,000 to 9000 and the culture deteriorated because of disuse, by the end of the 19th century Australia's coastal Aborigines had been decimated, and 50 years after Cook's exploration of the Antarctic icepack the once plentiful whales and seals had been virtually wiped out.

Mutiny and Romance in the South Seas: A Companion to the Bounty Adventure (1989) by Sven Wahlroos is a must for *Bounty* enthusiasts. Wahlroos, a Finnish-born psychologist who practises in southern California, describes his book as one that 'sets forth the known facts of the story and also points to those circumstances of which we cannot be sure'. He strongly feels that Ian Ball's *Pitcairn: Children of Mutiny* which is mentioned in this book's section on the *Bounty* saga is not an entirely reliable source of knowledge on the subject.

Modern Accounts

Thor Heyerdahl's *Kon-Tiki* is a contemporary nonfiction classic describing the 1948 voyage of a crew of Europeans aboard a Polynesian-style raft sailing from the coast of South America to French Polynesia. The purpose of the voyage was to 'prove' Heyerdahl's theory that Polynesians may have migrated from the South American continent instead of Asia. Whether or not you subscribe to Heyerdahl's ideas, the book is a great adventure story.

In *Moruroa Mon Amour – the French Nuclear Tests in the Pacific* (1977) by Bengt & Marie-Therese Danielsson, the authors trace the history of the bomb in French Polynesia and the socioeconomic effects the programme has had in Tahiti. Danielsson, who originally came to French Polynesia aboard the *Kon-Tiki*, has been the leading spokesperson against the nuclear testing programme and at times a lonely voice of conscience.

Tin Roofs & Palm Trees (1977) by Robert Trumbull is a serious socioeconomic/political overview of the South Pacific nations with particular emphasis on their emergence into the 20th century. Trumbull is a former *New York Times* correspondent and writes with authority on the subject. This is a good primer on the background of the modern-day South Pacific.

Tahiti, Island of Love by Robert Langdon is, as one of my esteemed colleagues says, one of the more 'popular' accounts of Tahiti's history. Though most likely out of print, it's worth looking for.

A Writer's Notebook (1984) by W Somerset Maugham is a collection of notes, journals and character sketches, some of which Maugham later used in his short stories and novels. Though the collection covers the period 1892 to 1944, 40 pages are devoted to his travels in the Pacific and include Tahiti, Samoa, Fiji and Hawaii. For Maugham lovers, the reading is fascinating.

Travel Guides

John McDermott, author of *How to Get Lost & Found in Tahiti* (Waikiki Publishing, Honolulu, 1979), is a retired ad man who likes to get 'lost and found' in the Pacific. His books are rambling, chatty accounts of his wanderings with his wife (the 'lady navigator') and contain some interesting tidbits of information if you don't mind wading through a lot of verbiage.

Tahiti Circle Island Tour Guide (Les Editions du Pacifique, Papeete, 1981) by Bengt Danielsson is the most complete historical tour guide available on Tahiti, or perhaps any South Pacific island for that matter. Exhaustively researched and sardonic in tone, it is available only in Tahiti.

Moorea (Les Editions du Pacifique, Papeete, 1983) by Claude Robineau with photos by Erwin Christian has the same format as the Marquesas book by the same publisher. Again, very good background information and great shots by Christian, but it's only available in bookstores in Tahiti.

Moorea – A Complete Guide (Millwood Press, Wellington, 1982) by James Siers is another background book on Moorea. Whereas the previous book is more concerned with history and culture, this guide reads more like a slick brochure or a travel edition of *Vogue*. It gives lots of practical information about shopping, where to eat, where to stay and what to do, and has very nice photography, but is very commercial.

Bora Bora E (Milas Hinshaw Productions, Hollywood, 1984) by Milas Hinshaw is a useful guidebook and map to Bora Bora. It contains information on all the restaurants, historical sites, hotels and so on. It's gossipy and entertaining, especially Hinshaw's unnerving experiences with tupa'pau (spirits). Hinshaw's most memorable quote is 'E tai oe i teie puta ia ite oe i te parau mau' (Read this book and know the truth). Decide for yourself.

The Marquesas (Les Editions du Pacifique, Papeete, 1982) by Greg Denning with photos by Erwin Christian is a comprehensive overview of the Marquesas with great photos by the renowned Tahitian photographer. It's about the best book available on the Marquesas. This book is sold only in Tahiti.

Island Tales

Eugene Burdick's *The Blue of Capricorn* (1977) is a delightful collection of short stories and nonfiction essays about the South Pacific. Burdick, a master of the craft and coauthor of *The Ugly American*, explores in particular white people's fascination with the tropics. It's one of the best collections of the South Pacific genre available.

South Seas Tales by Jack London is not London's most famous work but includes a few good tales including 'The House of Mapuhi', the slanderous 'story' of an avaricious pearl buyer. It's based on a real-life character with whom London had an axe to grind. The real-life person sued London and collected a handsome settlement.

Typee: a Real Romance of the South Seas; *Omoo: a Narrative of Adventures in the South Seas, a Sequel to Typee* and *Marquesas Islands* by Herman Melville are based on Melville's experiences on the islands.

Art, Culture, Archeology & The Tropics

Terence Barrow's *The Art of Tahiti* (Thames & Hudson, 1979) gives an overview of Polynesian art before European contact, with emphasis on Tahiti.

Noa Noa by Paul Gauguin is an autobiographical account of his life in Tahiti.

Tahitians – Mind & Experience in the Society Islands (1973) by Robert I Levy is a tome-like work written by an anthropologist for anthropologist types. It's a bit unwieldy but packed with all kinds of cultural information – a good reference book.

Exploring Tropical Islands and Seas – An Introduction for the Traveler and Amateur Naturalist (Prentice Hall, 1984) by Frederic Martini is not specifically on French Polynesia but is nonetheless a fine primer on the natural history of tropical islands. The title explains it all. Subjects covered include general island environment, coral reefs, marine life, geology and sharks.

For readers interested in hard-core 'Polynesian' archeology, two good books are: *Man's Conquest of the Pacific* (Oxford University Press, 1979) by Peter Bellwood and *The Prehistory of Polynesia* (Harvard University, 1979) edited by J D Jennings.

Those interested in following up on the

Tahiti Literati

Ever since its depiction as a Garden of Eden by 19th-century romantics, Tahiti has attracted not only missionaries and vagabonds but artists and writers as well. The writers who have sojourned in French Polynesia read like a Who's Who of world literature. Here is a summary of their varied but always piquant experiences.

Herman Melville In June 1842 the *Acushnet*, a Yankee whaler, dropped anchor off Nuku Hiva in the Marquesas. Aboard the vessel, 22-year-old Herman Melville couldn't wait to step ashore. He had already faced 1½ years of deprivation at sea and knew he wouldn't be returning home until all the whale oil barrels had been filled, perhaps two, three or even four years later. He and a friend named Toby stuffed a few biscuits inside their clothing and jumped ship. They hid in the deep, forested recesses of the island's interior, safe from the ship's crew, who would surely come looking for them. They hiked for days on end with little food and no shelter. The fact that Melville's leg was burning with infection made the trek even more excruciating. The two young men found their way to the Typee Valley, home of a tribe known for its ferocity.

Toby disappeared while looking for medical aid for his friend and Melville spent the next four months with the Typees, an experience that would be the basis for his first book, *Typee*. He was treated well by the Marquesans, who gave him a servant and royal attention from Mehevi, the chief. However, Melville was never sure of the natives' intentions. Was he being treated as a distinguished visitor or simply being fattened for the kill? After all, these people were cannibals.

Fortunately for world literature, Melville survived his sojourn with the Typee, during which he was held in a sort of protective custody. He dwelt with the Marquesans neither in bliss nor in terror. He observed closely and made some startling revelations. 'There were', said Melville, 'none of the thousand sources of irritation that the ingenuity of civilized man has created to mar his own felicity.' He noted that there were no debtors, no orphans, no destitute, no lovesick maidens, no grumpy bachelors, no melancholy youth, no spoiled brats and none of the root of all evil – money.

Melville adapted well, enjoying the company of a vahine named Fayaway and the companionship of the men. His foot, however, was still inflamed and spiritually he was isolated. He needed medical care but the Typees were unwilling to let him go. His situation was well known on the island and with the help of sympathetic natives and a captain who was hard up for crew members, he escaped by joining up with the

Herman Melville

Sydney whaler the *Lucy Ann*, which sailed to Tahiti.

Apparently the conditions on this vessel – inedible food, cockroach and rat infestation and rotten rigging – were so god-awful that upon reaching Tahiti Melville decided to join the crew members in a mutiny rather than continue. His fellow travellers – with such romantic names as 'Doctor Long Ghost' (the ship's surgeon!), 'Bembo' (a tattooed Maori harpooner), 'Jingling Joe', 'Long Jim', 'Black Dan', 'Bungs', 'Blunt Bill' and 'Flash Jack' – didn't need much persuading. When they refused to sail and complained to British Consul Charles Wilson in Papeete, Wilson decided against the mutineers and, with the support of the French Admiral Du Petit-Thouars, had them locked up. Melville was imprisoned in the Calabooza Beretanee, the local gaol. After his release six weeks later, he went to the remote village of Temae on Moorea (now near the airport) and talked the chief into allowing the women to dance the 'lory-lory' (the precursor of the tamure), an erotic, passionate performance that the missionaries had, naturally, forbidden.

Four years later Melville laboriously put together *Typee: a Peep at Polynesian Life*, which received immediate attention in America and Europe. Some critics hailed it, some doubted its authenticity, and others called it 'racy'. The missionaries (who weren't treated too kindly in the book) found it appalling. Both *Typee* and *Omoo* were outspoken tirades against the ruination of the Pacific by 'civilisation'. Why, Melville asked, should the natives be forced to participate in an alien church, to kowtow to a foreign government, and to adopt strange and harmful ways of living? In *The Fatal Impact*, Alan Moorehead writes that although Melville was 'possibly libellous and certainly scandalous in much that he wrote', his account of the 'sleaziness and inertia that had overtaken life' in Papeete in 1842 is remarkably vivid. Perhaps Melville was remarkably accurate as well. Moorehead says that many of the Tahitians – by this time caught between the missionaries, the whalers and finally the French – had 'lost the will to survive – the effort to adjust to the outside world had been too much'.

Pierre Loti Midshipman Louis Marie Julien Viaud, who later became known to the world as Pierre Loti, first came to Tahiti in the 1880s aboard a French naval vessel. His largely autobiographical book, *The Marriage of Loti*, brought him fame and is credited with influencing Paul Gauguin to come to Tahiti. In the book he describes his friendship with Queen Pomare IV and his all-consuming love affair with Rarahu, a young girl from Bora Bora.

Loti's book tells how he came upon Rarahu bathing in a pool (which still can be visited today) in the Fautaua Valley near Papeete. There he witnessed the girl accepting a length of red ribbon from an elderly Chinese as payment for a kiss. Rarahu was poor and this type of behaviour was not unusual for a girl of little means.

Nevertheless, as a result of what the incensed Frenchman saw, the Chinese in Tahiti suffered for years following the 1881 publication of *The Marriage of Loti*. Despite Loti's virulently anti-Chinese propaganda, the book did give an accurate account of life in Tahiti during the late 19th century.

Pierre Loti

Robert Louis Stevenson

Robert Louis Stevenson Robert Louis Stevenson arrived in the Marquesas with his wife and mother in 1888, which marked the first leg of his six-year voyage to the South Seas aboard the *Casco*. The South Pacific held him spellbound and in the Marquesas the health of the nearly always frail writer improved dramatically. He spent his days wading in the lagoon, searching for shells, or on horseback. The Stevenson clan were so impressed by the generosity and kindness of the locals that even Stevenson's mother, a staunch supporter of the missionaries, began to question whether such activities were actually beneficial to the natives.

From the Marquesas the *Casco* set sail for the Tuamotu atoll of Fakareva, where the Stevensons spent the balmy evenings trading tales with Donat Rimareau, the half-caste French governor of the island. The author's *The Isle of Voices* utilised Rimareau's tales to a great degree.

Tahiti was the next stop on the *Casco's* itinerary. The travellers found Papeete to have a 'half and halfness' between Western and Tahitian culture which they disliked and soon set sail for the other side of the island. There the Stevensons befriended a Tahitian princess (whom Pierre Loti had much admired) and a chief, both of whom helped them considerably. By this time Stevenson had become very ill, the family was short of money and the *Casco* needed extensive repair. The generous Tahitians, who offered the wayfarers food, shelter and moral support, were a godsend. The long stopover allowed Stevenson time to work and recuperate. Stevenson's wife wrote that the clan sailed from Tahiti for Honolulu on Christmas Day of 1888 'in a very thankful frame of mind'.

Somerset Maugham

Somerset Maugham Among the works of the English writer Somerset Maugham is *The Moon & Sixpence*, a novel based on the life of Paul Gauguin. During WW I, when according to Maugham 'the old South Seas characters were by necessity confined to the islands', he visited Tahiti to research the book. There he not only culled reminiscences of the painter from people who knew him but also learned more of writers like Loti, Brooke, Stevenson and London. Like those writers before him, Maugham was entranced by the magic of the South Seas and spent his time interviewing everyone who knew Gauguin, including businessmen, a sea captain, a hotel proprietor and others. In Maugham's words, he wanted to make the protagonist of his novel as 'credible as possible'.

Despite Maugham's enchantment with Tahiti, most of his short stories about the South Pacific — including 'Rain', which immortalised the prostitute Sadie Thompson — took place in Samoa. Of this the author commented, 'The really significant fiction of the world today involves a husband and wife relationship, the problems that lovers encounter and overcome, a cuckolded man, a jilted woman, an unrequited or pretended love for the other. From sexual conflicts we have our revenge and homicidal motives'. However, Maugham observed that in a place like Tahiti, 'where there are sexual licenses, excesses, the condoning attitude on infidelity, a tolerance of promiscuity, and an absence of sexual possessiveness, there does not exist the emotional tension that precipitates human drama...' In addition, Maugham asserted that 'Tahiti is a French possession, and the French with their *laissez faire* and *ménage à trois* tolerance of sexual philanderings and indulgences don't really provide believable fictional protagonists for any human triangle, story or play unless you want to make a comedy or farce out of the situation'.

Paul Gauguin's case, however, falls into a different category. When the artist came to Tahiti, 'the languor of this island, the Polynesian playfulness, the castrative sexuality that abounded there, could not save him from his ultimate and wretched fate. That of course was Gauguin's predetermined course of tragedy,' Maugham said.

Rupert Brooke In 1915, on a hospital ship off Skyros, the great soldier/poet of the Edwardian age, Rupert Brooke, died of food poisoning at the tender age of 28.

While visiting the west coast of the USA in 1913, Brooke had suddenly decided to tour the South Seas. He came to Tahiti in January 1914 and lingered there until April, nursing an injury caused by grazing against coral. During this time he fell in love with a beautiful Tahitian, Taata (who he called 'Mamua') and composed perhaps his three best poems, 'The Great Lover', 'Retrospect' and 'Tiare Tahiti'. According to biographer John Lehman, it was with Mamua that Brooke most likely had the only 'perfect and surely consummated love-affair of his life'. Wrote Brooke in 'Tiare Tahiti':

Mamua when our laughter ends,
And hearts and bodies, brown as white,
Are dust about the doors of friends,
Or scent a-blowing down the night,
Then, oh! then the wise agree,
Comes our immortality...

On returning to San Francisco Brooke's thoughts returned to Tahiti and his lover continued to haunt him. Months later, on his deathbed in the Aegean, he wrote in his last letter of instructions to a friend: 'Try to inform Taata of my death. Mlle Taata, Hotel Tiare, Papeete, Tahiti. It might find her. Give her my love'. Several years later, when Somerset Maugham came to Tahiti to research a book on Gauguin, Brooke's old friends still wept uncontrollably at the mention of his native name, 'Purpure', the only name they knew him by.

Rupert Brooke

Jack London

Jack London Perhaps the most controversial US writer of his day, Jack London came to French Polynesia in 1906 on the ill-fated voyage of the *Snark*. He first arrived in the Marquesas after nearly dying of thirst at sea when one of the crew members inadvertently left the water tap open during a storm. The Londons stayed on Nuku Hiva for several weeks, renting the house used by Robert Louis Stevenson. They also visited the Typee Valley, immortalised in Melville's *Typee*, one of London's favourite childhood books. London was, however, disappointed by what he saw. Melville's vision of 19th-century French Polynesia no longer existed and London referred to the natives as 'half-breeds', blaming the whites for the corrupting influence that had decimated the Marquesan race physically and spiritually. He spent his days feasting on tropical fruits, relaxing in the sun, collecting curios and trying to ward off huge wasps and *no-nos*, vicious flies that inflict a nasty bite.

Next stop was Tahiti, where London was greeted by the news that his cheques had bounced back home. To make matters worse, he did not get along with some of the French officials, and thieves stole many items from his boat. Perhaps this is why the writer did not speak of Tahiti in more flattering terms. In *The Cruise of the Snark* he wrote that: 'Tahiti is one of the most beautiful spots in the world', but that it was for the most part inhabited by 'human vermin'. He also took a dislike to a well-known pearl buyer, Emile Levy, and in *South Sea Tales* unfairly depicted the Frenchman as an avaricious businessman who cheated a native out of a huge pearl and then met a horrible death. London did not bother to change Levy's name or physical description in the story, and the pearl buyer was furious. Even the other residents of Tahiti, who were not terribly fond of the hard-driving businessman, thought London had gone too far. Levy successfully sued London, who had long since returned to the USA but paid dearly for his outpouring of venom.

Nordhoff & Hall James Norman Hall and Charles Nordhoff first met in the military service at the end of WW I when they were commissioned to write a history of the Lafayette Flying Corps. They were vastly different in temperament. Hall, a native of Iowa, was shy, optimistic and romantic. Nordhoff, raised in California, was outwardly more confident but pessimistic and sceptical. They distrusted each other at first, but their opposite natures were complementary and they eventually became the best of friends. Nordhoff convinced Hall that Tahiti was the place to go and write. When the *Atlantic* assigned them a piece on Tahiti and gave them an advance, they were on their way to the South Seas.

Years later, Tahiti had become their home and an outpouring of articles and books by the two ensued. They wrote some works separately but continued to work well as a team, and after their collaboration on a boy's adventure, Nordhoff proposed doing another book in the same vein. Hall refused but instead suggested an idea that became the most famous seagoing novel written in the 20th century – *Mutiny on the Bounty*.

During their initial research Nordhoff and Hall could scarcely believe that the most recent book on the *Bounty* incident had been published in 1831! No one had ever ventured to write a fictionalised account of the event even though it was the kind of story that begs to be transformed into literature. Based at the Aina Pare' hotel in Papeete, the two writers plunged into their work. From the British Museum they procured accounts of the voyage, the mutiny, Bligh's open-sea voyage and the bloody Pitcairn experience, along with copies of the court martial proceedings and the Admiralty blueprints of the *Bounty*. Both immersed themselves in 19th-century prose, which helped to set a common style. The resulting narrative was divided into three sections: the *Mutiny On the Bounty*, *Men Against the Sea* (Bligh's open-sea voyage) and *Pitcairn Island* (the adventures of Fletcher Christian, his mutineer cohorts and the Tahitians who accompanied them). The trilogy was completed in 1934, after five years of work. Fifty years and three cinematic versions later, the story still hasn't lost its charm and fascination.

Hall was buried facing Matavai Bay where the *Bounty* dropped anchor and where he and Nordhoff used to sit discussing their work. A bronze plaque on the grave is inscribed with a poem he wrote as a young boy:

Look to the Northward, stranger
Just over the hillside, there
Have you in your travels seen
A land more passing fair? ■

research in Huahine conducted by the venerable Yosihiko H Sinoto of the Bishop Museum should look for:

'Report on the preliminary excavation of an early habitation site on Huahine, Society Islands' in *Journal de la Société des Oceanistes* XXXI (1974): 143-86.
'Excavations on Huahine, French Polynesia' in *Pacific Studies* 3 (1979): 1.
'The Huahine Excavation: Discovery of an Ancient Polynesian Canoe' in *Archeology* 36/2 (1983): 10-15.
'Archeological Excavations of the Vaito'otia and Fa'ahia Sites on Huahine Island, French Polynesia' in *National Geographic Society Research Reports* 15 (1983): 583-99.

MEDIA

The local radio station, France Region 3, also known as Radio Tahiti, broadcasts in French and Tahitian. Along with local news and international news from the national French network, it features a pop music format with selections by French, US and Tahitian artists. The one television channel, which broadcasts in colour, carries drama, quiz shows, highbrow French programmes, interviews, locally produced news and footage from international correspondents. The station also broadcasts in Tahitian and French. A new development in Tahiti broadcasting is the privately owned radio stations. These include Radio Tiare, which broadcasts in French and has mostly a pop music format, as well as two smaller district stations in Papara and Papenoo.

Newspapers & Magazines

Scattered throughout Papeete are kiosks and bookshops selling the *International Herald Tribune* (flown in regularly from Paris) and the Pacific edition of *Time* and *Newsweek*, as well as French, German and other European publications. The kiosk at the Vaima Shopping Centre on the waterfront is a convenient place to browse.

French Polynesia is served by two daily French-language newspapers, *Les Nouvelles* and *Le Dépêche de Tahiti*, an English-language weekly, *Tahiti Beach Press*, which caters exclusively for tourists, and a new monthly publication, *Tahiti Sun Press*, published by US expat Al Prince. Prince covers the local scene extensively (often better than the French press) and has excellent travel trade reportage on hotels, airlines and tourism in general. The paper also has information on museums, special events and the like. The tabloid-style weekly is given away free at most hotels in French Polynesia.

A local French-language, general-interest magazine is *Tahitirama*, which has the TV scheduling. Three English-language magazines circulating throughout the Pacific are *Pacific Islands Monthly (PIM)*, *Pacific* and *Islands Business*. *PIM*, published in Sydney, is an excellent regional publication and a venerable institution in the Pacific, oriented mostly toward the old Anglo colonies. *Pacific* (formerly *New Pacific*), published in Honolulu, is a younger upstart that also covers the Pacific basin but has better reportage of former US Trust Territories and current US dependencies than its rival. *Islands Business* is a Fiji-based monthly magazine which attempts to cover business and political developments in the Pacific. In my opinion, since the 1987 coup in Fiji, management at *Islands Business* has struggled to maintain its objectivity, given what must be tremendous pressure to self-censure local reportage.

FILM & PHOTOGRAPHY

Photographers are permitted to take 10 rolls of film when they leave the islands. Should you need them, film and photographic accessories are readily available in Papeete's modern shops but they are much more expensive than you will be accustomed to. Colour prints can be developed from Kodacolor in one hour at QSS in Papeete's Vaima Shopping Centre. Agfachrome, Ektachrome 50 and Fujichrome R100 processing are also available at other places. The rule of thumb is to always take twice as much film as you think you'll need.

Keep in mind that daylight is very intense in the tropics so if in doubt when shooting film, underexpose. That is, if you really want that photo, shoot according to what your normal meter reading dictates and then shoot another at a third to one full stop under. It's always best, of course, to take photos at dawn or dusk for best lighting conditions.

Always keep film dry and cool, and have your camera cleaned if exposed excessively to the elements – the humidity and salt air can ruin sensitive photo equipment in no time. If you plan to go through customs at airports frequently, it's advisable to buy a laminated lead pouch for film, available in any photo shop.

When taking photos of the locals, smile and ask permission first. Most of the time people will be happy to let you photograph them but on other occasions some Tahitians may not want to be part of your future slide show.

HEALTH

Tahiti is malaria-free and inoculations are not required except for those arriving from an area infected with smallpox, cholera or yellow fever, which exempts 99.9% of visitors. Water is generally safe and plentiful in most areas but for the skittish there is always bottled water, Coca-Cola or Hinano beer. To date, I have never had problems with the drinking water anywhere in French Polynesia but have heard reports of visitors with water-borne parasites in the outer islands. It might be prudent to drink the local bottled water when in doubt. It is excellent and very popular with the French.

In some areas mosquitoes are pesky and numerous, ergo it is suggested that you bring a good insect repellent. During certain times of the year dengue fever, which is transmitted by mosquito, is rampant in the islands. Symptoms are flu-like, and include fever, chills and bodily pains. Though rarely serious, it is no fun and can dampen even the healthiest traveller's vacation. In the less expensive hotels and pensions it might even be a good idea to use a mosquito net.

In addition to modern clinics and hospitals in Tahiti many of the outer islands also have hospitals. These include: Moorea, Huahine,

Raiatea, Bora Bora, Maupiti, Rangiroa, Tubuai, Hiva Oa, Ua Huka, and Nuku Hiva. If there is no hospital on an island there will at least be a clinic (or a pharmacy).

For those who have never been in the South Seas, the extreme changes in humidity, food and other conditions may tax the system. The best advice is to take it easy for the first few days until you are acclimatised. Like good scouts you would do well to be prepared and bring sunscreen, Band-Aids, ice bag, baby powder/corn starch, Ace bandage, antacid, laxative, aspirin, cold tablets, cough syrup, antibiotic ointment and antihistamines.

Listed below are guidelines and suggestions gleaned from professional medical sources regarding several major concerns in the South Pacific. Excellent medical care is available in Tahiti so, if in doubt, don't hesitate to see a doctor.

Sunshine

No matter how hot it feels on a given day in the tropics the sun is less filtered by the atmosphere than in other climes and is much more potent. Damage can be done to skin and eyes so take heed. To avoid horrendous sunburn use a sunscreen. Tanning can still occur with sunscreen so don't be discouraged if you are not bronzed overnight. You will just peel sooner if you burn. A bad burn can ruin a vacation and a severe burn will require medical attention. A minor burn can be treated with a cool shower or compresses, soothing cream or steroids. An aspirin two or three times a day will also ease the pain. Some people are allergic to ultraviolet light, which results in redness, itching and pinpoint-sized blisters. For these unfortunates, clothing is the only answer. Fair-skinned people beware in the tropics!

Humidity

Humidity not only means discomfort but also the possibility of rashes caused by yeasts and fungi which thrive in the warm, moist environment. The problem is compounded by tight-fitting clothing rubbing against moist, hot skin. You don't have to be a doctor to deal with these difficulties. Keeping as cool and dry as possible is step number one. Loose-fitting clothing (cotton is best) is also a good idea, as are open-toed sandals. To reduce chafing, talcum powder or corn starch can be applied to body creases (under arms, on necks, under breasts, etc). If all else fails, medications are available to combat fungal and yeast rashes.

Bacterial Infections

Besides fostering the growth of fungi and other microorganisms, the tropics are a prime breeding ground for *Staphylococcus* bacteria. Commonly found on the skin, these little devils can multiply enormously under the right tropical conditions, especially if there is a cut, blister or insect bite releasing the fluids they thrive on. Infection can spread if you are not careful. To prevent this, wash the injury – no matter how insignificant – with soap and then treat it with antibiotic ointment and cover with a clean dressing.

Gastrointestinal Problems

Perhaps the most common complaint of visitors anywhere is the 'travellers' trots', which can stem from any number of causes. There are several things you can do to guard against this: one is to make sure all meals are cooked properly. Virtually all organisms that thrive at body temperature are killed in the cooking process. As mentioned earlier, water in French Polynesia is potable but if you have the slightest fears drink bottled water or soft drinks. Peel or thoroughly wash any fruit or vegetables purchased in a market. Peeling fruit yourself is always a good idea.

A word of warning about ciguatera, a form of poisoning from eating infected fish. It has been reported in French Polynesia and other areas such as Hawaii, Papua New Guinea and northern Australia, and was known to have infected Captain Cook's crew in 1774. The toxin that causes the poisoning is released by a microscopic marine organism living on or near coral reefs, particularly reefs that have been disturbed (eg by development). When fish eat the organism the toxin becomes concentrated in the head,

organs and roe of the fish. Symptoms of ciguatera include: diarrhoea; muscle pain; joint aches; numbness and tingling around the mouth, hands and feet; reversal of temperature sensation (cold objects feel hot and vice versa); nausea; vomiting; chills; itching; headache; sweating and dizziness. If you experience any of these symptoms after eating fish, contact a doctor immediately.

In general, eating seafood in the restaurants is as safe a proposition as anywhere in the world but it is not a good idea to eat any of the reef fish (those caught in the lagoons or on the reef) without a local opinion. In other words, if you catch your own fish, be sure and check with the local people before you cook it (cooking does not eliminate the toxin). It would also be wise to avoid eating fish that have come from a disturbed environment. Also, avoid eating the head, gonads, liver and viscera of fish.

Finally, avoid swimming, walking barefoot or collecting seafood from beaches or lagoons directly in front of settlements. Raw sewage is often dumped or piped into the nearest convenient grounds – ie, the beach that forms the villagers' front yard.

DANGERS & ANNOYANCES

Papeete is very safe by US big-city standards but there are still occasional reports of robberies. Some Tahitians are very poor and occasionally youths may resort to crime. Even though this is rare, visitors are urged to keep an eye on valuables as you would anywhere else in the world. Depositing jewellery and the like in a hotel safe is a good idea. Outside Papeete and on the outer islands there are relatively few problems.

Swimming & Snorkelling

Swimming in the lagoons and rivers is also a safe practice – shark attacks are rare indeed. However, every year there are tragic drownings. A few commonsense precautions are in order: don't swim in the ocean at night; don't wear bright jewellery when swimming or snorkelling; don't swim where fish have just been cleaned or fish remains have been thrown in the sea; and always be aware of the currents in the area where you are swimming. As a general rule, if the locals are swimming in a particular area it's probably safe for you.

When snorkelling avoid contact with sea urchins. In case you weren't aware, their long black spines can inflict a painful wound. Fire coral should also be avoided. You can recognise it by its relatively smooth, almost velvet-like surface and fawn colour.

When reef walking always wear some foot protection against the razor-sharp coral, shells and stone fish that lurk in the sand and gravel. The stone fish is normally about 25 cm long, rests on the bottom and resembles – yes, a stone. It is nearly invisible to the untrained eye and when you find one, hope that it isn't by accident. This creature has very venomous spines and coming into contact with it can be an excruciatingly painful experience. Fortunately stone fish are not very common.

ACTIVITIES

To call the Tahitians sports fanatics is an understatement. On Tahiti there are facilities for golf, bicycle racing, tennis, basketball, track and field, soccer and swimming. French Polynesia also participates in the annual South Pacific Games, a regional Olympics-like event featuring only South Pacific athletes.

Bowling

Those interested in bowling (yes, as in bowling alleys) may visit the Bowling Club in Arue (☎ 42-93-26), which is open Tuesday to Thursday from 5 pm to 1 am, Saturday from 5 pm to 2 am and Sunday from 5 to 10 pm. Depending on the time of day, games will set you back 200 to 420 CFP.

Squash

The Squash Club of Tahiti at the Hotel Matavai (☎ 42-67-67) is a private organisation but will accept guests who wish to play for 500 CFP per half hour.

Tennis

Tennis fanatics can play at any number of

hotels as well as nine private clubs. Most will accept guests for fees in the 250 to 400 CFP range. Clubs include: Fautaua Tennis Club (☎ 42-00-59, 42-38-66) in Pirae; Fei Pi Sports Association (☎ 42-40-60) in Arue; Excelsior Club (☎ 43-91-46) in Papeete; Chon Wa Tennis Club (☎ 42-01-31) in Mamao, Papeete; Club A S Dragon (☎ 43-31-13) in Papeete; and Club A S Phoenix (☎ 42-35-56) in Puunuia.

There are also less formal, 'local' clubs including the Pirae Tennis Club behind Pater Stadium, Tamarii Pater Tennis Club also near the stadium near the Fautaua River, and the J T (Young Tahitian) Tennis League (☎ 43-80-83) in Pirae.

Pirogue (Canoe) Racing

The closest thing to a national sport is *pirogue* (outrigger canoe) racing, which is highlighted during the Tiurai celebrations. Tahitians take great pride in the Polynesian tradition of canoeing and were shocked in 1981 when for the first time the visiting US club, Imua, trounced the leading Tahitian team in a major race.

Golf

At Atimaono in the Papara district, the Olivier Breaud International Golf Course is a 6352-metre par 72 and Tahiti's only course. The area was formerly a cotton plantation established during the US Civil War to provide Europe with the fibre then in short supply. The course was designed by Bob Baldock & Son, a Costa Mesa, California firm that has designed links throughout the USA and Mexico. It features expansive fairways, two artificial lakes and lush greens planted with hybrid Bermuda grass from Hawaii.

It is a 45-minute drive from Papeete and is open daily from 7 am to 6 pm year-round. The course has recently undergone a 100 million CFP renovation which includes a new clubhouse, restaurant, pro shop, pool, tennis courts and driving range. The resident pros are Raymond Tompsett and 'Kani' Tihoni Flores. Green fees are 2000 CFP for adults and 500 CFP per day for children under 18 years. Clubs can be rented for 2000 CFP per day. To get there call Hui Popo (☎ 57-40-32), a tour company that caters to enthusiasts and will pick you up at your hotel Monday to Saturday.

Horse Riding

Club Equestre de Tahiti (☎ 42-70-41) is in Pirae, Papeete, on the road to the Hippodrome. It's open Tuesday to Saturday from 8 am to 7 pm and Sunday from 8 to 11.30 am. The cost is 2500 CFP per hour and there are mountain trail rides.

L'Eperon de Pirae (☎ 42-79-87) is also in Pirae near the Hippodrome. It's open every day (except Monday) from 8 am to 7 pm and has mountain rides for 1800 CFP per hour.

Pony Club of Tahiti (☎ 43-70-41) is at the Hippodrome in Pirae. It's open Wednesday and Friday from 1.30 to 4.30 pm, Saturday from 8 am to 5 pm and Sunday from 9 am to noon. Fees are only 1000 CFP per hour.

Hotel Puunui Equestrian Centre (☎ 57-19-20) is on the premises of the hotel and is open daily. Rates are 1800 CFP per hour.

Scuba Diving & Snorkelling

Most of the islands of French Polynesia are bounded by reefs where tropical fish of every colour and description thrive. Snorkelling, easily learned, is safe and fascinating. Mask and fins (flippers) are readily available and reasonably priced – one of the few reasonably priced items in the entire territory. Fish watching is adequate on Tahiti and Moorea but better snorkelling is found on the outer islands where marine resources have been less affected by humans.

All scuba divers must have a certificate from a doctor indicating that the individual is in good health. A medical exam can be taken in Tahiti if the diver lacks the proper papers. Divers also need a certificate indicating the depth specifications allowed. A lead diver must have an international or a French licence allowing the person full authority to lead divers to designated depths.

The average water temperature in lagoons is 28 to 29°C. Outside the reef, temperatures range from 26 to 28°C.

Dive Specialists For the serious diver there are several dive shops and outfitters who will take you out.

Tahiti Tahiti Aquatique (☎ 42-80-42, 41-08-54), BP 6008, Faaa, Tahiti, is run by Dick Johnson. Adjacent to the Maeva Beach Hotel, this shop operates a variety of nautical activities including glass-bottomed boat trips, cruises and sailboat rentals. Johnson's guided scuba tours range in price from 8000 CFP per person (for rank beginners) to 5000 CFP (one to six people) and 2500 CFP (seven to 20 people). Underwater photography lessons are available. PADI (Professional Association of Diving Instructors) and CMAS (Confédération Mondiale des Activités Subaquatiques, or World Underwater Federation) certification courses are also available. Full PADI/CMAS certification takes about five days.

Tahiti Plongee (☎ 43-62-51, 41-00-62), BP 2192, Papeete is nine km from Papeete at the Marina Lotus and is headed by Henri Pouliquen. It is open seven days a week to divers of all levels. 'First dive' instruction and night diving are available; prices start at 2500 CFP per dive. Instruction is available in French or English. CMAS and PADI certification are available.

Yacht Club de Tahiti (☎ 42-23-55, 42-78-03/95), BP 1456, Papeete, calls itself Tahiti's 'first diving school' and has all equipment available, two dive boats, and a decompression chamber only three minutes by car from the premises. They offer bilingual instruction, night diving and diving outside the reef. Prices begin at 4500 CFP per dive and 5500 CFP per lesson. CMAS and PADI certification are available.

Hotel Beachcomber Parkroyal Diving Centre (☎ 42-11-10), BP 6014 Faaa, Tahiti, is a small dive operation equipped with a Boston Whaler. The cost is 2500 CFP per dive and there is an English-speaking instructor. PADI certification is available.

Moorea MUST (Moorea Underwater Scuba Diving Tahiti (☎ 56-17-32, 56-15-83), BP 336, Pao Pao, is adjacent to the Baie de Cook

Hotel. This is a well-established, experienced company which also has its own accommodation. They are equipped to take out groups of up to 12 divers on Zodiac rafts. The cost is 4500 CFP per dive. With instruction the cost is 6000 CFP per lesson or 20,000 CFP for four lessons. The instructors speak English and Spanish. CMAS certification is available.

Bathay's Club (☎ 56-19-19, 56-21-07), BP 1019, Papetoai, Haapiti, based at the Beachcomber Parkroyal in Moorea, has dive instruction as well as video camera and submarine scooter rentals. The cost is 5000 CFP per dive and 39,000 CFP for CMAS or PADI certification.

Scuba Piti (☎ 56-20-38), BP 1072, Papetoai, is at the Hotel Linareva in Haapiti. They organise two outings per day, every day except Wednesday, with a maximum of six divers. They are CMAS certified. The cost is 4000 CFP per dive. Incidentally, the Hotel Linareva is one of the most beautiful places to stay on the island.

Bora Moana Adventure Tours – Hotel Bora (☎ 67-70-33), BP 5, Bora Bora, is run by Erwin Christian, the well-known local photographer who has an exclusive contract with the Bora Hotel. He will take a maximum of six divers to both lagoon and open sea. The prices are 6000 CFP per dive inside the lagoon, 7000 CFP outside the reef and 4000 CFP for a resort dive. He is CMAS certified.

Bora Calypso Club (☎ 67-74-64), BP 259, Bora, is at Point Matira, the finest beach on the island. There are two dives daily (with reservations) and they can accommodate up to 20 divers. Rental of underwater cameras is available and certification is both CMAS and PADI. The cost is 5500 CFP per dive in the lagoon or 6500 CFP in the ocean.

Rangiroa Raie Manta Club (☎ 96-04-80), BP 55 Avatoru, Rangiroa, is run by Yves Lefevre. They offer dives twice daily, teaching and diving in the lagoon, the passes and outside the reef at a cost of 4500 CFP per dive. They can accommodate up to 24 divers

per outing. CMAS and PADI levels are available.

Hotel Kia Ora Rangiroa, BP 1, Tiputa, Rangiroa, provides diving in the lagoon, the passes and outside the reef as well as resort dives. The cost is 4500 CFP per dive, 5500 CFP for exploratory dives and 3500 CFP for resort dives. The instructor, Yves Lefevre, also runs the Raie Manta Club.

Manihi Manihi Blue Nui (☎ 42-75-53), BP 2460, Papeete, lead dives in the lagoon, the passes and outside the reef. Equipment includes a speedboat. Rates for dives inside the pass or in the lagoon are 3500 CFP for parties of one or two divers and 3300 CFP for groups of three or four. Ocean dives or night dives cost 4000 CFP. The instructor, Gilles Petre, speaks French and English.

Raiatea At Club de Plongee Uturoa (☎ 66-37-10), BP 272, Uturoa, Raiatea, is Michele Philippe, Raiatea's only dive operator. He transports divers in a large motorised outrigger and will pick up divers from yachts or hotels anywhere within the Raiatea-Tahaa area. He teaches as well as leads divers to any spot in the lagoon or the passes. According to Michele, Raiatea is 'virgin' territory for divers and there are a number of excellent sites near to shore, within five to 10 minutes of his pension. The cost ranges from 3000 CFP for guests of his pension to 4500 CFP per dive for non-guests.

Note Like all other prices in this book, costs for diving are subject to change. In other words, plan on things being more expensive than you had anticipated. Your best bet is to write to the dive operators you are considering and find out exactly how much it will cost. Some of the dive operators also run their own pensions (as in Raiatea or MUST in Moorea), some of which cater exclusively to divers. This usually means less expensive accommodation.

Windsurfing
This sport has become very popular in Tahiti over the last decade. With no lack of warm

water and gentle breezes in French Polynesia, it is an excellent place to windsurf for experts – neophytes may be another matter. Many of the hotels advertise windsurfing as an activity but you may find the equipment dilapidated or green with algae from lack of use. Coral heads in shallower areas of lagoons may present a real hazard to beginners who are not able to traverse deeper waters.

Deep-Sea Fishing

Deep-sea fishing has been a popular recreational activity for a certain class of visitor to French Polynesia for generations. This was a favourite pastime of US pulp western writer Zane Grey, who had his own fishing hideaway in Tahiti in the 1930s. By my reckoning there are over a dozen charter fishing boats in Papeete alone and charters are also available on Moorea and Bora Bora. For recommendations about vessels for charter, ask around.

Boat Hire

Charter boats can be hired for sport fishing (as well as speed boats for water-skiing). They don't come cheap but if you are concerned about price, you should not be in Tahiti in the first place. Game fish include marlin, sailfish, barracuda and other pelagics. Some of the resorts (such as the Beachcomber and Maeva Beach Hotels) have glass-bottomed boats for viewing undersea life out of harm's way.

Skydiving

Yes, folks, you can even skydive in paradise. For information call Club de vol Libre Polynesien (☎ 43-72-04).

ACCOMMODATION

An important step in reducing hotel food costs was implemented by the local government, which reduced import tariffs on booze and encouraged hoteliers to lower prices on food. This reduced prices dramatically on MAP (Modified American Plan; this includes three meals per day) and AP (American Plan; this includes breakfast and dinner)

programmes at various hotels as well as tabs at hotel bars. Although it varies from hotel to hotel the law has resulted in a 15 to 40% reduction in food bills. For example, one hotel in Moorea formerly charged 8000 CFP per day for three meals on its American Plan. It now charges 4500 CFP. Tipplers will be happy to know that instead of paying US$8 or US$9 for a shot of whisky, they will pay only US$5 or US$6.

That's the good news.

The bad news is that room prices for hotels in Papeete and in French Polynesia still fall into two general categories – expensive and very expensive. Aside from air-con, beach frontage, discos, restaurants and bars, upmarket resorts may provide tennis courts, swimming pools, bicycles and free snorkelling gear. Prices for this type of hotel range from US$150 to US$250 for a single.

On the lower end of the scale is accommodation for the budget-minded traveller. These are either older hotels that lost their lustre when the more modern resorts opened up, smaller family-operated pensions, or boarding arrangements with families. These do not afford all the luxuries but nevertheless are quite adequate for many people.

The smaller hotels may have air-con, pools and lovely gardens but not much else in the way of extras. Prices range from US$40 to US$80 for a single.

Hotel prices do not include 7% 'room tax' and – like all things in this world – are subject to change.

Just because hotels and pensions appear in this book doesn't necessarily mean they are good places to stay. Those that I liked or that were recommended to me are marked with an asterisk (*) and are commented upon.

For campers, the news is getting better all the time. There are now excellent facilities on Tahiti, Moorea and Bora Bora.

FOOD

Although the government has made a valiant attempt to bring prices down by slashing import duties on booze, these reduced prices apply only to special 'tourist menus' featured at hotels and some restaurants which have volunteered to go along with the revised pricing scheme. Most à la carte items retain their normal (usually expensive) price. The government is encouraging all restaurants to provide discounts in the future and this has occurred in many of the hotel restaurants.

There are four excellent varieties of food available in Tahiti: French, Vietnamese, Chinese and Tahitian. Tahitian fare is more or less the same as in the rest of Polynesia – fish, shellfish, breadfruit, taro, cassava (manioc), pork, chicken, yams, rice and coconut. Beef, very popular in Tahiti, is rare on most of the outer islands. Vegetables such as tomatoes and onions are grown on Tahiti and some of the outer islands, but are nonexistent on atolls. On most of the high islands, tubers such as manioc and taro are staples for the locals. Visitors soon find them bland and heavy. In the Tuamotus, where taro and manioc cannot be grown, rice, breadfruit and white bread are the main starches.

The dish most likely to be found on a French Polynesian meal table is *poisson cru*. This consists of chunks of raw fish marinated in lime juice or vinegar and salt and is usually topped with coconut cream, onions and oil. *Chevrettes*, found on most high islands, are freshwater shrimp. *Salade russe* is a potato salad with tiny pieces of beet. Taro and manioc are usually boiled and eaten as the main starch. Taro, which is served in large slices, contains significant quantities of fluoride and keeps teeth healthy. Young taro leaves, boiled and topped with coconut cream, resemble and taste like spinach. Finally, *poi* is a heavy, sweet pudding usually made with taro, bananas or papayas. It is served warm and topped with coconut milk.

One local fruit that no visitor should miss is the pamplemousse, a huge introduced species of grapefruit, most probably from Asia. Unusually sweet and tasty, the pamplemousse is available fresh in markets or you can buy the juice in litre-sized cartons. Occasionally you can find it fresh-squeezed in restaurants or cafes. Don't leave Tahiti without trying it.

The Polynesians who originally settled the islands brought with them bananas, bread-fruit, taro, yams and, strangely enough, the South American sweet potato. How the Polynesians got this last item is a mystery, but Dr Y H Sinoto of the Bishop Museum conjectures that Polynesian mariners made it to South America, perhaps traded with the locals and made their way back to Polynesia with the sweet potato. The missionaries later introduced sugar cane, cotton, corn, limes, oranges, guavas, pineapple, coffee and numerous other fruits and vegetables. Most Tahitians have adopted some eating habits from the French, including coffee, French bread, butter and canned goods. Unfortunately, it is a sign of the times to see them opening cans of Japanese tuna instead of fishing for the real thing.

ENTERTAINMENT
Cinemas
There are seven movie houses in Papeete and a number scattered in the larger rural areas. As you would expect, most films are French, or US dubbed in French. Admission is about 700 CFP.

THINGS TO BUY
Import duties imposed by the government are the most important source of Tahiti's income. Despite these tariffs, Tahiti's duty-free shops offer discounts on liquor, tobacco and perfume. For the fashion-conscious there are a number of boutiques with island-style and French clothing. Crafts, seashells and handmade shell leis sold in the market, at outdoor booths or at fairs make good mementos – and are perhaps the only local handicraft that is readily affordable. Other items such as carvings may be available on the outer islands. The best time to buy crafts is during fairs or festivals. The upstairs section of the market in Papeete is a good place to look for shell necklaces, carvings and basket wares.

If you have money to spend, black coral and the indigenous black pearl make even nicer acquisitions. Philatelists should stop at the special booth at the post office – French Polynesia issues beautiful stamps. And if you stay long enough in the islands you will undoubtedly adopt the local article of clothing called a pareu. This practical item is a brightly coloured wraparound cotton cloth worn by men and women and is sold in every store.

In Papeete you can purchase items from around French Polynesia: tie-dyed pareus from Moorea, black pearls from Manihi, wood carvings from Ua Huka, shell hatbands from Rangiroa, fine woven hats from Tubuai and tapa cloth from Fatu Hiva.

Although the market is an interesting place to look for souvenirs, quality is generally mediocre. Better to check out Manuia Curios, in a row of shops on Place Notre Dame, facing the cathedral. It's a source of better-than-average quality carvings as well as shells, bags and other woven goods. This shop is also one of the few places where you can get traditional Tahitian dance costumes.

One last word on shopping. Unlike other Oceanic or Asiatic countries, one does not haggle or bargain when shopping in the public market places in Tahiti. More often than not, the price you see is the price you get. Tahitians, though not so much the Chinese, might find it rude to haggle over prices. It does not appear to be part of their culture.

Pareus

The national costume for men and women is the pareu (par-ay-you), a rectangular piece of cloth about two metres long. It can be tied a number of ways but is usually wrapped skirt-like around the waist and worn with a T-shirt. Although Western men might at first cringe at the idea of wearing a skirt, they soon find that in Tahiti's often sweltering climate, a pareu is a practical item of clothing to wear around the house. Get hooked and you will find yourself bringing a few pareus back home. They come in a variety of colours and patterns, as well as several grades of quality.

In Papeete, a good place to look for fabrics is the square block or so area bounded by Rue Prince Hinoi, Rue De L'Ecole and Rue Colette. There are a number of fabric stores with colourful island patterns. For a fabric experience check into Chez Marcelle on Rue Colette just past the Mandarin Hotel.

Getting There & Away

AIR

Apart from those people who arrive on a cruise ship or by yacht, all visitors to French Polynesia arrive by air at the Faaa Airport near Papeete, Tahiti. Air services through Tahiti are generally operated using Tahiti as an intermediate stop between Australia or New Zealand and the USA, although there are also connections between Tahiti and Chile in South America via Easter Island. There are also some connections to other Pacific islands.

Airlines that fly into Tahiti include Air New Zealand, Lan Chile, Polynesian Airlines, Qantas, South Pacific Island Airways and UTA. Needless to say, the best fares can be found by travellers who shop around travel agents and check out the newspaper ads for discounted air tickets in the travel sections.

To/From the USA

The only departure cities from continental USA to Tahiti are Los Angeles and San Francisco. The carriers with the lion's share of passengers are UTA/Air France. Other airlines from the USA to Tahiti include Air New Zealand, Qantas and Hawaiian Airlines. A charter carrier, Minerve, also operates regularly out of San Francisco. Round-trip excursion fares from Los Angeles or San Francisco (during low season – 25 December to 15 June) to Tahiti are around US$950. From Honolulu (on Hawaiian), the round-trip fare to Papeete is around US$750. The best deal on the west coast is with Minerve which has weekly flights on Sundays out of San Francisco, costing from around US$650 (low season) to US$750 (high season). I am told they may become a regular scheduled carrier out of Los Angeles, but that has yet to be determined. For more information call them on (800) 323-4444. Reservations are handled by Char Tours.

Better deals are available, such as the circle-Pacific fares to New Zealand or to Australia which can be routed via Tahiti. Alternatively, discounted round-trip tickets to Tahiti can be found from 'consolidators' for around US$600 to US$700 from the US west coast, if you are prepared to shop around and look at the advertisements in the Sunday newspaper travel sections in major west coast cities.

The *New York Times*, the *LA Times*, the *Chicago Tribune* and the *San Francisco Examiner* all produce weekly travel sections in which you'll find any number of travel agents' ads. Council Travel and STA Travel have offices in major cities nationwide. The magazine *Travel Unlimited* (PO Box 1058, Allston, Mass 02134) publishes details of the cheapest air fares and courier possibilities for destinations all over the world from the USA.

To/From Australia

There are no great discounts on direct flights to Tahiti from Australia despite the relatively short distance. In fact, you could probably get a return ticket to Los Angeles via Tahiti for the same price as a return ticket to Tahiti only (unless you used a package plan, which would include accommodation in the cost). The other option is to make Tahiti a stopover on a round-the-world (RTW) ticket. Shop around and remember there are three pricing seasons for flights out of Australia – low, shoulder and high. Prices vary enormously according to the season, the length of validity of the ticket, the combination of destinations you choose on RTW tickets, and the agent.

The available combinations on an RTW ticket are almost endless. You could fly via Tahiti to the USA or Canada, for example, then to Europe, and ditto on return, or come back via Asia. You need to shop around and discuss possible itineraries with agents. A typical RTW ticket going Melbourne/ Bangkok/London/Los Angeles/Papeete/ Auckland/Melbourne would cost around

$2100. Continental/KLM offer a one-year RTW ticket with unlimited stops, returning via Asia, for around $2400.

Flying to America via Tahiti, you could pick up a three-month ticket with Air New Zealand from Melbourne to Los Angeles via Auckland and Tahiti for less than $1500. Qantas/Lan Chile offer a return six-month ticket to Chile with four stops including Tahiti for around $2400, or less than $2000 on a one-month ticket.

STA and Flight Centres International are major dealers in cheap air fares. Check the travel agents' ads in the Yellow Pages and in major newspapers, and ring around.

To/From New Zealand

The cheapest fares are probably with UTA. For example, you could get a 45-day ticket with UTA, from Auckland to Papeete, for under $1000 in the low season (January to June, or September to November), around $1250 in the high season (July, August or December), or a one-year ticket for around $1300 (low season) or $1500 (high season).

As in Australia, STA and Flight Centres International are popular travel agents.

To/From the UK

Few travellers are going to fly all the way to the South Pacific with a visit to Tahiti as their sole goal. Tahiti can, however, be easily visited en route to Australia or on a RTW ticket. Airline ticket discounters (bucket shops) in London offer RTW tickets which include Tahiti in their itinerary.

Flying round the world from London, a typical route is London/Los Angeles/Tahiti/Sydney/Fiji/Raratonga/Los Angeles/London, for around £1500. Or you could fly London/Bangkok/Cairns/Sydney/Tahiti/Los Angeles/London for around £1100. Flying to Australia only, London/Tahiti/Sydney/London would cost around £750. As with flights out of Asia, UTA is likely to be the operator through Tahiti although Air New Zealand flights may also be used from London (via Los Angeles).

Trailfinders in west London produce a lavishly illustrated brochure which includes air fare details. STA also has branches in the UK. Look in the listings magazines *Time Out* and *City Limits* plus the Sunday papers and *Exchange & Mart* for ads. Also look out for the free magazines widely available in London – start by looking outside the main railway stations.

Most British travel agents are registered with ABTA (Association of British Travel Agents). If you have paid for your flight to an ABTA-registered agent who then goes out of business, ABTA will guarantee a refund or an alternative. Unregistered bucket shops are riskier but also sometimes cheaper.

To/From Other Pacific Islands

There are surprisingly few connections between Tahiti and other Pacific islands. The ones that exist are not cheap. UTA flies between Noumea in New Caledonia and Tahiti with a one-way fare of around US$750. They also have a connection from Fiji, via Noumea, to Tahiti using Air Caledonie. The one-way fare is around US$1150. Air New Zealand fly Rarotonga to Tahiti for around US$350 one way.

There are also various excursion fares that span North America and the South Pacific. For example Air New Zealand has a US$1500 fare from Los Angeles to New Zealand with stopovers in Tahiti, Fiji or the Cook Islands. A similar ticket is available to Australia for around US$1600.

To/From Asia

For several years now one of the most popular tickets out of South-East Asia to the USA has been the southern loop through the Pacific.

Using Thai International, Qantas and Air New Zealand, you can fly Singapore /Jakarta/Sydney/Auckland/Fiji/Raratonga/Tahiti/Los Angeles for around Baht 27,500.

There are numerous ticket discounters in Singapore, Bangkok, or Penang in Malaysia, who sell tickets on this or similar routes. Hong Kong is the discount plane ticket capital of the region. Its bucket shops are at least as unreliable as those of other cities. Ask the advice of other travellers before buying a ticket.

STA, which is reliable, has branches in Hong Kong, Tokyo, Singapore, Bangkok and Kuala Lumpur.

To/From South America

Lan Chile connects Tahiti with Santiago, Chile via Easter Island. Flying to Tahiti and then connecting with this flight is the most direct, though not the cheapest, way to fly to South America from Australia or New Zealand. The one-way fare from Papeete to Santiago is around US$1150.

Package Plans

Packages may not appeal to the vagabond but they are the way most visitors travel to the South Pacific. The main advantage of using a package is that it will undoubtedly save you money on the air fare side of the travel equation. Naturally, the agent will make money on the 'land' and excursion end of the deal. After you have decided what island you'd like to visit and for how long, consult an agency that specialises in Tahiti. The agent should be able to answer questions such as: Does the hotel have a mountain or oceanside view? Will your accommodation be over the water, on the beach or in the garden? Is the hotel a super deluxe one or more moderate? How far away is the beach? A specialist will be familiar with the tour packages available and should be able to answer these questions so that there are no unhappy surprises.

A competent agent should also be able to prepare a tailor-made itinerary for the person who has special interests such as golf, snorkelling, diving, etc. In most cases US South Pacific specialists have toll-free telephone numbers and can advise you of the current air fare bargains and seasonal discounts. They should also have fares for interisland travel. Last but not least, a reputable agency can save you money. For US residents, I can recommend Manuia Tours (☎ (800) 532-3000) in San Francisco. It is

owned by a Tahitian family and they know their destination.

SEA

Unfortunately, the romantic days of catching a tramp steamer in the USA and working your way across the Pacific no longer exist. Unless money is no object, the prohibitive cost of taking ships long distances makes it much more feasible to fly. However, once you are in the islands it is still possible (although difficult) to take freighters from one South Seas port to another. Booking passage on a freighter entails going down to the dock and talking the vessel's skipper into giving you a berth. If there is room aboard and the captain likes your looks, you are in luck. On US-registered ships, hitching a ride is impossible unless you have sailor's papers. The schedule of cargo vessels coming into Papeete is posted at the waterfront branch of the immigration police adjacent to the tourist office. You can also island-hop by contacting private plane owners and negotiating with them for rides.

Yacht

For people with time on their hands and adventure in their hearts, travelling to Tahiti by yacht is also feasible. To become a crew member, go to Honolulu or one of the larger ports on the US west coast – preferably Los Angeles, San Diego or San Francisco – which are departure points for most Tahiti-bound yachts.

To find the boats headed in this direction, you must do some sleuthing down on the docks of the local yacht club. Usually notices are placed on yacht club bulletin boards by skippers needing crew members, or by potential sailors looking for a yacht. The best thing to do is ask around the docks or marine supply shops. Naturally, someone who has previous sailing experience, or is a gourmet chef or a doctor will have a good chance to get on as a crew member. A six-week sailing season starts during the last half of September, with a secondary 'window' opening in January and continuing through March.

If you are serious about getting on a yacht, it's best to start doing research at least six months ahead of time. Get to know the people you are going to sail with and help them rig the boat. Sailing time from the US west coast to French Polynesia is about a month, with nowhere to get off in the middle of the Pacific. Papeete is one of the major transit points for yachts in the entire South Pacific, and once you are there it is generally no problem for an experienced sailor to hitch a ride from Papeete to any point east or west.

Getting Around

Travelling to and within the islands of French Polynesia is not a difficult affair. Thanks to French largess the transport infrastructure is quite sophisticated. There are modern airstrips, well-paved highways, numerous boats and ferries, and a bus system that works. Visitors will find that most transport is reasonably priced and, despite the general 'manana' attitude, things generally run on time.

Because there is only one international airport in French Polynesia (Faaa near Papeete), a trip to the surrounding islands must begin on Tahiti. The two means of transport are air and copra boat. Travelling by air is the fastest and most efficient, but not necessarily the most economical. Although the local carrier, Air Tahiti (formerly Air Polynesie), flies to quite a few destinations, it does not go to all the islands.

Copra boats, on the other hand, do go to every inhabited island but take more time, and overall are a much cheaper form of transport than planes. On shorter routes they can be a great bargain and also give you the chance to meet some of the locals who will undoubtedly be journeying with you.

A third possibility is to combine air and sea transport. For example, if you want to visit Ahe, which has no air service, it is possible to book a flight to Manihi and then catch a speedboat from there to Ahe.

Air Tahiti has a minimum of two flights a week between the Marquesas and Papeete, and once a week between Rangiroa and the Marquesas. The schedule varies from season to season. There are also 'island hopper' flights within the Marquesas Islands.

AIR

Since French Polynesia's importance as a military base was established in the early 1960s, the government has developed an extensive air transport system serving all the distant archipelagos. Although it would be impractical to build runways on every island, most areas can be reached by flying to an island with an airstrip and then catching an outboard motor-powered skiff or interisland boat to the place you wish to visit. The major carrier, Air Tahiti, provides a well-run air service to every island group. For schedules go to the Air Tahiti office on Boulevard Pomare in Papeete or the Visitors' Bureau (Fare Manihini) on the quay. Several smaller airlines also charter planes or helicopters for visitors. The air fares chart in this book shows the prices in CFP for one-way flights to major destinations. There are additional flights so if you want to travel to an island not detailed check one of Air Tahiti's brochures. To calculate round-trip fares just double the one-way fare.

Travellers should note that the baggage allowance on interisland flights is only 10 kg. They will charge you without hesitation if your baggage is overweight.

In some cases flights to and from the outer islands are direct, while in others they are routed via Papeete. For example, you can fly directly from Huahine to Raiatea but to fly from Huahine to Rangiroa you must pass through Faaa Airport in Papeete. The type of aircraft used on most flights are the ATR 42s (hi-tech, twin prop, 46-seat). Nineteen-seat Twin Otters and smaller Britten-Norman Islanders are used on shorter routes. Air Tahiti has three different passes, good for 28 days, allowing one stopover for each island on a circular route. The three options, which have suboptions that are reminiscent of a Chinese menu, are:

- The Leeward/Windward Islands (Moorea/Huahine/Raiatea/Bora Bora) for 30,500 CFP.

- The Leeward/Windward Islands (Moorea/Huahine/Raiatea/Bora Bora) plus Rangiroa/Manihi or Manihi/Rangiroa for 45,500 CFP.

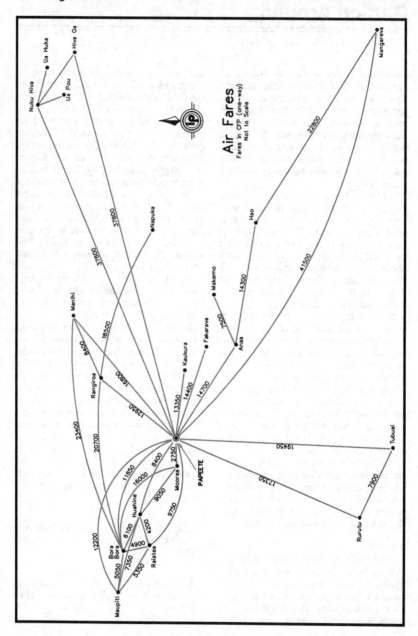

Air Fares
Fares in CFP (one-way)
Not to Scale

- The Leeward/Windward Islands (Moorea/ Huahine/Raiatea/Bora Bora) plus Rangiroa/Manihi or Manihi/Rangiroa for 50,500 CFP.

The difference between options two and three is that the lesser fare means swinging through the islands in one direction, starting in the Society Islands and finishing in the Tuamotus, whereas the more expensive fare allows you to start in either direction. Thus with option number two you can begin your journey from the Tuamotus or the Society Group.

For information on Air Tahiti in the USA, contact Tahiti Vacations (☎ (800) 553-3477). The staff are very knowledgeable and prepared to answer all your questions about French Polynesia. Ask for John Biggerstaff.

Tahiti Helicopter (☎ 43-34-26) and Pacifique Helicoptere Service (☎ 43-16-80) each have a helicopter service to Moorea from Faaa Airport. Pacific Helicopter also provides rides from Faaa on Sundays between 1 and 3 pm to Le Belvedere Restaurant, 550 metres above Papeete. The ride, aboard an Ecureuil chopper, costs US$46 and takes about 15 minutes. The company also has five-minute sightseeing tours over Papeete for US$24.

BOAT
Ferry

Despite the increase in air transport, interisland vessels remain a vital transport link for travellers and cargo to the outer islands. In many instances, interisland steamers or much smaller skiffs are the only way to reach isolated communities. If you don't mind roughing it, interisland boats are a wonderful way to travel and meet the locals. Make sure you allow plenty of time for this type of voyaging. Trips may range from a few hours to a few weeks and are generally inexpensive. Check the itineraries carefully before setting sail.

Boat schedules are simply not reliable. Like so many things in the South Pacific, they are subject to change. Departure and arrival times listed are only approximate. If you absolutely, positively *must* catch a vessel, especially on a remote island where communications are minimal, take a tip from the locals and camp on or near the dock. This will ensure your meeting the boat.

It is recommended that tickets be purchased at least half a day before the scheduled departure date. In the outer islands tickets can be bought on the dock. Keep in mind that meals are generally not served on board.

The following is a description of ferry itineraries and operator addresses, for ferries serving each of the island groups.

Society Islands There are four ferries serving these islands.

Taporo IV

Operator: Compagnie Francaise Maritime de Tahiti (☎ 42-63-93, 43-79-72), BP 368, Papeete (Fare Ute), Tahiti.

Port	Arrive	Depart
Papeete		Mon 5 pm
Huahine	Tue 2 am	Tue 3 am
Raiatea	Tue 5.30 am	Tue 7 am
Bora Bora	Tue 11 am	Tue 1 pm
Raiatea	Tue 3 pm	Tue 4 pm
Huahine	Tue 6 pm	Tue 7 pm
Papeete	Wed 5 am	Wed 5 pm
Huahine	Thu 2 am	Thu 3 am
Raiatea	Thu 5 am	Thu 7 am
Tahaa	Thu 9 am	Thu 10 am
Raiatea	Thu 11 am	Thu noon
Huahine	Thu 2 pm	Thu 3 pm
Papeete	Fri 3.30 am	Fri 5 pm
Huahine	Sat 2 am	Sat 3 am
Raiatea	Sat 5.30 am	Sat 7 am
Tahaa	Sat 9 am	Sat 10 am
Bora Bora	Sat noon	Sun 8 am
Tahaa	Sun 10 am	Sun 11 am
Raiatea	Sun noon	Sun 1 pm
Huahine	Sun 3 pm	Sun 4 pm
Papeete	Mon 3.30 am	

The *Taporo IV* can carry 160 passengers, 50 in cabins and 110 on deck. Voyage times are Papeete/Huahine nine hours, Huahine/Raiatea 2½hours, Raiatea/Bora Bora four hours, Bora Bora/Tahaa two hours, Tahaa/ Raiatea one hour. The fares in CFP are:

From/To	Deck/Cabin
Papeete/Huahine	1100/1540
Papeete/Raiatea	1300/1820
Papeete/Bora Bora	1500/2100
Papeete/Tahaa	1300/1820
Huahine/Raiatea	800/1200
Huahine/Tahaa	800/1200
Huahine/Bora Bora	750/1050
Raiatea/Tahaa	500/700
Raiatea/Bora Bora	800/1200
Bora Bora/Tahaa	800/1200

Temehani II

Operator: Société de Navigation Temehani, (☎ 42-98-83), BP 9015, Papeete (Motu Uta), Tahiti.

Port	Arrive	Depart
Papeete		Mon 5 pm
Huahine	Tue 1 am	Tue 2 am
Raiatea	Tue 5 am	Tue 8 am
Tahaa	Tue 9 am	Tue 10 am
Raiatea	Tue 11 am	Tues 1.30 pm
Huahine	Tue 3 pm	Tue 4 pm
Papeete	Wed 2 am	

Port	Arrive	Depart
Papeete		Wed 5 pm
Huahine	Thu 1 am	Thu 2 am
Raiatea	Thu 5 am	Thu 8 am
Bora Bora	Thu 10 am	Thu noon
Tahaa	Thu 1 pm	Thu 3 pm
Raiatea	Thu 4 pm	Fri 8 am
Huahine	Fri 10 am	Fri 11.30 am
Papeete	Fri 7.30 pm	

The *Temehani II* can carry 116 passengers including 27 in cabins. Voyage times are Papeete/Huahine eight hours, Huahine/Raiatea 2½ hours, Raiatea/Bora Bora two hours, Bora Bora/Tahaa one hour, Tahaa/Raiatea one hour. The fares in CFP are:

From/to	Deck/Cabin
Papeete/Huahine	1100/2200
Papeete/Raiatea	1300/2600
Papeete/Bora Bora	1500/2800
Papeete/Tahaa	1300/2600
Huahine/Raiatea	550/1100
Huahine/Tahaa	550/1100
Huahine/Bora Bora	825/1650
Raiatea/Tahaa	330/660
Raiatea/Bora Bora	550/1100
Bora Bora/Tahaa	550/1100

Raromatai

Operator: BP 9012, Papeete, Tahiti (☎ 43-90-42). Popular with locals and tourists alike, this vessel leaves Papeete twice weekly for a circuit of the Society Islands.

Port	Arrive	Depart
Papeete		Tue 7 pm
Huahine	Wed 4.30 am	Wed 5 am
Raiatea	Wed 7 am	Wed 7.30 am
Bora Bora	Wed 9.30 am	Thu 2 pm
Tahaa	Thu 4.30 pm	Thu 4.45 pm
Raiatea	Thu 5.30 pm	Thu 6 pm
Huahine	Thu 8 pm	Thu 8.30 pm
Papeete	Fri 4.30 am	Fri 7 pm
Huahine	Sat 4.30 am	Sat 5 am
Raiatea	Sat 7 am	Sat 7.30 am
Tahaa	Sat 8.30 am	Sat 8.45 am
Bora Bora	Sat 10.45 am	Sun 2 pm
Raiatea	Sun 5 pm	Sun 5.30 pm
Huahine	Sun 7.30 pm	Sun 8 pm
Papeete	Mon 4.30 am	

Fare: A deluxe cabin with three bunks is 25,500 CFP per night, 'tourist' cabin with four bunks is 6000 CFP per night, deck passage is 3800 CFP (entire trip) and interisland (between two islands) fare is 1000 CFP. The cost of a vehicle is 7200 CFP for the entire journey.
Note: The *Raromatai* transports both passengers and vehicles within the Society Islands. For those with sail/drive plans this would be the ferry to take.

Taporo I

Operator: Société Taporo Teaotea (☎ 66-32-29, 66-30-03), BP 68, Uturoa, Raiatea.
The vessel can carry 100 passengers. There are 12 cabins. Route: Raiatea/Maupiti/Raiatea.
Voyage length: six hours. Departs Raiatea Tuesdays and Thursdays at 10 am or 10 pm depending on the weather and the cargo, and arrives six hours later in Maupiti. Leaves next afternoon at 3 pm and arrives at Raiatea at 9 pm the same evening.
Fare: The cost is 850 CFP on deck and 1450 CFP for a bunk.

Tuamotu Islands Several ferries operate within the Tuamotus.

Cobia II

Operator: SNC Degage & Cie, Tahiti.
Route: Papeete/Kaukura/Arutua/Apataki/ Tikehau/Aratika/Toau. One voyage weekly, departs from Papeete on Mondays, returns to

Papeete on Thursdays. There is no phone so go directly to the docks and contact Mr Alfred Lochman to reserve a berth. Price is 3000 CFP per person, no meals served on board.

Dory

Operator: SNC Agineray & Cie, Tahiti.
Route: Papeete/Rangiroa/Ahe/Manihi/Apataki/Arutua/Kaukura. One voyage weekly, departs Papeete on Mondays and returns on Thursdays. No telephone reservations taken. To reserve berth contact Mr Afou Chongues dockside. Price is 3000 CPF per person, no meals served on board.

Manava II

Operator: STMI (Société des Transports Maritimes des Îles), Simeon & William Richmond, (☎ 43-83-84), BP 1816, Papeete, Tahiti.
Route: Papeete/Makatea/Rangiroa/Tikehau/Mataiva/Ahe/Manihi/Takapoto/Takaroa/Aratika/Kauehi/Fakarava/Toau/Apataki/Arutua/Kaukura.
Voyage length: 10 days. Prices range from 1800 to 3300 CFP depending on destination. No meals served and accommodation is strictly deck passage.

Rairoa Nui

Operator: Albert Tang (☎ 42-91-69), BP 1187, Papeete (Avenue du Regent Paraita), Tahiti.
Route: Tikehau.
Voyage length: four days, departs Monday, returns Friday.
Note: In the past, this vessel did not take tourist passengers, but check anyway to see whether this policy has changed. No phone reservations accepted. Reserve berth with Mr William Damas.

Tere Moana

Operator: Tere Moana Sarl (☎ 58-38-57).
Route: Apataki/Arutua/Kaukura/Fakarava/Toau/Faaite.
Voyage length: one week.

Maire II

Operator: Compagnie de Navigation Inter-Marquesas (☎ 43-33-29), Rue Colette, BP 2516, Papeete, Tahiti.
Route: Hao/Amanu/Vairaatea/Tureia/Mangareva/Marutu Sud/Reao/Pukarua/Tatakoto/Vaitahu/Nukutavake/Tamatangui.
Fare: Deck passage is 1700 CFP per day; cabin fare is 2200 CFP per day. Every two months the *Maire II* goes only to the Gambier Islands.
Voyage length: 12 days.

Saint-Xavier Maris Stella

Operator: Société de Navigation des Tuamotu SARL (☎ 42-23-58), BP 11366 Mahina, Tahiti.
Route: Papeete/Rangiroa/Mataiva/Tikehau/Ahe/Manihi/Takapoto/Takaroa/Arutua/Apataki/Kaukura.
Voyage length: eight days – two voyages per month. Fare is 3500 CFP for deck passage, including three meals per day.

Auura Nui II

Operator: Société de Transports Maritimes des Tuamotu (☎ 43-76-17), BP 9196, Motu Uta, Tahiti.
Route: Papeete/Anaa/Faaite/Tepoto Nord/Amanu/Hao/Marokau/Makemo/Taenga/Nihiru/Fangatau/Fakahina/Napuka/Puka Puka/Takume/Raroia/Katiu.
Voyage length: 20 days – one voyage per month. Fares range from 2000 to 10,000 CFP depending on distance travelled and type of accommodation (cabins are available). Three meals per day cost an extra 1700 CFP per person per day.

Vaihere

Operator: Société D'Entreprise Polynesienne de Navigation (☎ 43-76-17), BP 9196, Papeete (Motu Uta), Tahiti.
Route: Hereheretue/Anuanu Raro/Nukutipiti/Marutea Sud/Reao/Hao/Pukarua/Tatakoto/Aki Aki/Vaitahu/Nukutavake/Vairaatea/Tetamanu/Hikueru.
Voyage length: 20 days.

Kauaroa Nui

Operator: Mr Falchetto Philip SARL (☎ 57-22-07), BP 7368, Taravao, Tahiti.
Route: Papeete/Faaite/Katiu/Makemo/Raraka/Tetamanu/Fakarava/Makemo
Voyage length: four to five days – three voyages a month. Fare is 4000 CFP for deck passage and 7000 CFP for bunk. There is no food service on board but there is one small ship's store with food for sale.

Marquesas Islands The *Aranui*, the *Taporo V*, the *Tamarii Tuamotu* and the *Kahoa Nui* all serve these islands.

Aranui

Operator: Compagnie Polynesienne de Transport Maritime, (☎ 42-62-40), BP 220, Papeete (Motu Uta), Tahiti.
Route: Rangiroa/Takapoto/Hiva Oa/Ua Pou/ Ua Huka/Tahuata/ Fatu Hiva/Nuku Hiva/Papeete.
Voyage length: about 16 days.

The *Aranui*, French Polynesia's largest interisland freighter, was completely revamped in 1984 to accommodate 40 passengers for regularly scheduled service to the Marquesas Islands. Although other interisland boats (and air transport) are available, this is the only vessel specifically fitted for passenger traffic.

The 80-metre *Aranui* was built in Hamburg, Germany in 1967 and has three classes of air-con cabins as well as deck passage. First-class cabins include private shower and toilet facilities; 2nd and 3rd-class cabins share communal showers. The only real difference between 2nd and 3rd-class accommodation is a wash basin in 2nd-class cabins. Accommodation has been refurbished for tourists and is large considering the boat was never designed as a passenger vessel. Bunks and three showers are provided for deck class. The 'public' rooms consist of a small lounge with a modest library and selection of games, and a bar area on the upper deck.

The itinerary consists of three days in the Tuamotu Islands (Rangiroa, Takapoto and Arutua) and a 10-day swing through the Marquesas Islands (Nuku Hiva, Ua Pou, Hiva Oa, Tahuata and Fatu Hiva). Activities include fishing, a visit to a pearl 'farm', land tours and horse riding. The *Aranui* is still a working cargo boat and offers you an opportunity to visit the islands in comfort while seeing a slice of outer-island life. The ship has a French chef and the daily food includes plenty of fresh fish, lobster and shrimp. Meals are Tahitian, French and Chinese. The length of the voyage is 16 days. Prices vary between low and high season on all classes of cabins and all the 'A' cabins have individual prices. First-class accommodation costs from US$2330 to US$3160, 2nd-class from US$2144 to US$2360, 3rd-class from US$1750 to US$1920 and deck-class from US$1030 to US$1130. The price includes three meals a day. For more information in the USA call (415) 541-0674 in San Francisco.

Taporo V

Operator: Compagnie Francaise Maritime Tahiti (☎ 42-63-93), BP 368 Papeete (Fare Ute), Tahiti.
Route: Papeete/Tahuata/Hiva Oa/Nuku Hiva/Ua Pou/Papeete. Length: 15 days. Departs on Thursdays at 2 pm. Price for round-trip voyage with cabin-type accommodation and food is 44,000 CFP. Price for round trip with deck passage and food is 30,000 CFP.

Tamarii Tuamotu

Operator: Mme Vonkin c/o Kong Tao & Cie, (☎ 42-95-07), BP 2606, Papeete, Tahiti.
First Route: Papeete/Takapoto/Takaroa/Tepoto/Napuka/Ua Pou/Nuku Hiva/Hiva Oa/Ua Huka/Fatu Hiva. Return: Fatu Hiva/Puka Puka/Fakahina/Fangatau/Napuka/Tepoto/

Takaroa/Takapoto/Papeete.
Voyage length: one month – voyages every 40 days. The *Tamarii Tuamotu* reaches first landfall of the Marquesas Islands after seven days at sea. After first landfall, each succeeding island is visited daily. There are no cabins available on this vessel, only deck passage. Meals are available on board. Fares range from 7250 to 17,750 CFP depending on distance travelled. Fares include meals.

Kahoa Nui

Operator: Mr Philippe Tepea, (☎ 92-04-63, 92-03-96), BP 68 Taiohae, Nuku Hiva (Marquesas). This is an interisland vessel that travels exclusively around the Marquesas Islands. It sails once a month for a four-day voyage touching upon Ua Pou, Ua Huka, Hiva Oa, Tahuata, Fatu Hiva and Nuka a Taha. Prices range from 1000 to 2000 CFP depending on what island you are transiting to. In the unlikely event that you will have to use this vessel you will know how to determine the schedule.

Gambier Group The *Ruahatu* and the *Manava III* serve this group.

Ruahatu

Operator: c/o Mr Henri Grand (☎ 42-44-92), Motu Uta, Papeete, Tahiti.
Route: Hao/Amanu/Tatakoto/Pukarua/Reao/Marutea Sud/Mangareva/Tematangi/Vanavana/Turcia/Vaitahu/Vairaatea.
Fare: Deck passage is 6050 CFP.
Note: This vessel operates very irregularly within the Gambier Islands. Not the kind of boat to take if you have a schedule to maintain.

Manava III

Operator: Compagnie de Développement Maritime des Tuamotu, Mr Richmond Bene (☎ 43-32-65), BP 1291, Papeete, Tahiti.
Route: Hao/Vairaatea/Nukutavake/Marutea Sud/Puka Puka/Reao/Tatakoto/Vaitahu/Amanu/Eastern Tuamotus/Gambier Group.
Voyage length: 20 days.

Austral Islands In the Australs, look for the *Tuhaa Pae II*.

Tuhaa Pae II

Operator: Société Anonyme d'Economie Mixte de Navigation des Australes (☎ 42-93-67), BP 1890, Papeete (Motu Uta), Tahiti.
Route: Tubuai/Rurutu/Rimatara/Raivavae/Rapa.
Voyage length: about 15 days.

Cruises

For those who like the idea of exploring the islands by sea, and don't want to rough it, there is one passenger vessel that plies French Polynesian waters – the 134-metre motor sailor *Windsong* managed by Windstar Sail Cruises.

Cruising the islands has a distinct advantage for travellers who want their needs taken care of and are willing to deal with a 'structured' tour package. The disadvantage is that limited time is spent on the islands – obviously there is no opportunity to linger on the beach with a new friend when the boat is ready to leave.

The 150-passenger *Windsong* is a four-masted luxury motor sailer catering to an upmarket crowd of 30 to 40 people. Though reminiscent of an old-fashioned yacht there is nothing anachronistic about this boat. Its sails are operated by computer (eliminating the need for a crew), and high-tech gadgets such as VCRs and colour TVs are found in every room. The 75-cabin *Windsong* has the advantage of having a shallow draft, which means it can enter small coves and secluded beaches. Inside the vessel (built in France) is exquisitely detailed and crafted, using hardwoods such as teak. It's a class act, but then, you are paying for it.

The *Windsong* provides a comprehensive recreation programme for its well-heeled passengers. Sports equipment and instruction are available for water-skiing using Zodiac inflatable motor launches, and there

is windsurfing, sailing, deep-sea fishing, scuba diving and snorkelling. A Tahitian dive master is on board to provide scuba assistance, but passengers must be certified divers to use the diving gear.

Other on-board recreational facilities include a gymnasium with five exercise machines, a sauna and a masseuse, an outdoor pool with piano bar, a casino with about 10 slot machines and two black jack tables, skylighted disco and a video cassette and book library.

All 75 cabins are basically the same with only a slight difference in bed configuration. Most cabins have either two twins or a queen-sized bed, and 20 rooms provide a third bed. Rooms are all outside cabins, each with a colour TV, VCR, three-channel radio, minibar and refrigerator, safe, pull-out table, international direct dial telephone and sitting area. A far cry from the rusty bucket copra boats that were the only mode of transport in the old days.

The seven-day Tahiti cruise sails from Papeete after midnight and calls in at Huahine at 2 pm the next day. The ship sets sail again at 5 am the next morning. This schedule is repeated at each of the subsequent stops in Tahaa and Bora Bora, arriving at noon. When sailing conditions permit, the fourth day is spent on Maupiti or Tupai (Motu Iti) from 10 am to 5pm. On other occasions the ship either remains at Bora Bora for that extra day or proceeds to Raiatea and Moorea one day ahead of schedule. The price for the seven-day cruise begins at US$2195 per person, including use of all sports equipment. For more information call (800) 258-7245 in the USA.

Copra Boat

To book passage on a copra boat, walk down to where they are moored (past the naval yard in Fare Ute in Papeete) and see what boats are in port. You can obtain a list of all the copra boats and their destinations at the government tourist office. Chat with the skippers on the dock, double-check the current prices and determine where they are going and when they are departing. Often you have the options of either bringing your own food for the journey or eating the ship's fare; the difference in price can be substantial. Sometimes only deck passage is available, which means just that – sleeping, eating and drinking on deck with other islanders who have chosen the economy route. Keep in mind that a round-trip voyage may last a month or more. Also, jumping ship on an island that has no air service may turn out to be a long-term commitment – at least until another ship comes along.

A sea cruise on a copra boat can be appealing as long as things like rain, sea sickness, diesel fumes, engine noise, claustrophobia and huge cockroaches do not get on your nerves. On the other hand, the camaraderie, adventure, salt air, drifting, dreaming, guitar playing and drinking Hinano beer by moonlight are hard to beat.

Charter Boat
Rentals Revatua Charter Launch (☎ 43-28-21, 48-04-39) has tours to Tetiaroa, Moorea, Papeete Harbour and deep-sea fishing expeditions. Those interested in seeing the outer islands by motor launch might be interested in the motor yacht *Manavaroa*, which begins its itinerary in Raiatea then visits Huahine, Tahaa and Bora Bora. Call 66-20-62 for details and prices.

For people with more modest needs Tac Boat (☎ 42-28-65) has rentals of three to four-metre dinghies and outrigger canoes in Tahiti. They also have accessories such as fishing rods, underwater cameras, fins and mask, ice boxes, etc. Daily rental prices range from 5000 to 8000 CFP – call them for information. The office is next to the Maeva Beach Hotel.

ROAD
Except for the island of Tahiti, most areas do not have much paved highway. However, the roads that do exist are modern and well maintained. On all the islands there is a marvellous bus system consisting of owner-operators driving jitney-like vehicles known as 'le truck' – a triumph of small-scale entrepreneurial capitalism. Most French Polynesians cannot afford cars or motorcycles so these buses transport the majority of the population, especially on Tahiti where commuting to work in Papeete from the 'district' has become a way of life.

On the outer islands, where commuting is not so big a factor and the population density is much smaller, buses are less frequent. On these islands (such as Bora Bora, Huahine or Moorea) it definitely behoves the visitor to rent a car, motorcycle or bicycle for the day's sightseeing rather than depend on public transport. Taxis can be found everywhere but tend to be expensive.

The PK System
On larger islands like Tahiti and Moorea you can pinpoint your position on the map from the red-topped 'PK' km. stones along the inland or mountain side of the highway.

The
Society Islands

Introduction

The Society Islands are divided into two groups: to the east are the Windward Islands (Îles du Vent), which include Tahiti and Moorea; and to the west, the Leeward Islands (Îles sous le Vent) which comprise Raiatea, Tahaa, Huahine, Bora Bora and Maupiti.

The Society Islands were given their name by Captain James Cook, but the name originally referred only to the Leeward group. The English navigator Captain Samuel Wallis had already named Tahiti 'King George III's Island' and Moorea 'Duke of York's Island,' and Cook respected his predecessor's wishes. Later, however, both Tahiti and Moorea were included in references to the Society Islands.

But where did the name 'Society' originate? In Cook's own words, published in 1773, 'To these six islands (Raiatea, Tahaa, Huahine, Borabora, Tupai and Maupiti), as they lie contiguous to each other, I gave the names of Society Islands.' Thus the notion that the name referred to the Royal Society or the Royal Geographical Society is false.

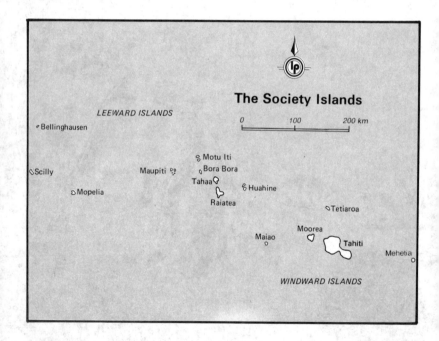

The Society Islands

LEEWARD ISLANDS

0   100   200 km

Bellinghausen

Scilly

Mopelia

Maupiti

Motu Iti
Bora Bora
Tahaa
Raiatea

Huahine

Tetiaroa

Maiao

Moorea
Tahiti

Mehetia

WINDWARD ISLANDS

Tahiti

Tahiti is the largest island in French Polynesia, with an area of 1041 sq km. Its shape can best be visualised as a figure eight on its side. The larger section of the island (Tahiti Nui) is connected to the smaller section (Tahiti Iti) by the narrow Isthmus of Taravao. The island's rugged terrain, crossed by numerous rivers and deep valleys, is marked by precipitous green peaks. The highest points are Mt Orohena at 2236 metres and Mt Aorai at 2068 metres, both eternally shrouded in wispy clouds. Because of Tahiti's mountainous interior, the vast majority of the population live on the coastal fringes. Politically, Tahiti is divided into 20 districts, most of which were formal tribal domains.

GETTING THERE & AWAY

Travellers arriving in French Polynesia by air will all arrive in Papeete. (See the Getting There & Away chapter for information about flying to Tahiti.) Papeete is also the central travel point for all of French Polynesia. From here flights fan out to the other islands; it is also the main port for copra boats which service the more remote islands. (See the Getting Around chapter for details of domestic flights and copra boat schedules. Or see the individual island sections for details of transport there from Tahiti.)

The addresses of airlines and helicopter services operating in and out of Papeete are:

Air New Zealand
　　Vaima Centre, Boulevard Pomare (☎ 43-01-70)
Air Tahiti
　　Boulevard Pomare (☎ 42-24-44)
Air Moorea
　　Faaa Airport (☎ 42-44-29)
Qantas
　　Vaima Centre, Boulevard Pomare
　　(☎ 43-06-65, 43-90-90 at the airport)
UTA
　　Boulevard Pomare (near Pitate Club)
　　(☎ 43-63-33, 42-22-22)
Air France
　　Vaima Centre (☎ 42-24-44, 43-20-00)

Hawaiian Airlines
　　Vaima Centre (☎ 42-44-38, 42-15-00)
Lan Chile
　　Vaima Centre (☎ 42-64-55/57 at the airport)
Minerve Corail
　　Immeuble Donald, Boulevard Pomare
　　(☎ 43-25-25)
Air Caledonie International (☎ 45-09-04)
Tahiti Conquest Airlines (charter carrier)
　　(☎ 43-84-25)
Tahiti Helicopteres (☎ 43-34-26)
Pacifique Helicoptere Service (☎ 43-16-80)
Heli-Tavake (☎ 41-01-00)

GETTING AROUND

Aside from renting a car in Tahiti, there are three modes of transport: le truck, taxis and hitchhiking.

To/From the Airport

Faaa Airport is 5½ km from Papeete. Le truck takes 15 minutes to town and costs 100 CFP. To get to town from the airport walk directly across the street and parking lot upon leaving Customs, climb two flights of stairs up to road level and cross the road. Look for a good spot to wait for the next Papeete-bound truck. Those who wish to walk should not follow the 'Papeete direct' signs unless, as my colleague Tom Huhti put it, 'they wish to dodge Fiat Pandas on the superhighway'. Reason being, the Papeete direct route will take you straight to a modern freeway, which bypasses an older, two-laned road, the latter being the normal truck route. It's simply not good for your health to be walking on a six-laned highway.

Note that there are also plenty of taxis. Taxi rates are set by the government and are fixed from the airport to each hotel.

Le Truck

The bus system known as le truck is the most practical and widely used form of transport on the island. The trucks, which are somewhere between jitneys and buses, have wooden benches that run the length of the vehicle, no shock absorbers, and speakers

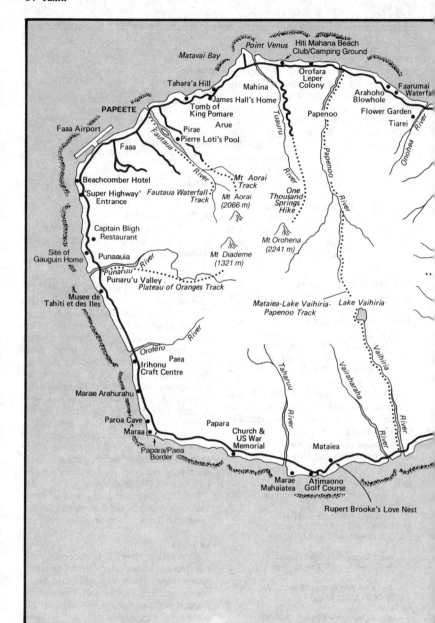

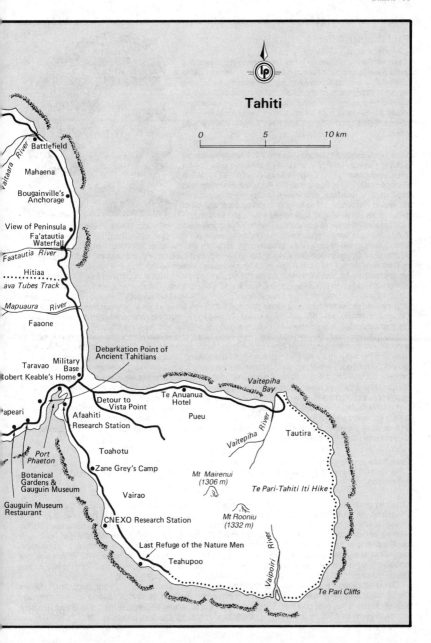

Tahiti

0   5   10 km

Vaitaara River
Battlefield
Mahaena
Bougainville's Anchorage
View of Peninsula
Fa'atautia Waterfall
Faatautia River
Hitiaa
Lava Tubes Track
Mapuaura River
Faaone

Debarkation Point of Ancient Tahitians

Taravao   Military Base
Robert Keable's Home

Vaitepiha Bay

Te Anuanua Hotel
Detour to Vista Point
Papeari
Afaahiti Research Station
Pueu
Vaitepiha River
Tautira

Port Phaeton
Toahotu
Zane Grey's Camp

Botanical Gardens & Gauguin Museum

Mt Mairenui (1306 m)
Te Pari-Tahiti Iti Hike

Gauguin Museum Restaurant

Vairao
CNEXO Research Station
Mt Rooniu (1332 m)

Last Refuge of the Nature Men
Teahupoo
Vaipoiri River

Te Pari Cliffs

Paul Gauguin & Tahiti

The reason why I am leaving is that I wish to live in peace and to avoid being influenced by our civilisation. I only desire to create simple art. In order to achieve this, it is necessary for me to steep myself in virgin nature, to see no one but savages, to share their life and have as my sole occupation to render, just as children would do, the images of my own brain, using exclusively the means offered by primitive art, which are the only true and valid ones.

When Paul Gauguin uttered these words five weeks before leaving France, he firmly believed that Tahiti was still an unspoiled paradise. On April Fool's Day in 1891, he left Europe and 69 days later arrived in Papeete. He left behind his Danish wife, Mette, and their five children in hopes that he would remain in Tahiti long enough to paint sufficient pictures for an exhibition that would establish his name.

Thanks to a letter of introduction to the local colonial administration, Gauguin was well received in Tahiti. He was wined and dined, and soon painted his first portrait in Tahiti for a fat commission. Unfortunately, the painting was unflatteringly accurate and it was his last commission for quite a while. At this point Gauguin decided it would be better to spend his time with the natives, and he moved into a Tahitian-style hut far from Papeete. Although disappointed at the little that remained of the native art and culture he had journeyed so far to see, Gauguin was happy to partake in village life. 'Koke', as he was known to the villagers, soon took a 13-year-old wife, Teha'amana, and spent his happiest year in Tahiti with her. The artist worked feverishly and by 1893 sailed back to France with 66 paintings and a dozen wooden sculptures for his planned exhibition. Unfortunately, nobody seemed to recognise Gauguin's genius, and his exhibition failed. To add to his troubles, Mette refused to see him again, he was assaulted and severely injured by a gang of sailors, and he contracted syphilis from a Paris dance hall prostitute. He departed for Tahiti once more and on arrival sought his Tahitian wife. She would have nothing to do with him, so he found another young girl. Despite poverty and constant suffering from the injury he had received from the sailors, Gauguin finished his masterpiece, *Where do we come from? What are we? Where are we going?*. He then swallowed an enormous dose of arsenic but vomited the poison and slowly recovered. His taste for life returned and he got a job with the public works department copying building plans, fathered a child, paid off his debts and devoted much time to writing anti-government editorials in local publications.

In 1901 Gauguin received an unexpected offer from a Paris art dealer who agreed to pay him a salary for every picture he produced. With his chronic money problems out of the way, Gauguin, still in search of paradise, decided to move to the isolated Marquesan island of Hiva Oa. Again he was disappointed with what he saw, and wrote:

Even if one is willing to pay high prices, it is no longer possible to find any of those splendid objects of bone, turtle, shell or ironwood that the natives made in olden times. The gendarmes have stolen them all and sold them to collectors.

Gauguin soon built himself the finest home in the Marquesas, which he dubbed the 'House of Pleasure'. He lived there with a 14-year-old vahine, Marie-Rose, who until then had been a resident of the Catholic mission school. With plenty of money to spend, Gauguin became well known for his wild parties and quickly incurred the wrath of the local clergy and the police. Meanwhile, his health declined further and his suffering necessitated the use of morphine. One morning a Marquesan neighbour found the artist lying on his bed with one leg hung over the edge. The visitor was not absolutely sure that his friend was still alive so he resorted to a Marquesan tradition – a bite on the head – to determine Gauguin's state. He then sang an ancient death chant.

Gauguin's legacy to modern art lies not in having introduced exotic subjects but, according to Bengt Danielsson, in having 'destroyed all existing conventions, dogmas, and academic taboos and rules that up to this time, had confined European artists to a narrow pedantic realism'. In Gauguin's own words, he provided future generations of artists with 'the right to dare anything'. ■

that blast Tahitian music and rock'n'roll. Each driver is an owner-operator who, like all independent truck drivers, must hustle to survive. The trucks have a few official highway stops (with canopies and benches), but generally they will pull over along any stretch of the road if you wave them down.

The trucks run on weekdays from the first light of dawn until about 10 pm. On Saturday they operate until midnight. Le truck runs on Sundays as well, though not as frequently. The main departure point for all trucks is the central marketplace in Papeete. To go west (towards Faaa Airport) you must catch le truck on the west side of the market. To go east (towards Pirae), catch a truck on the opposite side of the market. Drivers are always paid after the trip is completed. The fares range from 100 CFP (if you're going from Papeete to the airport – just under six km) to a maximum of 300 CFP to the other side of the island. Unlike taxis, you don't have to fear being 'taken' on le truck. The fare within a 20 km radius of Papeete is around 160 CFP.

Taxi

Compared with taxis in other locales, those in French Polynesia are very expensive. The government regulates taxi fares, and has established rates from Papeete to virtually every hotel and restaurant. Computerised meters have recently been installed in every taxi. This may cut down on blatant rip-offs but they are still expensive.

Inside the greater Papeete area the taxi fare should not exceed 900 to 1000 CFP, so be suspicious of anything much more than that for a ride within town. The tariff from town to the airport or vice versa is around 1600 CFP, except after 10 pm when the price goes up 50%. All other fares *double* from 10 pm to 6 am, and on holidays and Sundays the minimum rate may go up by 25%. Got all that? Quantum mechanics is simple compared with calculating Tahiti taxi fares.

Any complaints should be directed to OPATTI (the Visitors' Bureau). Although in theory taxi fares are regulated, some drivers may not adhere quite so strictly to the rules – especially if the passenger is a tourist.

Car Rental

For the visitor spending any appreciable time in Tahiti, or the person wishing to do an around-the-island tour solo, renting a car is a necessity. Aside from the the big names like Budget, Hertz and Avis there are smaller, good quality rentals – but consumer beware. Scrutinise the vehicle before you drive it away, lest you find nonexistent brakes or flat tyres. Depending on your choice of model, prices range from US$60 to US$120 per day or more. Rates are generally based on time plus distance and there is an insurance charge of 600 to 1500 CFP. Gasoline (petrol) is not included and it ain't cheap. A valid driver's licence issued in your country of residence is required.

I find Tahitian motorists uncommonly courteous compared with US or Continental drivers but they do have their own rules of the road so, when in doubt, drive very defensively. Watch out for French and Tahitian motorists who may insist on passing on blind curves, tailgating and turning without signalling. Beware also of children playing on the street, pedestrians who seem oblivious to traffic, and drunks on the weekends.

Car rental agencies are:

Andre
    Boulevard Pomare opposite the naval base in Fare Ute (☎ 42-94-04)
Avis Polynesie
    Rue Charles Vienot (☎ 42-96-49) and at the airport (☎ 42-44-23)
Budget
    (☎ 45-01-01, 43-80-79)
Daniel
    Near the airport, PK 5 (☎ 42-30-04)
Europcar
    Boulevard Pomare (☎ 42-46-16)
Hertz
    Rue Commandant Destremeau opposite the sports stadium (☎ 42-04-71) and at the airport (☎ 42-55-86)
Pacificar
    Rue des Ramparts near Pont de l'est in Papeete (☎ 41-93-93) and the airport (☎ 42-60-61)
Robert
    Rue Commandant Destremeau (☎ 42-97-20)

Hitchhiking

Hitchhiking is also possible, with varying degrees of difficulty for foreigners. The idea is to be as conspicuously non-French as possible. Although Tahitians enjoy meeting foreigners, hitching isn't as easy in Tahiti or Moorea as it used to be.

Papeete

The translation of Papeete is 'water (from a) basket', which most likely means that it was a place where Tahitians came to fetch water.

The population of greater Papeete is around 100,000. It is French Polynesia's only real city and continues to be a major South Pacific port of call for freighters, ocean liners and yachts. Business and government revolve around the town. It is the site of the high commissioner's residence, the Territorial Assembly, the post office, the tourist bureau, the banks, the travel agencies, movie houses, two hospitals, supermarkets, shops, hotels, nightclubs and restaurants.

Since the early 1960s Papeete has undergone a construction boom necessary to support its rising population (about 20,000 immigrants from France and 15,000 from the outer islands of French Polynesia) and modernisation. Although growth was inevitable, much of it can be attributed to the tourism infrastructure and France's nuclear testing programme, which resulted in increased population growth.

Unfortunately, the growth has been at the expense of some of Papeete's beauty. Despite new apartments and offices, however, the town still has the provincial charm of a French colonial capital – whitewashed houses, buildings of painted wood with large verandahs and corrugated tin roofs, narrow streets, parks, an outdoor market, street vendors and a profusion of odours ranging from pungent copra (dried coconut meat) to the aroma of frying steaks.

Papeete is designed for walking. The sidewalks and avenues are lined with vendors selling shell necklaces, straw hats, sandwiches, sweet fried breads, pastries and candy. The aisles of the Chinese shops are crammed with cookware, rolls of brightly coloured cloth, canned goods from New Zealand and the USA, mosquito coils and imports of every variety. You get the feeling that if you poke around long enough, you might discover a preserved 1000-year-old duck egg.

The best time to explore the narrow streets and browse through the stores is in the cool of the morning. Otherwise, fumes from automobiles and heat from the asphalt can be oppressive. A stroll through Papeete must be done in a leisurely manner and taken with several rest breaks at the many outdoor cafes and snack bars. There you can sit at tables shielded by canopies, sip the local Hinano beer, or eat ice cream and watch the procession of tourists and locals go by. On Sundays after 10 am activities cease and Papeete becomes a sleepy and provincial town.

HISTORY

At the time of Cook and Wallis, Papeete was a marshland with a few scattered residents and didn't attract too much attention until 1818 when Reverend Crook of the London Missionary Society settled there with his family. Papeete began to grow in earnest when Queen Pomare made it her capital in the 1820s and sailing ships began to use the protected harbour, which was a much safer anchorage than Matavai Bay to the north. By the 1830s it had become a regular port of call for whalers, and a number of stores, billiard halls and makeshift bars appeared on the waterfront to handle the business. When the French made Tahiti a protectorate in 1842-43 the military came on the scene, and in their footsteps came French Catholic priests and nuns.

In 1884 a fire destroyed almost half of Papeete, which resulted in an ordinance prohibiting the use of native building materials. Not much of consequence happened until 1906 when huge waves, the result of a cyclone, wiped out a number of homes and businesses. In 1914 two German men-of-war bombarded Papeete, sinking the only French naval vessel in the harbour.

INFORMATION

For information contact the Fare Manihini tourist office on Boulevard Pomare (on the waterfront). There is also an information office at Faaa Airport but it may be staffed by taxi drivers waiting for fares, rather than information officers. Best bet is the Fare Manihini office, which has excellent services. Airline offices, banks, the post office and other resources are all centrally located in Papeete, either on Boulevard Pomare or in the Vaima Centre.

Foreign Consulates

The addresses of the foreign consulates in Papeete are listed in the Facts for the Visitor chapter.

THINGS TO SEE

Marché Papeete

The centre of Papeete, the Marché Papeete (municipal market), covers one square city block and is between Rue 22 September and Rue Francois Cardella. In 1986 the 131-year-old market underwent a metamorphosis that changed it from a dark, crowded, seedy 'casbah' to a modern, well-lit, clean place of business. The old marketplace (a charming labyrinth of cramped, shabby stalls flavoured by accumulated tropical filth) was one of the last true South Pacific institutions left in Papeete. It was torn down and replaced by an airy, sunshine-filled, double-decked venue that local journalist Al Prince described as 'something out of the 19th-century gaslight era in Paris or the French Quarter of New Orleans'.

The 'new' market has been completely reorganised from the inside out and is much larger than its predecessor. Whereas in the old days fruit, flowers, watermelons and other produce would creep out of the market on major shopping days (like Sunday mornings), all selling now goes on within the market's walls. This is possible because of the two-tiered construction. The ground floor is reserved for flowers, taro, rootstalks

and daily catches of fresh seafood including bonito, mahimahi, albacore, lobster, shrimp, clams and other items. These are sold chiefly by Polynesians – an unwritten law here maintains that Tahitians may sell fish, taro, yams and other Polynesian foods; the Chinese sell vegetables; and Europeans and Chinese are the bakers and butchers. Downstairs, on the sidewalk, fruit and vegetables are displayed in the same traditional manner although the surroundings are aesthetically more sterile (but undoubtedly leaner). Although the environs are new, you can still stroll through the isles and find flower arrangements, bananas, pineapples, starfruit, coconuts, oranges, papaya, limes, mangoes, avocados, cassava root, lettuce, tomatoes, onions, carrots, beans, potatoes, cabbage and other items. No doubt there are still wary shoppers eyeing, squeezing, touching and scrutinising the merchandise.

The upstairs section, served by two escalators, is dedicated to handicrafts including woven pandanus hats, mats, bags and purses as well as shells, shell necklaces, larger shells, pareus and other clothing. There are numerous carvings such as tikis, bowls and ukuleles costing 50 to 200 CFP. Very few of the carvings are quality items. Prices for typical items are from 1000 to 1500 CFP for pareus and around 1500 CFP for hats.

Upstairs there is also a pleasant open-air snackbar which serves hamburgers, sandwiches, steak frites, poisson cru and other local dishes in the 500 to 700 CFP range. The eating area is breezy and some of the tables have canopies. Most of the clientele are local and it's an excellent spot for the weary shopper to have a meal.

The 'upper deck' provides an ideal place to take market photos without intruding on anyone's territory. In the old days it was very difficult to take shots of this fascinating institution because it was too dark and too jammed. This underlines the most striking improvement in the new regime – the space that now exists both for the consumer and the seller.

The best time to visit Marché Papeete is early Sunday morning when out-of-towners

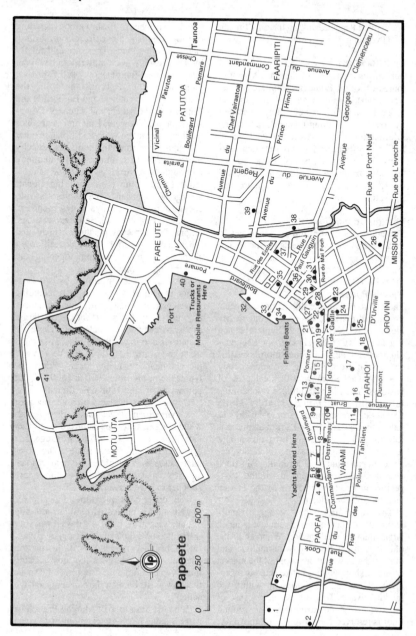

Papeete

0   250   500 m

PAOFAI

MOTU UTA

FARE UTE

PATUTOA

FAARIIPITI

MISSION

OROVINI

TARAHOI

VAIAMI

Port

Fishing Boats

Yachts Moored Here

Trucks or
Mobile Restaurants
Here

Rue du Commandant Destremeau

Boulevard Pomare

Boulevard Pomare

Rue de General de Gaulle

Avenue Bruat

Rue des Poilus Tahitiens

Rue du Cook

Avenue du Regent

Avenue du Prince Hinoi

Avenue du Chef Vairaatoa

Boulevard Pomare

Chemin Vicinal de Patutoa

Paraita

Rue Paul Gauguin

Rue des Ecoles

Rue du Mal Foch

Avenue Georges Clemenceau

Rue du Pont Neuf

Rue de L'eveche

D'Urville

Dumont

Taunoa

Chesse

Pomare

Commandant

1
2
3
4
5 6
7
8
9
10
11
12 13
14
15
16
17
18
19 20
21
22
23
24
25
26
27
28
29
30 31
32
33
34
35
36
37
38
39
40
41

1	Olympic Swimming Pool	22	Qantas/Air New Zealand
2	Stadium		(Vaima Centre)
3	Cultural Centre & Theatre	23	Cathedral
4	Foyer de Jeunes Filles de Paofai	24	Le Pescadou Restaurant
	(Girls' Youth Hostel)	25	Clinic Cardella
5	Church	26	Tahiti Budget Lodge
6	Tahiti Pearl Centre & Museum	27	Trucks to Faaa (Airport)
7	Pizzeria	28	Government Offices
8	Hospital	29	Market & Bus Stand
9	Hachette Pacifique (Bookstore)	30	Bank of Tahiti
10	Immigration Office	31	Trucks to Mahina (Point Venus)
11	Police	32	*Aranui* Dock
12	UTA/Air Polynesia Office	33	Customs, Immigration & Yachts
13	Bougainville Park	34	Tourist Office
14	Pitate Club	35	Polyself Cafeteria
15	Post Office	36	Trucks to Taravao
16	High Commissioner's Office	37	Town Hall
17	Territorial Assembly	38	Pacific Rent-a-Car
18	Chamber of Commerce	39	Baie D'Along Restaurant
19	Vaima Centre	40	Moorea Ferry
20	Bank	41	Interisland Vessels
21	Magazine & Newspaper Kiosk		

come to sell their goods, shop and attend church in Papeete. Don't be afraid to sample the exotic-looking fruits, vegetables and fish. The results will be satisfying.

Bus Stand

On the market's perimeter is the makeshift bus terminal where Tahiti's entire public transport system is centred. Amid the cacophonous streets, rumbling diesel-powered buses (known as 'le truck') blaring Tahitian music line up behind one another like cars on a freight train and inch their way up the road. Although the fume-filled, packed streets could be described as 'colourful', the road and sidewalks in the market area are terribly congested. Visitors should have no problem finding their way around. Trucks on Rue du 22 September head in the direction of the airport (towards Faaa) while those on the Rue du Mal Foch run in the direction of Hiti Mahana (towards Mahina and Pirae).

Waterfront

Several blocks from the market is the water-front, known as the quay. Formerly an array of clapboard warehouses and shacks, the area is now dominated by sleek shops and the four-laned Boulevard Pomare. On one side of the tree-lined avenue is a row of yachts several blocks long (mostly from the USA), beached racing canoes, fishing boats and ferries which deliver goods daily to nearby Moorea. On the other side of the road are business offices, shops, hotels, cafes, nightclubs, bars and the new Vaima Centre, a luxury residence and shopping centre. Walking along the quay you can see the yachts, watch the fishermen come in with their catch, and in the evening buy a meal from the many food vendors who gather in a huge parking area adjacent to the waterfront.

When the wind blows from the direction of the docks, Papeete's air is filled with the strong aroma of copra, the main export of the islands. To find the source of the smell, take a walk past the naval yard to Fare Ute (see map) where the copra boats are moored and where there is a coconut-oil processing plant. Here the vessels unload the crop they have picked up from the outer islands and exchange it for store-bought commodities. Watching the pallets containing beer, rice, drums of kerosene, sacks of flour, cases of canned butter and jugs of wine being loaded onto the rusty steamers gives you a feeling of the old days when all travel and trade were done by these boats. Try a sandwich and a bottle of Hinano at the nearby cafe where the stevedores and crew members congregate.

Continuing on past Fare Ute you will cross a bridge to Motu Uta, which was once an island in Papeete Harbour. Now, joined by two bridges, this area also has mooring spots for copra boats as well as marine servicing and dry dock facilities. This enclosing promontory serves to protect Papeete Harbour during inclement weather.

Territorial Assembly

Constructed in the late 1960s as the chamber of the democratically elected representatives of the French Polynesian government, this modern building sits directly over the source of the Papeete River. (The river has since been diverted to nearby Bougainville Park.) In this same area Queen Pomare had her home and eventually a royal palace which, in typical governmental fashion, was not completed until after her death. Nearby was an exclusive clubhouse for high-ranking military officers and civil servants where Gauguin (while he was still accepted) used to drink absinthe. The other important building occupying these grounds is the High Commissioner's residence.

Mairie (Town Hall)

The new *mairie*, or town hall, inaugurated in May 1990 by French President Francois Mitterand, is the newest landmark in Papeete. Despite its recent completion the building's design is based on the classic architecture of the old town hall, constructed in the last century. Located on Rue Paul Gauguin, it's well worth taking a look at.

Pouvanaa a Oopa Statue

Standing directly in front of the Territorial Assembly on Rue du General de Gaulle is a monument depicting Pouvanaa a Oopa, considered the greatest contemporary Tahitian leader. A decorated WW I hero and a coura-

geous Tahitian nationalist, Pouvanaa served as a deputy in Paris for the Tahitian Territorial Assembly. He was later jailed on what many believe were trumped-up charges by the metropolitan French government and exiled from his beloved Tahiti from 1958 to 1970. After his release (at age 72!) he served as a senator in the Territorial Assembly until his death in 1978.

Bougainville Park

Originally named Albert Park after the Belgian king and WW I hero, this park's name was later changed to honour the French explorer. On sunny days people usually occupy its concrete benches or enjoy the shade of its huge banyan trees. Of the two cannons prominently displayed, the one nearest the post office is off the *Seeadler*, the vessel skippered by the notorious WW I sea raider, Count von Luckner, whose boat ran aground on Mopelia Atoll in the Leeward Islands. The other belonged to the *Zelee*, the French navy boat sunk during the German raid on Papeete in 1914.

Melville's Calabooza Beretani

This is the site of the jail where Herman Melville was imprisoned in 1842. In his time here he gathered the grist for his second book, *Omoo*, and accurately described life during the early French colonial period.

Hats & Church

One traveller wrote to Lonely Planet and suggested that an entertaining way to spend part of Sunday is to go to church, listen to the hymns and study the women's hats.

ORGANISED TOURS

Tahiti's interior is one of the most beautiful (and seldom seen) attractions, making an inland tour a high priority.

Adventure Eagle Tours (☎ 41-37-63), run by William Leteeg, has a total of six tours, two of which are inland excursions – the 'Morning Mountain Tour' and the 'Mountain & Waterfall Tour'. Both visit 1400 metre-high Mt Marau, which entails a 4WD climb in a jeep wagon to see what Mr Leteeg calls

'Tahiti's Grand Canyon where no big buses can go'. The Mountain & Waterfall Tour also takes in Vaimahutu Falls and is a half-day trip, whereas the Morning Mountain Tour takes only two hours. The Morning Mountain Tour will cost you 4000 CFP; the half-day 'Mountain & Waterfall Tour' is 5000 CFP.

Mr Leteeg's other excursions are variations on circle island tours that read like a menu in a Chinese restaurant. Each tour has a selection of landmarks and you can pick and choose the items you wish to visit. These include the Gauguin Museum, the Vaihpahi garden and waterfall, the Papenoo surfing beach, the Fern Grotto of Maraa, Point Venus, the Arahoho Blowhole and other points of interest. He also has a city tour of Papeete which includes visits to the Black Pearl Museum, Lagoonarium and the Museum of Tahiti & Its Islands. These more conventional tours range in price from 3000 CFP for the 2½-hour 'Captain Cook Tour' to 4500 CFP for the 'Circle Island Tour'. Call William for more details.

Charter/Tour Boats

Revatua Charters (☎ 43-28-21, 48-04-39) has trips to Brando's private island (Tetiaroa), Moorea, sightseeing tours of Papeete's harbour area, and deep-sea fishing expeditions. The office is next to the Maeva Beach Hotel. Another company offering similar tours is Mers et Loisirs Nautical Activities Centre (☎ 43-97-99) with floating offices on Boulevard Pomare across from the post office. Their offerings include scuba diving, lagoon transfers between hotels in Tahiti and Moorea, day trips to Moorea, day tours to Tetiaroa, jet ski rentals, deep-sea fishing and excursions to Point Venus and Matavai Bay. Those of more modest means interested in renting a dinghy or outrigger for fishing, diving or lagoon exploration should call Tac Boat (☎ 42-28-65). They also rent fishing gear, snorkelling equipment and underwater cameras.

Bareback Charters

The popularity of bareback charters in Tahiti has grown tremendously over the last five years. This entails renting a fully provisioned boat for several days or, preferably, several weeks. Those who are not up to actually sailing the vessel on their own have the option of 'renting' a skipper or even a host or cook as well. Prices vary from season to season.

Mer et Loisirs (☎ 43-97-99) has six vessels available out of Tahiti. The prices (in CFP) are:

	April-December	January-March
Oceanis 350 and Sun Shine	231,000	182,000
Gibsea 372	266,000	203,000
Oceanis 390	280,000	224,000
Oceanis 430	336,000	266,000
First 455	406,000	322,000

PLACES TO STAY

Hotel reservations are not mandatory but can be made through your travel agent. Those who have booked 'packages' at the more expensive hotels will always get a cheaper rate than those who walk in and get the 'rack rate'. The prices listed are always the 'rack' or walk-in rate. Most prices are listed in CFP but some are listed in US dollars. Note that the less expensive hotels do not take telex or phone bookings from overseas countries but bookings can be made by writing directly to the hotel or in many cases by faxing. Usually there are vacancies year-round, with the exception of July. During the Bastille Day celebrations (starting at the end of June and lasting until August) it is virtually impossible to find a hotel room in Papeete. If you want to avoid crowds, this is not the time to come to Tahiti. Note that *all* hotels except OTAC (which runs the youth hostel across the road) charge the 7% tourist tax on top of the tariff.

Places to Stay – bottom end

To avoid any surprises, the traveller should be aware that paying for the 'bottom end' in Tahiti is like paying for the 'middle' in other areas.

Just a 10-minute walk from Papeete, the *Mahina Tea* (☎ 42-00-97) is your basic family-run, pension-style lodging. There are no frills or luxury about this place, but it is fairly clean, although reports are that local roosters can be aggravatingly noisy. It's in the Sainte-Amelie Valley, behind the gendarmerie. It has 14 rooms with double beds, six 'studios' with bathroom and kitchen, and two rooms with one bed. There is hot water from 6 to 11 pm. Rates are 3300 to 3500 CFP for singles/doubles depending on the size of the room. Rates drop if the guest stays more than two nights. Studios are available for monthly rent (90,000 CFP) only. Write to Vallon de Sainte-Amelie, BP 17, Papeete.

The newest and perhaps the only four-star accommodation in the budget category is the *Tahiti Budget Lodge** (☎ 42-66-82) in Papeete. About a 10-minute walk from Fare Manihini at the Tahiti Tourist Board, it's on Rue du Frere Alain, next to the College Lamenais. To get there from Boulevard Pomare walk down Rue du 22 September, cross Rue du Mal Foch and continue down Rue Eduard Ahne. It's a very clean, white-washed structure with a common dining area for 'home cooking'. There is also a snack bar.

By all appearances and reports this is a friendly place to stay, with excellent management. Beds cost 1500 CFP per night for shared rooms (three people), 3200 to 3500 CFP for private rooms with double bed and washbasin, and 4500 CFP with bath. An extra bed in larger rooms costs 1000 CFP. They meet travellers at the airport on most international flights. Aside from its popularity with travellers, Tahiti Budget Lodge is a favourite as a rooming house for French travellers working in Papeete. It is not by any means as inexpensive as other places but is well worth it for those who wish to avoid the more marginal lodging houses. For reservations write to BP 237, Papeete, Tahiti.

Around the corner from Tahiti Budget Lodge, on Rue du Pont Neuf, is *Teamo* (☎ 42-00-35), another low-budget place. It is a large, refurbished home with several dorm rooms that have eight bunks and self-contained baths and a few campsites on tiny lawns squeezed in between buildings. Beds range from 600 CFP in dorms to 3000 CFP for private rooms. There are several common

eating quarters and a large porch/sitting area. My take on Teamo was that it seemed OK but not as scrupulously maintained as some of the other hostels or pensions. At a cursory look, the facilities appeared to be fairly clean but at the time of writing the Tahiti Tourist Board had taken the establishment off its official list because it failed to pass a hygiene test. I have also heard that some travellers found it noisy.

One of the more reasonable places to stay in Tahiti (though not quite the cheapest) is the *Territorial Hostel Centre* (☎ 42-68-02, 42-88-50) on Boulevard Pomare, across the street from the Olympic pool and the OTAC, the cultural centre and library. It offers clean, dormitory-style accommodation. There are 14 rooms with three beds in each and three rooms with two beds. The cost is 3000 CFP for the first night and 2500 CFP for each additional night. The centre does not have kitchen facilities but there is a canteen which serves inexpensive meals. The doors are locked at midnight. For reservations write to M Jeffrey Salmon, Office Territorial d'Action Culturel, BP 1709, Papeete. You must have a student ID or youth hostel card to stay here. Large groups and organisations should make previous reservations, but this is not necessary for individuals, who are dealt with on a first-come first-served basis. Office hours are from 8 am to 5 pm Monday to Friday and from 8 am to noon on Saturday.

Pensions Staying with families can be an inexpensive and often enriching alternative to hotels. Sometimes it affords you a chance to see a side of Tahiti you would otherwise never experience. Note that the rates and services listed are more subject to change than other types of accommodation.

The *Chez Mirna* (☎ 42-64-11), BP 790, Papeete, is a few hundred metres from the Matavai Hotel on the fringes of Papeete in the Tipaerui quarter. They have two rooms with one double bed in each, and a communal bathroom, toilet and shower. The market and a phone are nearby. The cost per night is 3500/4500 CFP for singles/doubles. The minimum stay is two nights and a 5000 CFP deposit is required. Food is served upon request.

Places to Stay – middle

The *Matavai* (☎ 42-67-67, 42-61-69), BP 32, Papeete, was formerly the Holiday Inn but as far as I am concerned, once a Holiday Inn always a Holiday Inn. The 146-room hotel is on the outskirts of town and is popular with airlines, who put their flight crews up for the night there. Aesthetically awful. Prices are 9000/12,000 CFP for singles/doubles.

The *Royal Papeete** (☎ 42-01-29), BP 919 Papeete, is directly opposite the waterfront or 'quay' in the midst of Papeete's entertainment and shopping district. In its day it was one of the finer hotels but now is known mainly as the home of La Cave, one of the best nightclubs going. The 85-room Royal Papeete is not luxurious. In fact, its rooms are rather drab, but it's certainly adequate and is good for business people who need to stay 'in town'. Prices begin at 8000/8300 CFP for singles/doubles.

About two km from the heart of Papeete, the *Hotel Tahiti** (☎ 42-95-50, 42-61-55), BP 416, Papeete, was also one of the best resorts around in its heyday and still represents excellent (perhaps the best) value in its class. With 92 rooms and 18 bungalows, a swimming pool, an excellent restaurant and cordial English-speaking staff, it is a good choice for the visitor who wants good, clean accommodation but doesn't need the lap of luxury. The rates are 60,000/70,000 CFP for singles/doubles – perhaps the best price around for its class.

Prince Hinoi (☎ 42-32-77), BP 4545, Papeete, formerly the Ibis Papeete, has 72 air-con rooms and is located downtown, central to the nightlife and across from the quay. It is one of Papeete's newest hotels. The rooms are on the small side, but have a TV and video. Traffic noise could be a problem. Rates are 90,000 CFP for singles/doubles. The entire hotel is done in pastels.

Hotel Pacific (☎ 43-72-82), BP 111, Papeete, formerly the Kon Tiki, is moder-ately priced and located in the heart of Papeete on the Boulevard Pomare. In its former incarnation it was very tacky but it's now quite acceptable. There are 44 air-con rooms; the cost is 6500 CFP for singles/doubles.

Hotel Le Mandarin (☎ 42-16-33), which opened in 1988, is the newest hotel in downtown Papeete. With 37 air-con rooms, it provides colour TV and direct international dialling from the rooms. Tariffs begin at around 11,000/12,500 CFP for singles/doubles. It is within walking distance of the Papeete town hall, banks, boutiques, travel agencies, airline offices and the ferry docks.

Places to Stay – top end

In the 'suburb' of Pirae, the *Royal Tahitian* (☎ 42-81-13), BP 5001, Pirae, has 45 rooms with an ocean view and a black-sand beach popular with the locals. Although the beach was by no means 'trashed' I have seen cleaner ones. The crowd at the hotel was a mixture of French servicemen, Americans and Europeans. The rooms are well maintained and clean, and the grounds are expansive and manicured. Staff I encountered were friendly and courteous. Rooms start at 15,500 CFP for singles/doubles.

PLACES TO EAT

One of the best things about Tahiti is its restaurants. Thanks to the discerning palate of the French, Papeete is the only town in the South Pacific (with the possible exception of Noumea) where it is actually difficult to find a lousy restaurant. The main cuisines in Tahiti are French, Tahitian, Vietnamese and Chinese, or various combinations thereof. Prices range from reasonable to very expensive – US$10 to US$100 per person. The prices listed on the next page represent the cost of an average meal.

Good news on the price front is that some restaurants offer 'tourist menus' – special menus which are 20% to 40% less than standard fare. This has come about from a government programme aimed at lowering the price of restaurants by reducing import duties on food and booze for hotels and (participating) restaurants. Unfortunately, not all restaurants go along with the 'programme', so the lower prices only apply to particular menus at particular restaurants.

La Corbeille d'eau, Boulevard Pomare, French cuisine, considered to be the best French restaurant in Papeete, 5000 CFP.

Le Madrepore, Boulevard Pomare in the Vaima Centre, French cuisine, 4000 CFP.

Le Mandarin, Rue des Ecoles, Chinese cuisine, 2000 to 3000 CFP.

Jade Palace, Rue Jeanne d'Arc in the Vaima Centre, Chinese cuisine, 3000 to 4000 CFP.

Moana Iti, Boulevard Pomare, French-Tahitian, 2000 to 3000 CFP.

Le Baie d'Along, Avenue du Prince Hanoi, fine Vietnamese food, 2000 to 4000 CFP.

Le Pescadou, one block from Vaima Centre on Rue A M Javouhey, Italian food specialising in pizza – lively ambience and the best pizza in town, 750 CFP. It's perhaps the only restaurant open till midnight.

Scoubie Dou, around the corner from Le Pescadou, fast food Tahitian style, salads, sandwiches and the like. Owned by the same folks who own Le Pescadou.

Chez Vitu, next door to Le Pescadou, also owned by the same people who own Le Pescadou and Scoubie Dou. French and seafood specialities. Favoured by locals. Prices in the 800 to 1200 CFP range. Excellent.

Pizzeria, Boulevard Pomare, good pizza but lacks the atmosphere of Le Pescadou, 1500 CFP.

Acajou, on Rue Cardella, half a block from Boulevard Pomare near the market, is one of the all-time favourite cheapo eateries. Red chequerboard tablecloths, cosy, cave-like environs. Good place for breakfast. Prices range from 400 CFP for an omelette to 1000 CFP for steak or chicken.

Waikiki, Rue A Leboucher, good and inexpensive Chinese-Tahitian food, 1500 CFP.

Polyself, Rue Gauguin, next to the Bank of Polynesia, caters to the lunchtime office crowd – Chinese-Tahitian cafeteria-style food but consistently good, 1000 CFP.

Le Bistrot du Port Avenue Bruat, an outdoor cafe under shady trees, good seafood, French cuisine and local dishes.

Restaurant Tehoa, corner Rue du Mal Foch and Rue Eduard Ahne behind the market – tasty, inexpensive Chinese and European food, 500 to 1000 CFP. Friendly.

Restaurant Cathay Rue du Mal Foch (near Restaurant Tehoa), good, cheap Chinese food from 580 to 900 CFP.

Le Snack Paofai, corner of Rue Cook and Rue du Commandante, inexpensive snacks for 250 to 400 CFP and meals at 800 CFP. Open from 6.30 am to 5.30 pm daily.

La Suope Chinoise, behind the town hall. More good Chinese food, reasonably priced, 680 to 1000 CFP.

Chez Gerard, Avenue Prince Hinoi, French/seafood cuisine, 700 to 1000 CFP.

Chez Roger, a small cafe a few doors down from Manuia Curios, serving espressos, bakery items and the like. From 250 to 1000 CFP.

Market Area Budget Places

Some of the least expensive restaurants in the vicinity of the market include *Chez Roti*, *Acajou*, *Waikiki* and a few others. They are all quasi-Chinese restaurants/takeaways with prices in the 400 to 1500 CFP range. Their speciality is a dish called 'maa tinito', a mixture of red beans, pork, fresh vegetables and whatever else the chef feels like throwing in. These are real local dives and chances are you won't find tourists in there.

While in the neighbourhood you may want to stop at *La Marquisienne*, an excellent patisserie on Rue Colette near the corner of Rue Paul Gauguin, in the same block as the Mandarin Hotel. Nearby is one of Papeete's few public toilets, on the corner of Rue Colette, directly opposite the Mandarin Hotel.

Trucks or Roulettes

These places are on the waterfront parking lot opposite the upper end of Boulevard Pomare. These vans, decked with colourful, electrically lit signs, serve the best inexpensive meals in town, with prices in the 600 to 1000 CFP range. Even if you are not planning to eat, just walking around the various vans is a treat. Some of the owners have put a great deal of effort into ornately painting and decorating the vans to fit gastronomical themes ranging from pizzerias to creperies. One of the 'pizzerias' on wheels is complete with a hearth-like oven. The best time to go is in the evenings. Depending on the roulette you choose, dishes include grilled chicken, steaks and fish piled high with 'pommes frites' (chips), pizza and Chinese food. There are also vans specialising in ice cream, omelettes, and several that serve only crepes with toppings that include Grand Marnier, chocolate and honey. They are open after 5 pm every day and are very popular with locals as well as visitors.

Outdoor Cafes or Al Fresco Bars

These are at the upper end of Boulevard Pomare, opposite the Moorea Boat Dock. Near the sleazier discos on Boulevard Pomare, these are the hangouts of what travel guides refer to as 'colourful' people – soldiers, sailors, French Legionnaires, prostitutes (of all persuasions), transvestites, pimps, transsexuals and perhaps a lost tourist. These charming places are also great to hang out and watch the world go by while sipping an espresso, a glass of wine or perhaps a Hinano. Typical of the bars in this category are *Tiare Tahiti Bar*, *Jasmin Cafeteria* and the *Taina Bar*. They are a must for aspiring novelists and post-beat poets.

'Tourist Menu' Restaurants

The following restaurants in Papeete have adopted the government's policy of a 'tourist menu': *Acajou* (the high-priced one near Vaima Centre), *Le Baie d'Along*, *Le Bou-gainville*, *Le Jade Palace*, *Le Mandarin*, *La Pizzeria*, *Le Gillardin* and *Le Manava*.

ENTERTAINMENT

Clubs range from sleazy servicemen's clip joints to posh discos. However, before you step out, prepare to spend some cash. The cheapest beer in town is at least 300 CFP (a large bottle of Hinano in a supermarket costs around 130 CFP, just for your information) and the price of a cocktail ranges from 600 to 800 CFP. On a weekend night most clubs extract a cover charge of at least 1000 CFP, which includes a drink. Papeete is a small town, and most places are within several minutes' walking distance of each other.

Undoubtedly the friendliest places in town are the rollicking working-class bars where the common people come to unwind with conversation and a few beers. The bars are noisy, crowded, smoke-filled dens that usually have a trio or quartet hammering away on ukuleles and guitars. These places seem formidable at first because of the mass of people packed inside. Once you're in and flash a few smiles, however, the locals will be quite amiable.

Someone will most likely buy you a beer

Moonglow and a freighter's lights reflect from the rippling waters of the harbour. A warm south-east trade wind blows through the narrow streets and ruffles the bright print dresses of vahines as they walk in pairs towards the neon signs.

On the street, young sailors with crew cuts and tight-fitting jeans leer at the girls, banter in French and puff away at Gauloises cigarettes. Behind them, the pulsating disco beat of the Blackjack Club blares into the night. A painted, mini-skirted Tahitian in stilt-like platform shoes stands at the doorway and peers into the street.

Across the Boulevard Pomare, on the quay, the US yachts are moored neatly in a row. Inside the lighted cabins you can make out the figures of people eating dinner and sipping wine from plastic cups. Occasionally a denim-clad youth will slip out of a darkened yacht, cross the street and disappear into the maze of lights and people.

Down the Boulevard Pomare, near the bus stop, several old women with sleeping babies at their sides sit cross-legged on pandanus mats and weave crowns of pungent tiare Tahiti beneath fluorescent street lamps. Later they will peddle their fragrant creations in restaurants, nightclubs, bars and streets.

Over at the Pitate Club, across from the Monument de Gaulle, the band has started to play a Tahitian-style foxtrot and couples are slowly filing in. At the bar sit four crew members of a Chilean naval ship. The young men, who have been two months at sea, ogle the women and squirm self-consciously on their orange plastic seats. The Tahitian women eye them; some whisper to their boyfriends that they will try to hustle a few drinks from the *popa'a* (foreigners). ■

and ask where you're from and whether you're married. For some reason, Tahitians are extremely curious about one's marital status. If you have no spouse, they will shake their heads and say, 'Aita matai (no good). Maybe you find a nice vahine from Tahiti.' You might also be questioned about a person they have met from the same area. 'You know Jimmy from Los Angeles? He come here two years ago. He nice man.'

Expect to be chided a little if you go to working-class bars. Tahitians are generally polite, but often the visitor bears the brunt of their jokes. Laugh along. One evening at a local dive, several Americans were fortunate enough to be entertained by one drunken Tahitian comedian who alternately plunked away at a ukulele and told outrageous jokes. He was bringing the house down. The routine was entirely in Tahitian, and the Americans were the butt of every joke.

Dance Halls

For the average Tahitian, the dance halls (as opposed to the discos) are the most popular places to go. All the dance halls have amplified sound systems and bands that play the same Tahitian waltzes, foxtrots, rock'n'roll and music for the sensual tamure, the hip-shaking dance which has been known to cause palpitations in otherwise healthy men. Watching the tamure being performed by the bronze-skinned, sultry-eyed Tahitian beauties for the first time is a memorable experience. The dancers gyrate their hips to a breathtakingly rapid beat while their feet and shoulders remain perfectly still. Though originally an Eastern Polynesian (Tahitian and Cook Island) dance, the tamure has become a pan-Polynesian phenomenon.

Of the dance halls, the classiest is La Cave, beneath the Royal Papeete Hotel. La Cave has more of a ballroom atmosphere than the dance halls. Virtually everyone in Tahiti dances, sings, plays guitar, or does it all. Music and dance play an extremely important role in Tahitian culture. To not take part in this is to miss a large slice of the Tahitian experience. The Maeva Beach Hotel has a free music and dance performance.

Continuing on the dance hall circuit, down the socioeconomic ladder from La Cave is Le Pub on Avenue Bruat and, adjacent to it, the Pitate on Boulevard Pomare. Sporting garish red lights and movie posters on the ceiling, the Pitate is the most popular club among working-class Tahitians. At the door sits a bouncer with fists the size of hams. During the course of the evening couples file past him and disappear into the parking lot across the street, only to return several minutes later. There is, as one local put it, very little pretension at the Pitate.

Discos

These seem to have a universal character – flashing lights, a pulsating beat and a high decibel level. There are three types of discos in Papeete: the seedy B-grade hangouts frequented by French sailors; those popular with transvestites (and French sailors); and the posh 'straight' discos.

The first category, located on the waterfront near the naval yard, should be avoided. The second variety, which includes the Piano Bar, its neighbour, the Topless Club and the Bounty Club, have the 'loosest' ambience in town and attract a mixed crowd of tourists, locals, servicemen, gays and straights. Everyone is accepted here, and you can spend the evening dancing or watching the assorted types filter in and out through the swinging doors. The Piano Bar and the Topless Club are meeting places for mahus (transvestites), and feature strip shows with female impersonators. The Topless Club specialises in transvestites who have had hormone injections and like to show off their acquired charms. The Piano Bar, however, is the older, more famous institution.

Leaving the Piano Bar behind, you can try the 'straight' discos which include the Lido, Star Circus, Le Retro, Club Too Much (formerly the Rolls Club) and the ultra-posh Mayana – all places to be seen for the young and the restless. The Mayana caters to a younger, 'teenybopper' crowd; Le Retro's patrons are usually older. All the clubs are near the waterfront or the Vaima Centre area, within a few minutes' walk from each other.

When it's time for the show to begin, the music stops and patrons gather in a semicircle before the mirrored wall of the stage like schoolchildren awaiting a puppet show. With vaudevillian flair, the owner announces the entrance of Gigi, and the disc jockey cranks up Donna Summer or Michael Jackson to a deafening level. From stage left emerges Gigi, knees pumping and bottom swaying, making her way to a solitary bar stool in the middle of the dance floor.

She stands over six feet tall in her five-inch chromium-plated shoes and is wearing a skimpy leopard-skin outfit. Strands of hair from her wig fly in all directions as she bumps and grinds her way across the stage and contorts her body on the stool. Meanwhile, the audience is in rapt attention. The women giggle, the French sailors leer, and the tourists try hard to be nonchalant. Within a few minutes into the next song, Gigi's clothing has been peeled off and a drunk Tahitian teenager is sitting near her groping for her G-string. He is harmless and nobody pays attention to him. With a casual but deft flick of the wrist, Gigi removes even the G-string and disappears backstage.

At the tables, the hum of conversation resumes. Several uniformed sailors, still covered with acne, are animatedly flirting with a mahu. Although her demeanour and husky voice mark her as a transvestite, there are other mahus who are not so obvious. Often the transvestites rival the women in their beauty, an occurrence which, since the time of Cook, has led to some surprising discoveries by unwary visitors. ■

Drinks

On Saturday night, a quiet cocktail can be had at La Jonque, a remodelled boat anchored across from the Pitate. Major hotels in the area, like the Tahiti Beachcomber Parkroyal and the Hyatt Regency, have a tranquil ambience if you are not up to the nightclubs. When the bars close (after 2 am) you can continue drinking and dancing at the Princess Heita in Pirae or head to the roulettes for a bite to eat.

Around the Island

In the pre-European days Raiatea and Huahine were the most important islands in the Society Islands group. It was only after the Europeans came that Tahiti became the centre of trade and eventually the focus for colonisation. Consequently, Tahiti is the most densely populated and the most developed island and, with the exception of archaeological sites (mostly on Huahine), has the most to see.

Tahiti has one main road that circles the major part of the island (Tahiti Nui), but comes to a dead end in the outer reaches of the smaller part of the island (Tahiti Iti). The main roads are well maintained, but tend to be narrow and overcrowded.

When driving around the island, you cross the halfway point at the Isthmus of Taravao (PK 60). From there you may either complete the circle or explore one of three dead-end roads in Tahiti Iti.

For the reader interested in an in-depth overview of the historical sights around the island, Bengt Danielsson's *Tahiti Circle Island Tour Guide* is the definitive book on the subject. Most of the information for the Peninsula, South Coast and North Coast sections in this chapter was gleaned from it and I owe the author a tremendous debt for compiling facts that would otherwise be very difficult to come by. The guide is available at most bookstores in Tahiti.

ORGANISED TOURS
Te Pari Excursions

For those who would like to get to the back country without too much effort, there are several options, one of which is Te Pari Excursions (☎ 57-19-20), BP 7016, Taravao, based at the Hotel Puunui. They depart from the Hotel Puunui Marina aboard an outrigger canoe and bring visitors to the Te Pari Cliffs as well as the other natural attractions. The trip, which lasts from 9.30 am to 3.30 pm, includes a picnic on the beach. Rates are 2500 CFP per person – a minimum group of eight is required.

Helicopter Tours

For the better-heeled, helicopter tours from Pacific Helicopter Service (☎ 43-16-80, 43-28-90) can be taken to the remote Maroto Valley at the island's centre. The price is 4000 CFP for the 30-minute round-trip flight.

Adventure Eagle Tours

Travellers who like bushwhacking along mountain roads in 4WD vehicles should call William Leteeg (☎ 41-37-63) at Adventure Eagle Tours. William has a variety of mountain tours on the island of Tahiti and his reputation is good. For more details see Organised Tours, in the Papeete section, this chapter.

ACTIVITIES
Trekking

Upon your arrival in Tahiti the verdant hills beckon, but venturing into the bush can be a dangerous proposition unless you know what you are doing and where you are going. Torrential rain can swell streams into rivers and 'easy-to-find' trails can be overgrown with vegetation in no time. It's always best for the serious hiker to be accompanied by a guide. In many instances it's also best to rent a 4WD to get to the trail head.

Despite the requirements, Tahiti has a variety of excellent trails and guides for hire. Here are six treks of varying difficulty. Many, but not all, require guides.

If you plan to do extensive hiking it is suggested that you bring a sleeping bag, backpack, gloves, utensils (bowl, knife, fork and spoon) and food supplies. Recommended food is dried fruit, concentrated milk in a tube, soup, chocolate, etc.

Mataiea/Lake Vaihiria/Papenoo This two-day, across-the-island hike via Lake Vaihiria (Tahiti's only lake) begins on the south coast, crosses the island's ancient volcanic crater and ends in Papenoo on the north coast. Allow 45 minutes by 4WD to the Mataiea trail head. Hikers should be in good physical condition and a guide is required.

Mt Aorai The trek begins at the end of the Belvedere restaurant road (near Papeete). This is a two-day hike and a guide is required. Small fares have been built for hikers along the trail.

Fautaua Waterfall For this day trip up the Fautaua Valley take an ordinary car to Bain Loti (of Pierre Loti fame) and walk for three hours to the waterfall. A guide is not necessary but permission is needed from the Service des Eaux et Forêts.

One Thousand Springs Hike This is a comparatively easy hike and no guide is required. Take Mahinarama Road (near the Hyatt Regency) to the end (about five km) and walk for two hours to the springs. From this junction it is possible to climb Mt Orohena (Tahiti's highest) but naturally a guide is required for such an undertaking.

Plateau of Oranges (Punaru'u Valley) Take a car to Punaauia (about 15 km from Papeete) and enter the Punaru'u Valley road to the trail head (one to two km by car). Walk to Tamanu Plateau – an eight-hour hike. Trekkers should be in good shape and a guide is required.

Lava Tubes Start at PK 40 (east coast) and 4WD it for about eight km. It's a two-hour walk to the lava tubes. The walk is easy but a guide is required.

Guides The Tahiti Tourist Board recommends several guides who regularly lead hikes to the hinterlands. Two of these are Zena Angelien and Pierre Florentin.

Zena Angelien (☎ 57-22-67), BP 7426, Taravao, leads a variety of different treks on the peninsula separating Tahiti Iti and Tahiti Nui but her speciality is *Le Circuit Vert* (The Green Route). This entails a three-day hike around the *sauvage* coastline of Tahiti Iti including the mist-shrouded Te Pari Cliffs. You do not have to be a triathlete to participate but hikers should be in good physical condition. The trip includes walks through

Top Left & Right: Tahitian performers in national dress (RK)
Bottom Left: Basket-weaving contest during Tiurai (RK)
Bottom Right: Tahitian warrior at Tiurai celebrations (RK)

Top: Marquesan family (GH)
Bottom: Fruit-carrying competition on Huahine (RK)

thick jungle, wading waist deep across untrammelled rivers and streams and hiking precipitous bluffs. The scenery is breathtaking and sights include marae (ancient temples), burial caves, grottoes and petroglyphs. Zena will take a minimum of five and a maximum of ten people. Those feeling a bit insecure will be relieved to know that Zena always takes her two-way radio, is insured and has medical training. Backpacks and tents are available. The cost is 11,000 CFP per person. Zena will provide custom hikes for those with special needs or schedules.

Pierre Florentin Pierre runs Tahiti Special Excursions (☎ 43-72-01), BP 5323, Pirae, and is reputedly an experienced guide who brings visitors almost exclusively to Tahiti's interior valleys and mountains. He visits seven different locales in Tahiti and his hikes vary in degree of difficulty. Trips are scheduled only on weekends or holidays.

The longest trek is a three-day hike to Mt Orohena, French Polynesia's highest peak (altitude 2241 metres), in the district of Mahina. Vistas include the Papenoo, Punaru'u and Tuaru valleys, Tahiti's east coast and the Tahiti Iti Peninsula. The cost is 45,000 CFP for a party of eight (maximum). Pierre also has a two-day hike along the Tahiti Iti Peninsula, walking in a northerly direction around the Te Pari Cliffs and the Fenua Aihere wilderness to Tautira village. The price is 30,000 CFP for a party of up to eight.

Another two-day hike, recommended only for those in excellent physical condition, is to the summit of Mt Aorai (altitude 2066 metres). The trek includes a visit to the Fare Ata refuge and a magnificent vista of Papeete and Moorea. The cost is 30,000 CFP for a party of up to eight. Most people do not even know about the Hitiaa Lava Tubes but Pierre will take you there. Located on Tahiti's south-east coast, the Lava Tubes are underground burrows with streams meandering through them. There are also panoramic views of the peninsula. The cost is 15,000 CFP for party of up to eight.

For a pleasant day trip one might consider a visit to the Papenoo Plateau on Tahiti's east coast. The valley has several easy to reach plateaus with a plethora of orange, grapefruit and avocado trees. Swimming is at the foot of Topatari Waterfall. The rate is 16,000 CFP for a group of eight.

Finally, there are two half-day trips, to Fautaua Waterfall near Papeete and to the Plateau of a Thousand Springs. Of the two half-day trips the hike to the springs is the more difficult. The waterfall trip costs 16,000 CFP and the springs hike is 15,000 CFP – both for groups of up to eight.

Note that transport is not included, but is available for 1500 CFP per person (round trip). Sleeping bags and backpacks may be rented from Mr Florentin.

PLACES TO STAY

For information on hotel reservations, prices and so on, see Places to Stay in the Papeete section of this chapter.

Places to Stay – bottom end

The *Hiti Mahana Beach Club** (☎ 48-16-13), BP 11580, Mahina, Tahiti is a quality, low-budget dorm/camping area that has become the model in the local tourism industry for this niche. Operated by Coco and Pat Pautu (he's Tahitian and she's American), the beach club is a combination camping ground and dormitory on nine acres adjacent to a black-sand beach in the Mahina district. The owners appear to be earnest in providing good service and an amiable environment but at times are harried by the sheer numbers of travellers they must deal with.

The 'dorm' is actually a two-storey, century-old mansion (once owned by an American) which has both communal and private rooms with bath, as well as cooking facilities, refrigerator, dining room, lounge and plenty of breathing space. The ambience is nice and the atmosphere is very international. Campers have four acres of lush garden at their disposal as well as amenities such as bath, refrigerator, clothes line, bicycle, reading room and barbecue.

The 'Club' is very accessible by le truck yet far enough from town to be away from the urban blight. The cost to travel there from town is about 240 CFP one-way. The Club also offers good swimming, picnicking, snorkelling, windsurfing and excursions. Banks, grocery stores, inexpensive restaurants and fresh produce can be purchased nearby. Reasonably priced sandwiches and hamburgers are available on the premises.

The cost of camping is 700 CFP per person. Note that tents are no longer rented but mattress, sheet and pillow are around 400/800 CFP for singles/doubles. Dorm accommodation at the White House is 1500 CFP per person. Private room with bath is 3000/6000 CFP for singles/doubles, plus daily charges of 300 CFP for linen and 100 CFP for towel. The price for breakfast is 400 CFP, dinner is 1200 CFP and barbecues (on Fridays at noon and in the evening) are 2100 CFP. On Sundays the *Maa Tahiti* feast is 3200 CFP. Activities such as windsurfing cost 4000 CFP for half a day's rental and 6000 CFP for the whole day. Visitors who are not lodging or camping at Hiti Mahana are required to pay 300 CFP per day for the use of facilities.

To get to Hiti Mahana Beach Club from the airport look for the Hiti Mahana rep at the visitor information desk, where free cups of coffee are available for newcomers. If no one is there take a truck from the airport to the market (about 100 CFP) and transfer to any Mahina-bound truck. Pay the driver ahead of time (240 CFP) and tell him to let you off at Hiti Mahana. Although it's a few km off the main road (past the Point Venus turn-off), the driver will take you directly there.

Note that after 4 pm the trucks stop running and you will have a tough time returning, at least on public transport. The lack of inexpensive transport after 4 pm is perhaps the biggest problem with staying at Hiti Mahana.

Pensions The *Chez Michel et Armelle* (☎ 58-39-18) at PK 15 in the Punaauia district, is on the ocean side of the road. This place provides one room with a double bed and private bathroom. Amenities include outrigger canoe, and windsurfing and snorkelling equipment. The rates (with breakfast) are 4000/5000 CFP for singles/doubles. The price is halved for children aged five to 12. The chalet costs 5000 CFP per day for singles/doubles and 1000 CFP per extra bed.

Chez Tea* (☎ 58-29-27) at PK 17.5 next to the sign that says *'tatouage'* (tattoo parlour) on the ocean side looks like a winner – if you can get in. The owner, Tea Hirshon, usually has long-term tenants so it's suggested that you write to her at BP 13069, Punaauia, to see what's on the agenda. She has three comfortable, very funky bungalows filled with art. The place has a very bohemian feel. There is also a nicely landscaped garden and access to the beach. The cost is 4000 CFP per person.

Chez Vaa (☎ 42-94-32), BP 828, Papeete, is in Punaauia, at PK 8 on the mountain side in the Nina Peata neighbourhood. Her place – one room with double bed, communal bath (hot water) and pool – has been described as 'very clean' and I am told she is a very nice person. The daily rates are 4000/4500 CFP for singles/doubles, including breakfast.

Chez Coco (☎ 42-83-60), BP 8039, Puurai, Faaa, Tahiti has been around for years but at the time of writing had been taken off the list of approved hostels by the Tahiti Tourist Board because of poor hygiene. I've also heard that some of its management may harass female clients. Coco Dexter has two bedrooms, each with single beds, and four additional mattresses which can be used in the house. There are communal bathroom facilities and a swimming pool. Rates are around 1500/3000 CFP for singles/doubles. Excursions are also available on request.

Fare Nana'ao* (☎ 57-18-14) is one of the newer additions to the mid-level pension scene and was recommended to me by several people in the know. At the far end of Tahiti, in Faaone (PK 52) on the ocean side, it features six very original bungalows from available natural materials, mostly wood and stone. The owners, Monique and Jean-Claude Michel, emphasise that 'the shape of the walls, the support beams, the doors and windows are determined by the natural shape and contours of the trees and stones'. Though none of the bungalows are conventional by any means, one is actually built in a tree. Prices (for doubles) range from 4000 CFP in the tree house or 4500 CFP for a bungalow on the shore, to 5000 CFP for bungalows with full kitchen, and 6000 CFP for the largest bungalow with kitchen and inside bath. All other rooms have an outside bath. You pay extra for food and activities such as sightseeing, sea tours, sailing and the like. Transport to and from the airport is 2000 CFP. Those with a taste for the unusual or the bohemian may find Fare Nana'ao to their liking.

Fare Maroto Relais (☎ 43-65-87) is perhaps the most remote lodging in Tahiti because of its location in the centre of the island, high in the Papenoo Valley where the Vaituoru and Vainavenave rivers converge. Although it affords a splendid view of the valley and adjacent mountains, Relais was never meant to be an alpine resort. Rather, it was erected as housing for construction workers who built a nearby hydroelectric dam. It's fairly basic, as you might expect for construction crews. There is a sturdy concrete structure with ten rooms, each containing four bunks, a terrace and bathroom with hot water. There are also three concrete 'bungalows' each with two bedrooms, a single bed, living room, terrace and private bath.

For groups of fewer than eight people rates are 5500 CFP per person for a room, 8500 CFP per person for a bungalow, and three meals cost 5500 CFP per person per day; for groups of eight or more, meals are 5000 CFP per person. Individual meals cost 2500 CFP. A deposit is required for reservations. One more thing: you need to rent a 4WD vehicle to get there. If your idea of a vacation is tropical mountain scenery, check it out.

Places to Stay – middle

The *Te Anuanua Hotel** (☎ 57-12-54), BP 1553, Papeete, is highly recommended,

especially for its excellent food, and is considered one of the best small hotels on the island. Its only drawback is the price. Located in the countryside on Tahiti Iti in the district of Pueu, it is far from the hustle of Papeete. They have three bungalows with two rooms per bungalow. The layout includes a double and a single bed, private bathroom and balcony. There is also one 'bungalow suite' with a single and a double bed, two bathrooms with tubs and a refrigerator. The amenities here include bicycles, windsurfing, lagoon and mountain tours. The daily rates are from 6000 to 8000 CFP for singles and 7000 to 9000 CFP for doubles. Credit cards are not accepted so bring plenty of cash.

The *Tahiti Country Club* (☎ 42-60-40, 43-08-29) is on Punaauia Hill, two km from the airport and six km from town. Formerly part of the Ibis chain, it is now part of the Tahiti Resort Hotels chain. It has 40 rooms; the ground floor rooms have air-con and the upper floor rooms have ceiling fans. Each room has a refrigerator and TV. Further amenities include tennis courts and water sports. It is not luxurious but it is decent. The rates are 9500/11,000 CFP for singles/doubles. For reservations the postal address is BP 576, Papeete.

Princess Heiata (☎ 42-81-05), BP 5003, Papeete, is best known as an after-hours club on the weekends for revellers who don't think the party is over when the nightclubs close. It has 25 rooms and 11 bungalows and is about five km from Papeete going east towards Pirae, near a black-sand beach. Prices are around 7000/8000 CFP for singles/doubles.

Next to the Tahiti Beachcomber, about seven km from Papeete, *Te Puna Bel Air* (☎ 42-82-24), BP 354, Papeete, is reasonably priced and adequate. It has 48 modern motel-style rooms and 28 thatched bungalows with overhead fans. The hotel has a freshwater pond-cum-swimming pool with ferocious-looking but perfectly harmless eels. It also has spacious gardens and a good restaurant, and is near the beach. Sundays feature a Tahitian feast followed by dancing to a local band. Prices start at 8000/9000 CFP for singles/doubles.

Hotel Puunui (☎ 57-19-20), BP 7016, Taravao, is on a grassy hillside in Taravao, about 65 km from the grime of Papeete. Its 54 'junior suites' are modern but whoever designed them must have been on loan from the US Army Corps of Engineers. On the outside the rooms appear more akin to ammunition bunkers than hotel rooms. They do, however, command a spectacular view. There are two restaurants on the premises, a pool, two tennis courts and all the water sports. The hotel did not seem particularly occupied when I visited there. Most of the people on the premises appeared to be day trippers. There is also a beach and a marina belonging to the hotel on the shore with all the requisite nautical sports activities. Rates for 'junior' suites are 10,000 CFP for singles/doubles.

Places to Stay – top end
The *Tahiti Beachcomber Parkroyal** (☎ 42-51-10), BP 6014, Faaa, Tahiti, a 202-room resort two km from Faaa Airport and eight km from Papeete, is a compromise between city and town – close enough to enjoy Papeete but far enough away to avoid the hustle. It is considered the best large 'resort' hotel on Tahiti. Located on the water, it features the usual assortment of water sports and cruises as well as 185 standard rooms and 17 air-con, over-the-water bungalows. Its management poured US$5 million over several years into refurbishing the rooms, and the bar/restaurant and conference hall were totally revamped. Prices begin at 21,000/25,000 CFP for singles/doubles. The Beachcomber also has an extensive water sports pavilion with glass-bottomed boat, snorkelling, outrigger canoe excursions, scuba diving, sunset cruises, windsurfing, water skiing and all the other nautical sports.

About nine km from Papeete (just down the road from the Beachcomber), the *Maeva Beach* (☎ 42-80-42), BP 6008, Faaa Airport, was one of the first luxury hotels in French Polynesia. It has 230 rooms, one of the best restaurants on the island (the Gauguin) and

is on the beach. It feels more like a European hotel than any resort on the island. Prices begin at 18,600/20,700 for singles/doubles. The beach at this hotel is an excellent place to swim and there is a water sports centre (Tahiti Aquatique) with all the requisite activities such as diving, snorkelling, glass-bottomed boat, sport fishing charters, windsurfing and harbour cruises.

Hyatt Regency Tahiti (☎ 48-11-22), BP 1015, Papeete, formerly the Tahara'a Hotel, is perched on a summit named 'One Tree Hill' by Captain Cook and overlooks historic Matavai Bay. The hotel is on the boundary of the Arue district about eight km outside Papeete. Below the hotel is a gorgeous black-sand beach; above, the view of the bay is spectacular. The rates start at 23,000 CFP for singles/doubles. Though the quality of accommodation is mediocre when one considers the cost, the sheer physical beauty of the location may make up for other shortcomings.

Tetiaroa* (☎ 42-63-02/03) is the name of the atoll resort owned by Marlon Brando. The string of 12 islands (10 of which are bird sanctuaries) are a 20-minute, 60-km flight from Faaa Airport in Tahiti. In my opinion, they are archetypically beautiful South Pacific islands, complete with blue lagoon, blinding white-sand beach, swaying palm trees and warm trade winds. Tetiaroa is also one of the better travel bargains in French Polynesia. If I had a week to spend in French Polynesia with a close friend, Tetiaroa would definitely be one of the places I'd seriously consider.

Although 'resort' is a loosely used term, usually conjuring up images of strangely shaped swimming pools, sickly sweet, red tropical drinks with tiny parasols stuck in them and bored-looking waiters, this does not apply to Tetiaroa.

Brando purchased the atoll in 1965, put a few modest fares (local accommodation) up and left it in its natural state. I was told by the former manager, a venerable Tahiti hand named Alex, that Brando ordered the builders not to use insecticide or chemicals of any kind in constructing the fares. They didn't.

Because the islands were a bird sanctuary and a former island retreat for the Pomare dynasty (the royal family which sought refuge from the puritanical missionaries) he assumed that doing as little as possible to alter the place was the best policy. He was right. To put up fancy digs on Tetiaroa would have destroyed the whole funky atmosphere, which the island still has.

Brando's private paradise is not for everybody, however. One gets the feeling he does not want it to be. The island is for self-contained people who like to read fat novels, bask in the sun or swim. Alex called it a 'decompression chamber' that provides basic amenities in a superb natural environment.

The biggest attraction is a visit to one of the bird islands where half a dozen species of sea bird nest. The birds (such as crested terns, bobbies, fairy terns, grey terns, frigate birds, etc) seem relatively unafraid of humans and it's possible to walk up to their nests.

One of the best things about the island is its proximity to Tahiti. Jump on a plane and 20 minutes from the largest urban centre in the south-east Pacific, and you are there. The 'resort' consists of about 12 fares constructed from local wood with thatched roofs and simply fashioned furniture, and beds that are comfortable but not fancy. One is given a kerosene lamp (to use after the generator goes off) and a mosquito coil. Other amenities include a circular outdoor bar with fishing floats of every nation hanging from the beams and a very orthodox dining hall that serves basic food.

One and two-day excursions are available to the island from Papeete or Moorea. Included in the one-day trip is a visit to Bird Island and archaeological sites on the island. Scuba diving is available at an extra charge. Package deals begin at US$400/740 for singles/doubles (including three meals) and air fare for two nights and two days. Every extra day costs US$135/230 for singles/doubles. You can also get to the island via charter boat on a day trip from Tahiti for approximately 15,000 CFP, which includes round trip, three meals, tour of a copra village, picnic and visit to Bird Island. (See Charter/Tour Boats, in the Organised Tours section ealier in this chapter for information.) The postal address is BP 2418, Papeete. In the USA, you can reserve space at Tetiaroa by calling (800) 922-6851.

PLACES TO EAT

Pirae
The Le Belvedere, a 'tourist menu' restaurant, is perched on a mountainside near Papeete – great view day or night. It serves French food at 2500 CFP and specialises in Fondue Bourguignonne (meat fondue). Ring them (☎ 42-73-44) for free transport.

Arue
The Dahlia, at PK 3.3, is a decent Chinese restaurant with a median price of 800 to 900 CFP.

Pamatai
The Maribaude has an oceanside view. They offer French cuisine at 3000 to 5000 CFP. Excellent.

Punaauia
At Coco's you can get seafood at 3000 to 6000 CFP and is near the ocean (PK 13). There is also a US-style bar, L'Auberge du Pacifique, offering seafood for 3000 to 5000 CFP (PK 11.2).

Two restaurants that have adopted the 'tourist menu' are Acajou and L'Auberge du Pacifique.

Faaa
The Le Gauguin is at the Sofitel Maeva Beach (PK 7.5). The cuisine is French, at 3000 to 6000 CFP. Excellent.

Le Grand Lac, PK 4.5, is on the ocean side, and offers some of the best inexpensive Chinese food around, at 580 to 900 CFP.

Papara

Constructed on the water, *Le Petit Mousse* (PK 32.5) makes for a nice Sunday afternoon dining outdoors. It serves North African food at 2500 CFP.

The *Nuutere* and *Vahine Moena* restaurants have adopted the 'tourist menu'.

Mataiea

The *Vahoata* (PK 42.9) is famous for its Tahitian feasts on Sunday. The restaurant is a 'tourist menu' one and the food is Tahitian, at 2500 CFP.

Papeari

The *Restaurant-Bar Musée Gauguin* (PK 60) has excellent French food and pleasant surroundings at 2500 to 4000 CFP. It's another 'tourist menu' restaurant.

BEACHES NEAR PAPEETE

One naturally associates Tahiti with beaches, and there is no shortage of sand on this tropical island. Unfortunately, most of it is not the powdery white substance that many people who come to Tahiti expect. There are some fine white-sand beaches in French Polynesia but they are not on Tahiti (don't say I didn't warn you).

Just two miles north of Papeete, near the Royal Tahitian Hotel in Pirae, is a black-sand beach fringed with ironwood trees, palms and shrubs. Offshore is a beautiful view of Moorea. The beach has a nice local atmosphere but could be cleaner. Further north, at the foot of the Hyatt Regency in the Arue district, is one more black-sand beach, perhaps the loveliest on the island. Just a few km further north of the Tahara'a is the Point Venus area, popular with picnickers because of a shady grove of palm and ironwood trees and an excellent beach. If you keep going in the same direction for another 12 km, at PK 22 you will find a very nice black-sand, half-moon beach just past the Arahoho Blowhole. It's a winner.

If you start from Papeete, going in the other direction, the best beach nearest to town is near Maeva Beach Hotel in Faaa. A hundred metres or so offshore is a pontoon anchored in three metres of water, about 100 metres from the barrier reef. It makes for great sunbathing and a 360° panorama. Keep in mind there's no shade on the pontoon.

To find a white-sand beach you must go south of Papeete – about 10 to 15 km – to the 'high-rent' district of Punaauia. Access to the beach is through the former Hotel Tahiti Village. Although there are fine homes adjacent to the hotel area no one will chase you off their frontage – the general public have sunbathing and swimming rights to practically all the beaches in Tahiti. A few more km down the road will put you in Paea, which has more beaches and some of the best surfing conditions on the island. Surfing was the ancient sport of Polynesian kings, who rode the waves in to these very shores 1000 years ago. In fact, it was none other than the Tahitians who brought surfing to Hawaii, when they migrated there in the 11th and 12th centuries.

Aside from Paea, other surfing areas can be found just south of Pomare's Tomb, south of Point Venus and beyond the Papenoo River towards the Arahoho Blowhole. (All these areas are on the north coast highway.)

NORTH COAST: PAPEETE-TARAVAO

Pirae (1.5 km, Papeete)

As you drive out of Papeete on Avenue George Clemenceau (the beginning of the north coast road) you will enter Papeete's suburb of Pirae, home of Tahiti's President Gaston Flosse. Pirae is also headquarters for the Centre du Expérimentation de la Pacifique (CEP) the agency responsible for nuclear testing on Mururoa in the Tuamotus. The massive complex is on your left. This huge bureaucracy, which employs thousands of French Polynesians and metropolitan French, is a source of French pride, though perhaps their sentiments are not shared by all Tahitians. France's independent nuclear arsenal, 'force frappe', was developed during the days of de Gaulle. French Polynesia was chosen as a testing ground when Algeria (a former French colony used as a nuclear testing ground) became politically unsuitable.

Unlike the many vocal nuclear activists in other nations, French people of all political persuasions accept the policy of an independent nuclear striking force and the CEP has not been a centre of controversy since the mid-1970s, when many Tahitians rallied round the cries for independence from France. On the contrary, many Tahitians are paid quite well for their work in this often hazardous form of employment.

On the main road in Pirae there is a market area where shell necklaces, jewellery, clothing and other souvenirs are sold. Le truck regularly makes stops so it is quite accessible from Papeete.

Fautaua River & Pierre Loti's Pool

(2.5 km, Papeete)
Pierre Loti was the pen name for Julien Viaud, the French merchant marine whose book *The Marriage of Loti* describes the love affair of a Frenchman and a native girl (see the Tahiti Literati section in the Facts for the Visitor chapter). The pool where he first saw the enchanting Rarahu (the novel's heroine) is several km up the Fautaua River Valley. Unfortunately this romantic spot on the river is now covered with concrete but is marked by a bust of the author. Bain Loti is also the trail head for a three-hour hike to the Fautaua Waterfalls (see the Activities section in Around the Island, this chapter).

Tomb of King Pomare V (4.7 km, Arue)

A sign on the ocean side of the road marks the access road to the tomb. The Pomare line rose to power as a direct consequence of the European discovery of Tahiti. The first of the lineage, Pomare I, used members of the ex-*Bounty* crew, who were armed with guns, to defeat his enemies. Pomare I's son and successor, Pomare II, was crowned at a temple just a few feet away from the site of the present-day tomb where the Protestant Church now stands. During the ceremony a *Bounty* crew member, James Morrison, reported that three human sacrifices were made on behalf of the new king.

In 1812 Pomare II became the first Tahitian convert to Christianity and after three years managed to convince the populations of Moorea and Tahiti (with the use of arms where necessary) to follow his example. In his religious zeal Pomare II constructed a temple larger than that of King Solomon out of breadfruit tree pillars, palm fronds and other local materials. The Royal Mission Chapel, as it was called, was about 230 metres long (longer than St Peter's in Rome!), 18 metres wide and could hold 6000 people. Pomare II died in 1821 at the age of 40 from the effects of alcohol and soon afterwards the Royal Mission fell into disrepair. Today a 12-sided chapel built in 1978 stands where the Royal Mission once did.

The tomb itself was constructed in 1879 for Queen Pomare, who died in 1877 after a reign of 50 years, during which her country became a French colony. The Queen's remains were removed a few years later by her son King Pomare V who, feeling that his end was near, apparently wished to occupy the mausoleum by himself. Pomare V lived on a stipend supplied by the French government, and died in 1891 at the age of 52; in true Pomare tradition, he drank himself to death. (An account of his funeral is given by Paul Gauguin in *Noa Noa.*)

Local tradition has it that the object on the tomb's roof – which misinformed guides say represents a liquor bottle (which would have been a fitting memorial to Pomare) – is actually a replica of a Greek urn.

James Norman Hall Home/Museum

(5.4 km, Arue)
Look for the old Hall residence on the mountain side of the road. Nordhoff and Hall (see the Tahiti Literati section in the Facts for the Visitor chapter), authors of the *Bounty Trilogy, Hurricane* and *The Dark River*, probably did more to publicise Tahiti in the 20th century than any other writers. Hall died

at his Arue home in 1951 and is buried on Herai Hill just above. The Hall residence is now a museum which can be toured daily (except Mondays) from 9 am to 5 pm. Admission is free. The Pu Maohi Art Centre is also here.

Hyatt Regency Tahiti & One Tree Hill
(8.1 km)
Pull into the hotel parking lot and walk a few metres to the cliff, which affords a magnificent view of Moorea and Matavai Bay where Wallis and Cook once anchored. Wallis originally called this piece of real estate 'Skirmish Hill' because he bombarded the Tahitians gathered here with cannonballs from his ship. Cook later changed the name to 'One Tree Hill' because of the solitary *atae* tree that grew here at the time. When the hotel was built in 1968 the owners kept the Tahitian name. The Hyatt Regency (formerly the Tahara'a Hotel), which hugs the bluff like a gull's nest, has recently been refurbished.

Point Venus & Matavai Bay
(10 km, Mahina)
Turn left towards the ocean at the sign marked 'Point Venus' (on the same corner as a large store). Drive about one km to the parking lot. This area has all the natural amenities – shady trees, a river, beach and exposure to cooling trade winds – and makes a wonderful picnic ground. Near the beach area, towards Papeete, note that a local outrigger canoe racing club stores its vessels here. There are also a few souvenir shops near the road.

In the early days of Tahiti's history this tiny point of land was used by some of the most important visitors of that era – Captains Wallis, Cook and Bligh. Until the 1820s, when Papeete became a more popular port of call, all visiting ships anchored in the area. Although Wallis, Tahiti's discoverer, landed here in 1767, it was Captain Cook's expedition in 1769 that was to give this piece of land its name.

Cook was sent by the Royal Society of England to record the transit of Venus which,

theoretically, would enable scientists to compute the distance between the earth and the sun – a figure that would be an invaluable tool for navigators. On 3 June 1769 the weather was good and the transit was recorded by the best instruments available at the time. Unfortunately the best equipment of the day was not accurate enough and Cook's measurements were for nought. His journey was still a success, however, because of the many new species of flora and fauna gathered by the other scientists on the trip. Cook also anchored off Matavai Bay in 1773, 1774 and 1777 during his second and third voyages of exploration.

During the *Bounty* episode in 1788, Captain Bligh also landed here, collecting breadfruit plants to use as a cheap source of food for the slave population in the West Indies. His landing became grist for Hollywood, which came up with three different cinematic interpretations in 1935, 1962 and 1983. According to Danielsson, during the shooting of the 1962 *Bounty* version with Trevor Howard and Marlon Brando, a sequence was filmed on Matavai Bay featuring thousands of Tahitian extras welcoming the visitors ashore. The director, wishing to portray the Tahitians in their former glory, had the Tahitian extras don long-haired wigs and false teeth before the filming to compensate for attributes most of them no longer possessed.

Wallis, Cook and Bougainville were once honoured by non-figurative wooden sculptures placed at Point Venus in 1969. However, the monuments, along with the quaint Museum of Discovery, were swept away by a storm several years ago. Bligh, the third navigator to visit the area, was not remembered by any monument. In the same area where the above-mentioned sculptures once stood, you will see an abstract monument which Danielsson describes as a 'needle pointing to heaven'. This commemorates the arrival of the first Christian missionaries on Point Venus in 1797. Dispatched by the London Missionary Society, they abandoned their mission in 1808 and did not re-establish themselves until 1817.

Though they worked actively for the British annexation of the islands, the British missionaries were eased out of Tahiti after the French takeover in 1842. The missionary era came to an end in Tahiti in 1963 when an independent Protestant church run by Polynesians was formed.

About 50 metres north-east of the Missionary Society memorial is a monument enclosed by an iron railing. According to the text on its bronze plaque (which has now disappeared), the column was erected by none other than Captain Cook in 1769 and refurbished in 1901. However, not only was the monument not built by Cook (it was a product of the local public works department), it is not on the spot where Cook made his astronomical observations (which took place between the river and the beach).

Finally, the most visible (existing) landmark on Point Venus is the lighthouse, constructed in 1868 despite the 1867 date perhaps overoptimistically inscribed on the entrance.

Hiti Mahana Beach Club & Camping Ground (10.5 km, Mahina)

This camping ground/dormitory is the best thing to happen to low-budget travel in Tahiti. It is run by a savvy couple (Coco & Pat Pautu), and the operation offers inexpensive and clean lodging. The atmosphere is friendly, international in flavour, and about half an hour (depending on traffic) from downtown Papeete by le truck. Highly recommended. (For more information see the Places to Stay section in this chapter.)

Orofara Leper Colony (13.2 km, Mahina)

Prior to WW I, victims of leprosy were ostracised from communities and chased into remote areas away from the population. By government decree, in 1914 the Orofara Valley was set aside as a 'leper colony' for all those in Tahiti who suffered from the dreaded disease. Until the development of sulphur drugs there was little the French Protestant mission treating the lepers here could do. Nowadays it is possible in most cases to cure the disease and allow patients to go home. According to current statistics, approximately two out of 1000 French Polynesian citizens suffer from leprosy.

Papenoo Village & Valley (17.1 km)

Papenoo is a typical rural village, the type that has rapidly disappeared since the end of WW II. Many of its homes are built in the old colonial style, with wide verandahs. The Catholic and Protestant churches and mairie (town hall) are all along the highway. Past the village, a new bridge (the longest in Tahiti) spans the Papenoo River. The Papenoo Valley, the biggest on the island, was formed by an ancient crater. The river's mouth (where the bridge is located) is the only hole in the crater wall. Continuing up the Papenoo Valley you will come to the trail head that leads across the island (see Trekking, in the Activities section in this chapter).

Arahoho Blowhole (22 km, Tiarei)

Beneath a steep cliff about 200 metres before the road turns towards Tiarei is one of Tahiti's biggest roadside attractions – the Arahoho Blowhole. Actually there are at least two blowholes, one on the ocean side, the other unmarked and on the shoulder of the road. Perhaps it does not rate as one of the world's great blowholes, but it is clearly the most accessible (if not the only one) in Tahiti. Through countless years, battering surf has undercut the basalt shoreline and eroded a passage or tube to the surface. When waves crash against the rocks, the result is a geyser-like fountain of sea water and a shower for onlookers – even if they are standing on the highway. Several metres away from the blowhole is a small, crescent-shaped black-sand beach. It's a good spot to picnic. There are also several vendors selling coconuts, *mape*, a delicious Tahitian chestnut and, if it's the right season, *rambutan*, a wonderful red-spined fruit native to Asia.

Faarumai Waterfalls (22.1 km, Tiarei)

Just past the blowhole is a marked 1.3 km dirt road leading to the three Faarumai

Waterfalls. Park in the lot near a bamboo grove and walk the several hundred muddy metres to Vaimahutu, the first fall. If you look carefully you'll notice star fruit, guava and mape on the trail. Be sure and bring a swimsuit and insect repellent. Try standing underneath the falls for a natural high. The other two falls are accessible – one is a five-minute walk, the other 30 minutes (see Trekking, in the Activities section in this chapter).

Gardens & Copra Plantation
(25 km, Tiarei)

This is a private reserve but you can park and from the road see the lily ponds and accompanying flora that thrive in the area. The coconut plantation here, only one of many around Tahiti and its neighbouring islands, was once an important source of cash for the average Tahitian. Although harvesting copra (dried coconut meat) is still a vital occupation for islanders outside Tahiti, it is of secondary importance in an economy that now relies on tourism, governmental bureaucracy and small businesses as money-earners.

Battlefield (32.5 km, Mahaena)

The annexation of Tahiti by France in 1843 sparked armed resistance among Tahitians, and guerrilla warfare continued until the rebellion was crushed in 1846. The most important battle of this war was fought at Mahaena on 17 April 1844. The battlefield stretched from the beach southward to the present-day church and city hall. Heeding the advice of British sailors and French army deserters, Tahitians dug three parallel trenches and awaited their French adversaries. Two French warships appeared and a force of 441 men stormed the Tahitian position, which had approximately twice the defenders but lacked the weapons of the French. When the dust cleared, 102 Tahitians were dead; the French had lost only 15 men. After this blow the natives realised that guerrilla warfare was the only alternative and they continued to operate from bases in the bush until their main stronghold was captured in 1846.

Bougainville's Anchorage
(37.6 km, Hitiaa)

Look out to sea and note the two islets, Vairiararu and Oputotara. The former has a few trees and the latter just brush. Bougainville anchored at Oputotara in April 1768; a plaque at the bridge in the nearby village commemorates the event. Although cultured to the bone, Bougainville was not much of a sailor. His choice of this particular anchorage, which lacked the proper shelter and wind conditions, was not the best. He managed to lose six anchors in 10 days and nearly lost the ships as well. Believe it or not, soon after this debacle some Tahitians actually salvaged one of the anchors and gave it to the King of Bora Bora as a gift. Captain Cook later took possession of it in 1777.

Bougainville will probably be best remembered for his glowing account of Tahiti, later published in France, where he lauded the Tahitians' hospitality and sexual freedom. Well versed in the classics, he called Tahiti 'New Cytheria', after the island birthplace of the Greek goddess of love, Aphrodite. To this day, the myth lives on.

Vista of Peninsula (39 km, Hitiaa)

From here you have a splendid view of Tahiti Iti, Tahiti's panhandle.

Fa'atautia Waterfall (41.8 km, Hitiaa)

You can pause at the bridge to take photographs. This site was chosen by US film maker John Huston to make a cinematographic version of Herman Melville's *Typee* but due to his first commercially unsuccessful Melville flick, *Moby Dick*, the scheme was abandoned.

Military Base & Junction
(53 km, Taravao)

Military and police installations have existed here since 1844 when the French guarded the isthmus to prevent marauding guerrillas from filtering down from the peninsula to the main part of the island. The old fort (within the army camp) still stands. Since then, the site has served as a gendarmerie, an internment camp for Germans fortunate enough to be on the island during WW II and, most recently, a military base. Nearby is a large Catholic church with a most imposing facade and also the junction for the two roads leading to the peninsula. Note that the north and south coast roads do not meet – to get around the far end of the island you must hike.

PENINSULA: TARAVAO-TAUTIRA
Detour to Vista Point (0.6 km, Afaahiti)
Take the turn-off at the sign on your right, just before the school. There are pastures complete with grazing cattle and the seven-km road leads to a summit. Hike the rest and take in a gorgeous panorama of Tahiti.

Te Anuanua Hotel (9.8 km, Pueu)
This is a highly recommended, inexpensive hotel run by a local family (see Places to Stay in the Around the Island section).

Vaitepiha River (16.5 km, Tautira)
Great place for a swim.

Vaitepiha Bay (18 km, Tautira)
Captain Cook's second expedition almost met its doom near Tautira in 1773. One morning the esteemed navigator awoke to find his two ships drifting perilously close to the reef. Apparently the crew had been too busy entertaining Tahitian visitors the evening before to notice. The ships eventually did run aground, but were saved by smaller boats that kedged the larger vessels off the reef. Cook lost several anchors in the confusion. In 1978, by sheer luck, one of the anchors was located and brought to the surface. The event was properly celebrated by locals and the crew of movie producer David Lean, who was on location to promote a new version of the *Bounty* episode. Although the film was never made, the anchor can be seen at the Musée de Tahiti et des Îles.

This bucolic setting was also the scene of a confrontation between the British and the Spanish. Angered by the English presence in the Pacific (which the Spanish felt was theirs to plunder) the Viceroy of Peru was ordered by his King to send a ship to Tahiti. He promptly sent the *Aguila*, commanded by Boenecha which, after having the misfortune of striking a reef, anchored in a lagoon about three km from Tautira Village and formally 'took possession' of Tahiti for the King of Spain.

Less than a year later, on his second voyage of discovery, Cook wound up in the same vicinity and soon heard about the landing of the dastardly Spanish. In 1774 Boenecha returned to the area with two Franciscan priests in an effort to give the savages a little religion. The mission failed miserably. Captain Boenecha soon died and the priests, scared witless of the Tahitians, erected a veritable fortress to keep the curious natives away. The *Aguila* returned at the end of 1775 with provisions but the priests would have none of the missionary life and gladly sailed back to Peru.

Cook came back to Tautira on his third voyage in 1777 and found the padre's quarters still in good condition. The house was fitted with a crucifix which bore the inscription 'Christus vincit Carolus III imperat 1774'. On the reverse side of the cross Cook ordered his carpenter to carve 'Tertius Rex Annis 1767, 69, 73, 74, & 77'. By this time, Bengt Danielsson writes, 'both England and Spain had realised that Tahiti was an economically as well as strategically worthless island and gave up their costly shows of force'.

One hundred years later Tautira was the temporary abode of Robert Louis Stevenson, who anchored the *Casco* here in 1888 (see Tahiti Literati, in the Facts for the Visitor chapter). He was taken in by local royalty and stayed for about two months, calling Tahiti a 'Garden of Eden'. Although on assignment for the *New York Sun* to write about the cruise, he spent his time in Tautira working on 'The Master of Ballantrae', a Scottish horror story. Upon returning to

England, Stevenson's mother sent a silver communion service to the local Protestant church, where it is still being used.

PENINSULA: TARAVAO-TEAHUPOO
Research Station (0.5 km, Afaahiti)
This atmospheric research station was constructed during International Geophysical Year (1957/58) to study the ionosphere.

Zane Grey's Fishing Camp
(7.3 km, Vairao)
Although the author of *Riders of the Purple Sage* and 60 other pulp westerns spent his life cranking out stories about the old American West, his real passion in life was deep-sea fishing. From 1928 to 1930 he spent many months in Tahiti with his cronies catching marlin, mahimahi, sailfish and other sport fish. Like Melville's protagonist in *Moby Dick*, Grey dreamed of landing his own version of the white whale and on 16 May 1930 he finally did – a four-metre, 454-kg silver marlin that probably would have weighed 90 kg more had not the sharks ripped off so much flesh.

Describing this episode in *Tales of Tahitian Waters*, Grey gives us an insight into French colonial mentality. He relates that French officials had the local chief spy on the Americans because they thought the fishermen might actually be surveying the area for the US government, which perhaps had designs on taking over Tahiti as a naval base. Said Grey, 'The idea of white men visiting Tahiti for something besides French liquors, the native women, or to paint the tropical scenery had been exceedingly hard to assimilate.'

Hotel Puunui (6 km, Vairao)
The Puunui, recently purchased by the government, sits high atop a hill and looks like a collection of military bunkers or artillery batteries rather than a hotel complex. Take the several kilometre entrance road and note that the land is covered with all sorts of crops – mango trees, beans, tomatoes and other edibles. The reason for taking the road to the top is the spectacular view of the narrow isthmus that divides Tahiti Nui from Tahiti Iti.

Maui's Footprints on the Reef
(8.5 km, Vairao)
Tradition has it that on this very spot the great Polynesian hero Maui slowed down the sun in order to provide time for the Tahitians to cook their food before it got dark. Maui accomplished this by braiding a rope of pubic hair from his sister Hina, lassoing the sun, and tying the unwieldy ball down to a boulder on the beach. To prove the tale, Maui's footprints are still visible on the reef.

CNEXO Oceanographic Research
Station (10.4 km, Vairao)
The ponds you see here are for breeding shrimp – one of the many ambitious projects of CNEXO (Centre National pour l'Exploitation des Océans), a French government agency.

Last Refuge of the Nature Men
(18 km, Teahupoo)
Years ago the 'nature men', as Danielsson refers to them, were a common fixture throughout Tahiti, but as civilisation marched on, this remote area became their last refuge. The best-known of these rugged individuals, who perhaps bore a strong resemblance to the US underground comic book character 'Mr Natural', was Ernest Darling. According to Danielsson, Darling 'lived stark naked, slept on the ground with his head pointing north, and produced an endless stream of pamphlets, extolling the virtues of nudism, vegetarianism, abstinence, pacifism, Christian Socialism and phonetic spelling'.

SOUTH COAST: TARAVAO-PAPEETE
Home of Robert Keable
(55.5 km, Papeari)
Look carefully among the mango trees on the hill and you will see the former home of English writer Robert Keable. Although not a household word today, Keable produced

two religious novels, *Simon Called Peter* and *Recompense*, which sold a combined total of 600,000 copies in the 1920s. Obsessed with the question of why Tahiti and Tahitian women held so much attraction for white men, he provided his own answers in two more books: *Tahiti, Isle of Dreams* and *Numerous Treasure*. Keable's well-maintained home is in its original 1920s condition.

Debarkation Point of Ancient Tahitians
(52 km, Papeari)
Traditional accounts say that this was the first place where the ancient Polynesians settled over 1000 years ago. Because of this, families chiefly from this district have always had the highest prestige among their counterparts in the other districts of Tahiti. The present-day village is known for its beautiful gardens and roadside produce stands. The Papeari inlet has a number of oyster beds and fish traps.

Botanical Gardens & Gauguin Museum
(51.2 km, Motu Ovini)
The Botanical Gardens were established in

1919 by Harrison Smith, a physics professor who at age 37 left the Massachusetts Institute of Technology to dedicate the rest of his life to botany in Tahiti. He introduced to the islands a range of tropical shrubs, trees and flowers from throughout the world, and some became important local products. My favourite among these is the huge, delectable grapefruit known as the pamplemousse, which originated in Borneo. Smith did not merely putter around in his own garden but generously gave seeds and cuttings to Tahitian farmers to help them improve their own crops. After his death in 1947 the garden was willed to another botanist and, through the help of US philanthropist Cornelius Crane, was given to the public.

The massive gardens are laced with footpaths that wend their way through acres of well-tended palms, hibiscus, elephant ears, bamboo, bananas and many other species. There were also several Galapagos turtles brought to Tahiti in the 1930s which were given to author Charles Nordhoff's children. At the time of writing two of the turtles are still living.

The gardens, which you may find more

Gauguin Museum

interesting than the Gauguin Museum, were spruced up in 1990 for the visit of President Mitterand of France. The entrance fee just for the gardens is 250 CFP.

Opposite the garden grounds is a modern, circular building – the Gauguin Museum – with exhibits chronicling the life of Tahiti's most famous former resident. The walls are covered with documents and photographs from the Gauguin era, along with reproductions of his works. Ironically, the Gauguin Museum contains no original works by Gauguin. The finest original paintings exhibited are those by Constance Gibbon Cummings, an English woman who stayed in French Polynesia for six months in 1877. She has left us with some exquisite landscapes of Tahiti and Moorea. For sale at the gift shop are excellent reproductions of her paintings and the works of other artists who lived on the island.

Outside the museum note the two-metre-tall *tiki* (statue) from Raivavae in the Austral

group. Those in the know say it has a curse attached to it, as do many tikis removed from their original surroundings.

Although modern-day Tahiti is very different than it was during Paul Gauguin's time, the joyous and perplexing moods of Tahitians that he captured on canvas are still displayed today on every street corner in Papeete.

Perhaps as a metaphor for Gauguin's broken dreams, the museum is dimly lit and run down, and the postcards and souvenir T-shirts are overpriced. Despite the pathetic state of the museum, Gauguin fans will not want to miss it.

Those taking le truck to the museum from Papeete and its environs should start their trek early in the morning. The last le truck heading back towards town is at 1 pm and believe me, it's a long walk back. Bring along some insect repellent when you visit – the mosquitoes can be a nuisance. There is a separate entrance fee of 450 CFP for the museum.

Gauguin Museum Restaurant
(50.5 km, Papeari)
On the ocean side of the road, the restaurant is excellent and meals are priced in the 1000 to 1500 CFP range.

Vaihiria River & Lake (48 km, Mataiea)
The Vaihiria River originates from the lake of the same name – Tahiti's only lake. At 500 metres above sea level, it is bounded on the north by 1000-metre cliffs which make up the southern wall of the Papenoo crater. The lake is known among locals for its large eels and nearby plantations of *fe'i* (mountain bananas). It is accessible with the aid of a guide, but there are cascades visible from the road (for more information see Activities, in the Around the Island section in this chapter). Keep an eye out for the nearby Vaima Bath, a very popular bathing area for locals along the banks of the river, just off the road. The bathing area has been improved recently – it's a good place to stop and cool off.

Mataiea Village (46.5 km, Mataiea)

After living briefly in Papeete, Paul Gauguin moved to this village in October 1891 and lived here until May 1893. He rented a bamboo hut, found a vahine and painted such masterpieces as *Hina Tefatou* (the Museum of Modern Art, New York), *Ia Orana Maria* (the Metropolitan Museum of Art, New York), *Fatata te Miti* (the National Gallery of Art, Washington, DC), *Manao Tupapau* (Albright-Knox Art Gallery, Buffalo), *Reverie* (the William Rockhill Nelson Gallery of Art, Kansas City) and *Under the Pandanus* (the Minneapolis Institute of Art).

Twenty-three years later, when Somerset Maugham came to the village culling information about Gauguin's life for his novel *The Moon & Sixpence*, he discovered three painted glass doors in the wooden bungalow belonging to Gauguin's landlord. These paintings by the great artist had never been discovered. Most of the paintings had been mutilated by children's play but Maugham picked the best one up for 200 francs and painstakingly shipped it back to Europe. Near the end of his life he sold the forgotten door at Sotheby's for a cool £13,000.

Rupert Brooke's Love Nest

(44 km, Mataiea)

Shortly before WW I Rupert Brooke jumped on a boat in San Francisco and headed for Tahiti 'to hunt for lost Gauguins'. He ended up in Mataiea, rented a bungalow, and instead of discovering lost French painters found his first and only true love. Mamua inspired one of his best poems, 'Tiare Tahiti'. Brooke eventually left Tahiti with a heavy heart and several years later died on a hospital ship off Gallipoli, a casualty of the war. His beloved Mamua fell three years after that, a victim of Spanish influenza.

Olivier Breaud International Golf Course, Atimaono (41 km, Papara)

Although today this area is a golf course, the cotton plantation that once covered what today are fairways and sand traps had a tremendous impact on Tahiti's population and history. The story begins not in Tahiti but in the USA, which in the early 1860s was in the midst of a bloody civil war. This war not only caused bloodshed in the USA but in Europe created a shortage of the cotton that usually came from southern USA. The demand for this commodity gave Scottish wine merchant William Stewart, who made a living importing liquor to the South Pacific, the idea of growing cotton in Tahiti. He acquired land in Atimaono, the only area in Tahiti capable of large-scale agricultural development and, with the help of blackbirders (slave traders), he recruited labour. This did not work too well, so coolie labour from China was used and thus the seeds of the powerful Chinese community in Tahiti were planted. Working conditions were atrocious and violence tempered by the guillotine was the rule of the day.

Despite the awful circumstances, by 1867 1000 hectares of high-grade cotton were planted and the harvest lived up to Stewart's dreams. In the meantime he had built a huge villa and spent his evenings as the king of the roost, entertaining Tahitian high society. However, there was a catch. The Civil War had ended and with it the shortage of cotton from the USA. Stewart could not compete with his US counterparts, who were geographically much closer to Europe, and he plummeted into bankruptcy. He died at the young age of 48. About half the Chinese coolies elected to stay and the rest is history.

Site of Marae Mahaiatea

(39.2 km, Papara)

The access road to the ruins of this once great temple is posted on the highway. Today the marae is only a huge pile of boulders but early European visitors (such as Captain Cook) were astounded by its dimensions (about 90 metres long, 29 metres wide and 15 metres high) and its architecture. Not only did the builders need a considerable amount of skill to construct the temple, they had to do so without the benefit of iron tools. Danielsson claims it was once the most spectacular monument in Tahiti. The temple's fall into decay is not only the fault of nature – apparently the old temple was used by William Stewart as a source of stones for his building projects down at the cotton plantation a few km away. In the words of J C Beaglehole, the great biographer of Cook, whom Danielsson quotes in describing the fate of the marae, 'Nature and human stupidity combine as usual to wipe out the diverse signs of human glory.'

Protestant Church & US Civil War Memorial/Seashell Museum

(36 km, Papara)

In the graveyard of this Tahitian church lie the remains of a former US Consul and Yankee hero of the Civil War. The inscription on the stone tells the story of Dorence Atwater, who at age 16 joined the Union Army, was captured by rebel scouts and served time in three Confederate prisons until he was sent to a hospital where he ended up as a clerk recording the deaths of Federal prisoners. Fearing that the Confederates were not keeping accurate records, he copied the lists and escaped, bringing them to the attention of the federal government. Atwater was buried here because in 1875 he wed the beautiful 'princess' Moetia of the local chief's family which had ruled the district for generations.

Close by is the Seashell Museum, or *Musée du Coquillage*, open seven days a week from 8 am to 5 pm. Admission is 300 CFP for adults and 200 CFP for children over four years of age.

Border Between Papara & Paea (29 km)

The districts of Paea and Papara have the least amount of rainfall and are among the most desirable areas in Tahiti to live in. Note the fine homes on the coast (owned mostly by whites) and the quiet lagoon and beaches, sheltered by a barrier reef. Just prior to Paea is the Maraa Fern Grotto.

Maraa Grotto (28.5 km, Paea)

The cave here, always a stop on the visitor's itinerary, has no traditional importance. Its only meagre significance is that it is an optical illusion – it seems to be smaller than it is. The area is, however, popular as a stop and has been improved to accommodate more cars and picnic-goers.

Marae Arahurahu (22.5 km, Paea)

Danielsson writes that this particular marae (there's a sign on the main road at the turnoff) had no great historical importance, but it so captured the imagination of Dr Sinoto of the Bishop Museum that he completely reconstructed the shrine. The rectangular pyramid is about the size of a tennis court and has a flat top with a wooden platform where animal and human offerings were left for the gods. The marae is now used occasionally during the Tiurai festival in July as a stage for re-enactment of ancient rituals such as the 'Crowning of a King' ceremony or similar events. The temple is in a lush valley bordered by steep cliffs.

Irihonu Craft Centre (20 km, Paea)

At the mouth of the Orofero River are three buildings housing the workshops of artisans (all members of the Paea Craft Association) who still practice the traditional arts of the islands, woodcarving and mat-weaving, as well as a skill introduced by missionaries – quilting. The varied arts and crafts are on sale at the centre, which is supported by the local Paea government. In the past few years there has been a resurgence of interest in the old Polynesian arts, a trend that will, hopefully, check the disappearance of traditional skills.

Near the craft centre is a popular surfing spot. Surfing is a sport the Tahitians have practised since time immemorial and brought with them to Hawaii. During the missionary years surfing was prohibited (surfboards were ridden naked in those days) and it wasn't until the 1960s, after Tahitians had visited Hawaii by plane, that the sport made a comeback. The same beach was also the site of a marae where in 1777 Captain Cook witnessed a human sacrifice.

This area was also the scene of an important battle in 1815 that pitted Pomare II, by then a Christian convert, against the heathen forces of the Teva i Uta clan. Pomare's well-armed Christian soldiers, aided by white mercenaries, overran their adversaries but with true Christian mercy spared the enemy from unbridled revenge. Pomare spared human life but unfortunately all the artistic treasures – the wooden and stone carvings – were either tossed into the fire or destroyed, leaving future generations with very little in the way of Tahitian art. One of the results of this episode is that modern-day artisans carve tikis which are copies of works from the Marquesas Islands or those of the New Zealand Maoris.

Musée de Tahiti et des Îles

(15.1 km, Punaauia)

Opened in 1978, the museum is an excellent introduction to Tahiti and the entire spectrum of French Polynesian culture. You can get there by taking a right turn (coming from Papeete) at the sign posted at the junction of the gas station and market and continuing toward the beach for another km or so. Though damaged in the cyclone of '83, it was later revamped and remains the finest

Pomare II

and most modern museum in the South Pacific. It consists of four sections:

- Milieu natural – flora, fauna, geology and Polynesian migration exhibits. Many of the displays include sophisticated, electrically operated diagrams and instructional aides.
- Traditional Polynesian culture – homes, costumes, religion, games, dances, musical instruments and ornaments.
- Post-European era – displays illustrating Cook, Bougainville, Wallis, Pomare dynasty, missionary period and Chinese population.
- Outdoor exhibits – a botanical garden, consisting of plants that Tahitians brought with them (such as taro, 'ava, yams, medicinal herbs), and the Canoe Room – traditional outrigger and dugout canoes.

In addition to the museum's exhibits of traditional arts and crafts there is a wonderful collection of paintings and prints. Most of these will be available for viewing in the Exhibition Building, which has rotating shows ranging from artists like Webber (Captain Cook's artist) to modern-day Tahitian painters, sculptors and potters who otherwise would not have the means of displaying their works. Exhibitions will not be limited to local art but will show works from throughout the Pacific and the rest of the world.

The building will also be the home of special events programming such as demonstrations of tapa-making, mat-weaving, instrument-making, traditional dances and exhibits illustrating the latest archaeological excavations.

No visitor to Tahiti with an interest in the island's culture should miss the museum. Hours are 9 am to 6 pm daily except Monday. The entrance fee is 300 CFP.

Punaru'u Valley (14.8 km, Punaauia)

Beyond the bridge was once a fortress built by the French during the Tahitian uprising of 1844 to 1846. The site is now used as a TV relay station. The road up the valley leads to a trail (see Activities, in the Around the Island section) to the Tamanu Plateau where oranges grow in profusion. In the 19th century Tahiti was a large exporter of oranges to New Zealand and – believe it or not – to California.

2+2=4 Primary School & Site of Gauguin Home (12.6 km, Punaauia)

A 19th-century French landowner donated the land for the school and had the above mathematical equation inscribed at the entrance. According to Danielsson, the planter, dubious about the propriety of introducing the French educational system to Tahiti, figured that if nothing else the children would learn at least one thing of value.

Just south of the school, in an area now subdivided, is the site of a home where Paul Gauguin lived from 1897 to 1901 and produced about 60 paintings. Among these are *Where Do We Come From* (the Museum of Fine Arts, Boston), *Faa Iheihe* (Tate Gallery, London) and *Two Tahitian Women* (the Metropolitan Museum, New York). Note that this 'landmark' is merely the site of Gauguin's former home – the structure is long gone.

Captain Bligh Restaurant

(11 km, Punaauia)

Formerly known as the Lagoonarium, this is a decent restaurant which used to be combined with a small aquarium. The aquarium end of the attraction was shut down but the restaurant still thrives. It's open daily, except on Monday, from noon to 2 pm and after 7 pm.

Yachties and other visitors needing large quantities of groceries should be aware of the 'euromarche', the huge new supermarket off the freeway in Punaauia. This discount mart, along with a similar new market in Pirae called Tropic Import, are the cheapest places in French Polynesia to buy groceries. These new stores are such bargains that it is actually less expensive for residents of the outer islands to take a ferry (with automobile) to

Tahiti, stock up on groceries and return to their home island, than to buy from a local grocer. Because of the lack of competition, the retail mark-up in Tahiti was horrendous until the supermarkets entered the scene.

Sofitel Maeva Beach (8 km, Punaauia)

Just beyond the 'super highway' entrance, Maeva Beach is a popular 'local' beach. Nearby is the Sofitel Maeva Beach, one of the largest and oldest hotels on the island. It has Tahiti Aquatique, a great water sports centre with scuba diving, snorkelling, glass-bottomed boat and harbour cruises.

'Super Highway' Entrance

(7.8 km, Punaauia)

At this point the motorist can either take a modern four-laned freeway and zoom back to Papeete, or travel down the old coastal highway.

Tahiti Beachcomber (7.2 km, Punaauia)

The site of the present-day Beachcomber (which has one of the best cuisines on the island) is called Tata'a Point. In times past it was a holy place where the souls of the dead were said to depart to the nether world.

Tahiti – Faaa International Airport

(5.5 km)

Tahiti's Faaa Airport is as modern as any in the world, but still has distinct Tahitian touches like barefoot kids, rotund Tahitian women selling leis and perhaps an unattended dog sleeping near the ticket counter. The airport's 3½-km runway was constructed by filling in a lagoon. Prior to its completion in 1961 Tahiti was served by passenger vessels and New Zealand TEAL flying boats. Amenities at the airport include: two banks that open for an hour before international flights depart and for an hour after arrival; a post office which keeps regular business hours; an OPATTI (Tahiti Tourist Board) information booth which opens for arriving international flights; and a snack bar with restaurant.

There is a *consign* (storage area for

luggage) and shower facilities for transit passengers; three duty-free shops and a (non-duty-free) boutique, Manureva, which has fashions, souvenirs and a newsstand. The Gallerie Leonard da Vinci is an art gallery.

There are two car rental offices (Hertz and Avis) and offices for Air New Zealand, Qantas, Lan Chile, Continental, Air France, Hawaiian Airlines, Air Moorea and Air Tahiti. In separate buildings are offices for Tahiti Helicopter and Tahiti Conquest Airlines, both charter carriers. Note that the office for Air Moorea is in a separate wing from the international and Air Tahiti offices and is adjacent to Tetiaroa's office.

Across from the airport is a fare where women sell purses, hats, shells, flower and shell leis for departing friends and relatives. It's a good, inexpensive place to pick up souvenirs.

Moorea

Lying 19 km west of Tahiti is Moorea, the only other major island in the Windward group. It covers an area of 132 sq km and has a population of nearly 9000. After Tahiti, it is the second most popular tourist attraction and has witnessed a great deal of tourist development over the past few years. Moorea is quick and easy to reach from Tahiti – shuttle flights leave every 30 minutes from Faaa Airport and ferries depart from Papeete four to six times daily.

Moorea, which means 'yellow lizard', is a name taken from a family of chiefs which eventually united with the Pomare dynasty. The island is serrated with sharp peaks that command deep cleft valleys, which were once centres for vanilla cultivation. Nowadays, pineapple has replaced vanilla as the biggest cash crop. Seen from the air, Moorea is encircled by a lagoon of translucent green and is fringed by an azure sea. It has a triangular shape, one side with two large but shallow bays (Cook's Bay and Opunohu Bay).

Moorea is famous for its tie-dyed pareus which are sold on the island or in Tahiti.

HISTORY
Archaeological evidence in the Opunohu Valley suggests that people were living on the island as early as 1600 AD, which corresponds with the oral history of the valley. At the time of Cook's return in 1774, there was internecine fighting among the islands' chiefs and warfare with tribes on neighbouring Tahiti. The battles continued for many years and the arrival of the missionaries in 1805 actually helped the Pomare dynasty gain power in Tahiti by supplying arms and mercenaries in return for support. After Pomare I conquered Tahiti, Moorea (which had been his refuge) became no more than a province of the Tahitian kingdom. During the latter half of the 19th century, colonists arrived and cotton and coconut plantations began to spring up. Vanilla and coffee cultivation came later, in the 20th century.

INFORMATION
New and very welcome to the island are the locally run Moorea Tourist Bureau offices at the airport, the ferry dock and adjacent to the Baie de Cook Hotel. Office hours are from 7.30 am to 3.30 pm daily. The office at the ferry terminal opens at 8 and 10.30 am, corresponding with the arrival of the ferry. The tourist bureau and many of the hotels provide a free booklet called 'Welcome to Moorea' which you should pick up. It contains airline and ferry schedules, phone numbers of hotels and restaurants, travel tips and a great map.

Useful Phone Numbers
Fire Department	(☎ 56-20-18)
Police Station	(☎ 56-13-44, 56-10-36)
Hospital	(☎ 56-23-23)
Pharmacy	(☎ 56-10-51)
Visitors' Bureau	(☎ 56-29-09)

ORGANISED TOURS
Moorea Safari Tour (☎ 56-20-41, 56-19-13), run by Ronald Sage, takes visitors by 4WD on excursions through the interior. The itinerary includes a swim in a river, a visit to a bamboo forest and vanilla, coffee and pineapple plantations deep in the highlands. The trip is well worth it for those who wish to see the interior. Safaris can be booked through the Activities Centre. The 'safari' departs morning and evening and the cost of the tour is 4000 CFP per person.

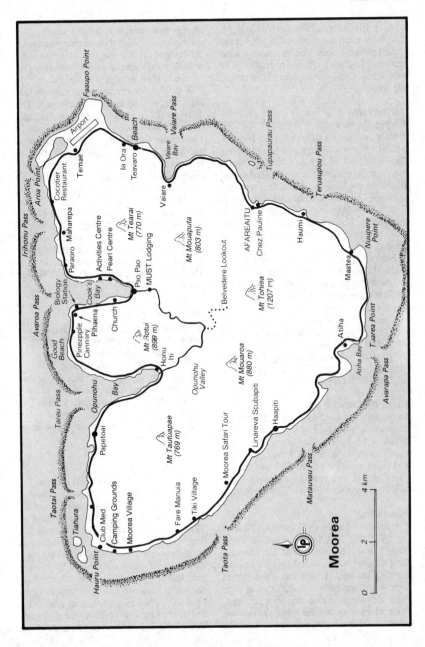

Faaupo Point

Irihonu Pass

Aroa Point

Avaroa Pass

Tareu Pass

Taotai Pass

Hauru Point

Tiahura

Taota Pass

Matauvau Pass

Avarapa Pass

Tjarea Point

Teruaupou Pass

Nuupere Point

Tupapaurau Pass

Vaiare Pass

Airport

Cocotier Restaurant

Temae

Maharepa

Pararoro

Activities Centre

Pearl Centre

Biology Station

Pihaena

Church

Pineapple Cannery

Good Beach

Opunohu Bay

Papetoai

Camping Grounds

Club Med

Moorea Village

Fare Manuia

Tiki Village

Moorea Safari Tour

Linareva Scubapiti

Haapiti

Ia Ora

Teavaro

Vaiare Bay

Vaiare

Ia Ora Beach

Pao Pao

Cook's Bay

MUST Lodging

Honu Iti

Opunohu Valley

Belvedere Lookout

AFAREAITU

Chez Pauline

Haumi

Maatea

Atiha

Atiha Bay

Mt Tearai (770 m)

Mt Mouaputa (803 m)

Mt Tohiea (1207 m)

Mt Rotui (899 m)

Mt Mouaroa (880 m)

Mt Tautuapae (769 m)

Moorea

0   2   4 km

Inner Island Photo Tours (☎ 56-20-09, 56-13-26 has excursions twice daily (8 am and 2 pm) aboard a Jeep Cherokee to the inner reaches of Moorea. The price is 4000 CFP per person. Call Mr Alex Roo a Haamataerii for details.

ACTIVITIES
Diving
Divers are well looked after in Moorea. MUST (Moorea Underwater Scuba Diving Tahiti) (☎ 56-17-32), run by Philippe Molle, has exploratory dives for experienced divers, night diving and facilities for teaching novices. The cost is 4500 CFP per dive or 20,000 CFP for five dives. The tariff includes equipment. Lessons are also available for 6000 CFP per session or 20,000 CFP for four lessons.

Scuba Piti (☎ 56-20-38), owned by Jean-Luc and Cathy Arnau, also teaches beginners the basics as well as taking out the experts. Their forte is underwater photography. The price is 4000 CFP per dive.

Bathy's Club Moorea (☎ 56-19-19, 56-21-07) is based at the Beachcomber Parkroyal. They are fully equipped with photo gear, video cameras and underwater 'scooters'. The price is 5000 CFP per dive or 20,000 CFP for five dives.

Glass-Bottomed Boat
Excursions on a glass-bottomed boat for snorkelling and shelling in the lagoon are given by Mr Hiro Kelley at the Hotel Bali Hai. For more information call (☎ 56-13-59). Boat rides are 1500 CFP per person (once daily) and snorkelling tours leave twice a day at a price of 3000 CFP per person.

Parasailing
The brochure put out by Polynesian Parasail (☎ 56-19-19) says in no uncertain terms 'Don't miss this spectacular Experience'. Despite what seems to be hype, I'd have to say they are right. What's more, you do not have to be a triathlete to do it. Based at Club Med, the service is overseen by a US expatriate who makes sure his employees adhere to strict safety guidelines. For those who

always have wanted to try this activity (but were a bit intimidated) this is the place to do it. One is lifted from the deck of the boat like a feather and dropped gently back down on the deck when the tour is complete.

The operator struck me as very professional, leaving no margin for accidents. The chute, which is launched from the boat like a kite, provides the participant with an utterly spectacular view from as high as 150 metres above sea level. The experience is silent to the point of being eerie, yet thoroughly enjoyable. The vessel used is the *U'u'pa*, an immaculate, high-tech speedboat.

The company also provides 1½-hour island tours which include background information on the history, geology and culture of French Polynesia. From the boat visitors can often see fish, sea turtles and, if you're lucky, dolphins. The price of the tour is 2500 CFP. The price of the parasail 'flight' is 4500 CFP. Check it out.

Other Water Sports
Deep-sea fishing enthusiasts can arrange boat rentals or half-day trips by speaking to Alain Hequet at Club Med.

Those interested in water-skiing, jet skiing and aqua six (a sort of surface submarine used for viewing underwater life without getting wet) activities can contact the Ia Ora Hotel (☎ 56-16-41) or the Beachcomber Parkroyal (☎ 56-12-90) for information on these watersports.

Horse Riding
Rupe Rupe Ranch (☎ 56-15-31), across the road from the Nelson & Josianne camping ground, is run by Rene Denis, an enthusiastic Connecticut Yankee and 20-year veteran of Moorea. She knows and loves her horses and they show it. The ranch, a charming, rambling, old-style farmstead, is worth taking a look at. Beach rides are handled by a wrangler. Rides are scheduled at 8, 10 am, 2.30 and 4 pm. Rates are 2500 CFP for hour-long rides and 3500 CFP for 1½-hour rides.

Tiahura Ranch (☎ 56-28-55) near Moorea Village has daily rides at 8, 10 am, 2.30 and

4 pm. Rates are 1500 CFP per hour or 2000 CFP for 1½ hours.

Centaure Ranch (☎ 56-18-65) near the Ia Ora Hotel has rides at 8, 10 am, 2.30 and 4 pm. Prices are 2000 CFP for hour-long rides and 2500 CFP for 1½-hour rides.

PLACES TO STAY
Places to Stay – bottom end
Haapiti The *Hotel Residence Tiahura** (☎ 56-15-45) is quite popular with 'local' tourists from Papeete and is often booked up on weekends. The scale of the place is small, the gardens are well manicured and the feeling is intimate and family style. There is also a restaurant, with prices ranging from 800 to 1800 CFP on the grounds. There are 24 thatched-roof bungalows, 18 with kitchenettes. Other amenities include a pool and snorkelling gear. Prices are 3500 CFP for a bungalow without kitchenette and 4500 CFP with cooking facilities.

If you come looking for Billy, owner of *Chez Billy Ruta* (☎ 56-12-54), Haapiti, PK 28, chances are you will find him underneath the chassis of a bus or some other vehicle. A very genial guy, he appears to be a full-time mechanic, puts on tours, dance shows and also happens to run an accommodation place. Billy's 11 bungalows are on the water but are very basic. Because he is consumed with his vehicles, tours and dance shows, I got the impression that his hotel business does not get the kind of attention it deserves. Its basic advantage is the comparatively low price. Rates start at 3000 CFP for A-frame type facilities.

Pao Pao *Chez Albert** (☎ 56-13-53, 56-19-28) is one of the best in the bottom-end category. It is a small, family-run affair with 19 clean (albeit sterile) units, some equipped with kitchenettes. Stores and restaurants are nearby. Guests have to stay for a minimum of two nights. Rates are 3000 CFP for singles/doubles, 4000 CFP for triples, 6000 CFP for four people and 7000 CFP for five. Albert also has car rentals starting from 4000 CFP and scooters from 2500 CFP with

'illimited mailleg' (unlimited mileage?). Albert has a plethora of tours and 'photo safari' expeditions ranging in price from 1000 CFP for an 'interior island tour' to 1500 CFP for a 'combined circle island tour and interior island tour with shopping'.

Afareaitu Eight km from the airport, *Chez Pauline* (☎ 56-11-26) has seven rooms and a small restaurant. It is the oldest family-run accommodation on the island and famous for its 'local' ambience and its restaurant. You can eat there without being a guest but be sure and call ahead of time to reserve the meal. Prices for accommodation are 2500/3500 CFP for singles/doubles.

Camping Travellers should note that the prices listed for the various camping grounds are subject to change more than other types of accommodation. This is because occasionally there are 'price wars' between the owners in an effort to compete for the pocket books of travellers. This can work to your benefit.

Haapiti *Nelson & Josianne* (☎ 56-15-18), PK 27, Haapiti, is situated on a broad swath of land, shaded by coconut trees and fringed by a thin strand of white-sand beach. The camping ground is approximately one hour by le truck from the Moorea ferry dock. The facilities are clean, well kept and well appointed. They do, however, fall short on kitchen facilities, which cannot accommodate the large number of travellers staying here. The common eating area was also rather small, and the common bathing area/toilets were clean. There are two rows of barracks-like dorms, each with five rooms that sleep two; four 'fare' units with one double bed; three bungalows with two bedrooms (a few hundred metres down the road from the campsite) with kitchenette and private bath with hot water; five beach cabins with two single beds; and a single large bungalow with a double and single bed, private bath and kitchen.

I was told by travellers that the bungalows

near the beach are preferable. Naturally, camping is permitted and many travellers choose to set up tents on the grounds. Prices begin at 500 CFP per person for campers (BYO tent), 1200 CFP per night for a 'barracks bunk', 2500 CFP for the fare units (with mosquito nets) and 4000 CFP for beach cabins. The three large bungalows down the road from the campsite are 5000 CFP and are first rate. On weekends they are generally occupied by local tourists from Papeete. If they are not occupied, grab them.

There are daily boats to the nearby *motu* (coral islet) for snorkelling, which is free of charge. Nearby there is also a small store, Magasin Rene, and attached to it is an inexpensive cafe, Snack Michel, which has hamburgers and other basic fare in the 600 to 800 CFP range. Nearby is a good pizzeria and a patisserie as well. The only complaint I've heard about the camping ground is with management. If you decide to stay here bring your patience and goodwill with you. From all reports, and my own observations, Josianne can be abrasive – perhaps she should consider hiring a person with better 'people skills' to act as host. Two days is the minimum stay.

Moorea Camping * (☎ 56-14-47) PK 27.5, Haapiti is about half a click down the road from their competitors, Nelson & Josianne, and is also on the beach. Managed by an easy-going older man by the name of Viri, the vibes here are friendly and the facilities are first rate. It might be said that Moorea Camping is the 'Avis' of French Polynesian camping grounds – they try harder. The shower and baths were the cleanest I'd seen in any camping ground in the islands. Another nice touch was the vending machines that dispense beer and soft drinks in the common eating area which, incidentally, faces the beach. The cooking facilities are clean and adequate, but not spectacular.

Although Moorea Camping is half the size of Nelson & Josianne there is still room for 30 tents. Other accommodation includes a large, very clean dorm unit with six rooms, each with four bunks, and a large bungalow with 12 rooms, each with a double bed.

Prices are 500 CFP for the dorm bunks and 1000 CFP per room in the large bungalow. Camping is 300 CFP (BYO tent).

Temae *Chez Coco's (Madou)* (☎ 56-17-16) is the least preferable of the camping grounds. Though located near the best beach on the island, in a shady grove of coconut palms, it is not well maintained. To get there take the road opposite the post office for two km in the opposite direction from Teavaro Beach. Look for Magasin Helene and you are there. Facilities include a shack of a dorm that sleeps eight and a few private rooms covered with woven palm fronds. The floors are covered with coral gravel. I would discourage travellers from sleeping in rooms with palm fronds because they attract insects – especially centipedes, one of my least favourite creatures. If you do sleep in these facilities, double check your clothing and shoes the next morning for unwanted guests that may want to slither into your life. Bathing facilities are very basic and substandard. On the positive side, the manager provides free drinking nuts and papayas to travellers. The tariffs are 1000 CFP for a room or dorm, 500 CFP for camping and 700 CFP for tent rental.

Lodging in Private Homes This is a subcategory of low to mid-range accommodation run by entrepreneurial islanders who rent out rooms or homes, often with self-contained (kitchen) facilities. While not strictly hotels, they are not really pensions either. The great advantage of these properties is privacy. Some are located in exquisite surroundings as well. They are generally less expensive than hotels but don't confuse 'less expensive' with 'cheap'. The style of accommodation ranges from comfortable to spartan.

For visitors who don't need a restaurant on the property, do not need maid service and like the feel of staying in someone's home, rather than being another anonymous 'guest' in a hotel, this might be the ticket. Many of these places require minimum stays of several days and almost always provide linen, but no towels. If you are at all considering this type of property, BYO towels. Naturally it's advisable to check out a property personally before you plunk down your bags.

Haapiti If you happen to round the curve at PK 30 and see a large smiling woman carrying a mobile phone, chances are you have reached *Fare Manuia** (☎ 56-26-17). Run by the ever-pleasant Jeanne Salmon, this accommodation has three well-appointed bungalows on a wide grassy point near the beach. A colleague of mine called these the 'Cadillacs of the bungalow set' and I would have to agree. The largest unit, on the beach, can house up to six people, while the smaller fares sleep four. All are self-contained with kitchens and private bath with hot water. Linen is provided but BYO towels. They are a good bet for families or couples. Prices are 6000 CFP for a garden bungalow, 7000 CFP for a (four-person) beach bungalow and 10,000 CFP for the largest unit. The minimum stay is two nights and no credit cards are accepted.

Papetoai The *Village Faimano** (☎ 56-10-20), BP 1676, Papeete, is at PK 14 and has six 'local' style airy bungalows, all with kitchen facilities. The environs are very Polynesian. There is nothing presumptuous about Faimano, which makes it one of my favourite places to stay. There are lots of shady trees and fresh ocean breezes. The management are very laid back (what else would you expect?) and leave you to your own devices. Another nice element is the proximity to a white-sand beach/swimming area right on the property. Four of the 'fares' are one-bedroom affairs with one double bed and a single. There are also two larger bungalows with two bedrooms each. Some of the units have private bath. There is no hot water here. Prices range from 7500 CFP for bungalows sleeping two or three people to 10,500 CFP for the larger units which sleep four to six. Linen is provided but no towels. The proprietor, Hinano Feidel, offers discounts for longer stays. Check it out.

Chez Nani* (☎ 56-19-99, 42-97-67), Papetoai, BP 67, Papeete, is at PK 14.5, about 50 metres from Hotel Moorea Lagoon. It has three bungalows with kitchen, double bed, single bed and bath. The setup is similar to Village Faimano, though slightly less 'traditional'. Still, the natural environs are exquisite and Chez Nani is worth a look. Prices are 7000/8000 CFP for doubles/triples. Food is available on request. There is a nice beach/swimming area just steps away from the bungalows. Sheets are provided but BYO towels. The proprietor is Maeva Bougues.

Chez Francine (☎ 56-13-24), at PK 14.5, Papetoai, is a single home with two bedrooms, each containing two single beds and private bath (with hot water). One of the rooms has a kitchenette. Each of the rooms can be rented out separately. A room with kitchenette is 5000 CFP, or 4000 CFP without cooking facilities. Discounts are provided for long-term renters. Note that Chez Francine is a neighbour of Chez Nani so when checking one out you may want to look next door as well.

Pao Pao The *MUST Lodging* (☎ 56-17-32, 56-15-83), Pao Pao Valley, Papetoai, BP 336, Moorea, is exclusively for divers using MUST. Don't try to find it by yourself – it's not far off the beaten track but is difficult to locate if you don't know the island well. Rather, find MUST's headquarters on the jetty near Baie de Cook Hotel and have them take you there. Accommodation is a two-roomed home on a banana plantation – lush bucolic environs. The house has one communal bathroom with hot water. The tariff, 6000 CFP per night, includes three meals The minimum stay is six nights. Call Philippe Molle for more information.

Chez Dina (☎ 56-10-39), 13 km from the airport in Pao Pao, is set behind Boutique Dina on the mountain side of the road. It has three very spartan (we're talking borderline basic) bungalows with one double bed in the 'living room' and one single bed in the mezzanine, kitchenette and communal bathroom. Perhaps the nicest thing about Chez

Dina is the setting, in the shadow of the mountains. The cost is 3000 CFP per bungalow. Activities include snorkelling and outrigger canoes. Chez Dina accept credit cards.

Places to Stay – middle
Haapiti The *Moorea Beach Club* (☎ 56-15-48) Haapiti, Moorea, was formerly the *Climat de France Moorea* and is of fairly new construction. It is a 40-room, 46-bungalow lodging on the beach. It has modest bungalow-style accommodation and a two-storey row of units, which are very spartan considering the price. Amenities include a restaurant, bar, windsurfing, snorkelling, a swimming pool and tennis. Tariffs begin at 9500 CFP for doubles.

Just down the road from Moorea Camping is *Moorea Village** (☎ 56-10-02), Haapiti, Moorea. It has 50 very basic Tahitian-style bungalows (15 with kitchenettes), a pool, bar, restaurant, tennis and volleyball facilities, and a beach. Though fairly massive in scale compared with other properties on the island, the people I spoke to with children in tow enjoyed the environs, which are clean and well tended. In particular they felt the self-contained units represented good value, though they seemed in need of painting and perhaps upgrading. Prices begin at 6000/7000 CFP for singles/doubles.

Linareva* (☎ 56-15-35) BP 205, Temae, Moorea, is one of the most impressive lodgings I have ever seen in all of French Polynesia. The grounds are immaculate. The classic, thatched fares are truly elegant and furnishings include rattan beds, polished wooden floors and, unexpectedly, TVs. Linareva provides a seclusion which would be very conducive to 'honeymooners'. There are 12 units which can house two to seven people. Prices begin at 6800 CFP for doubles for garden bungalows and top out at 11,800 CFP for 'ocean shore' bungalows.

Moored directly off the hotel grounds is a floating bar/restaurant known appropriately enough as Le Bateau. The interior of the vessel, formerly an interisland boat, is all hardwood embellished with plenty of brass

nautical antiques, and has a great view of the reefs and the high peaks nearby. The restaurant fare ranges from 1200 to 1900 CFP and has 'happy hour'from noon to 2 pm and 4 to 6 pm. Each bungalow has a bathroom, kitchen, plates and utensils, towels and bedding. Occupants may use the canoes, barbecue and raft. Linareva is also the site of Scuba Piti, a local dive establishment. Hence, many of the occupants tend to be divers.

Fare Matotea (☎ 54-14-36), PK 28.7, Haapiti, has eight bungalows with kitchen and bath (with hot water). Five of the bungalows have one bedroom with a double bed and two sofa beds; the other three bungalows have two bedrooms with one double bed and two single beds. Prices begin at 7200 CFP. Two nights is the minimum stay required.

Hauru A good, moderately priced hotel/restaurant/bar is *Les Tipaniers* (☎ 56-12-67), BP 1002, Moorea, run by a very nice Italian woman who doubles as a fine chef. The hotel is near Club Med. Some of the 21 units are equipped with kitchenettes. There are free outrigger canoes and excursions. Prices start at 7500/10,000 CFP for singles/doubles. This place still has a reputation as one of the better restaurants on Moorea but in my opinion it has gone down in quality.

The *Hibiscus* (☎ 56-12-20), BP 1009, Haapiti, Moorea, has 30 bungalows, roughly half with kitchenette. There are two double beds, private bath and space for an extra cot. It has a restaurant, snack bar, pool and beach. Rates begin at around 5000 CFP for singles/doubles. On the grounds of the hotel is Ceasario Pizzeria, which has a great outdoor setting and terrific food. Don't miss it.

Cook's Bay The *Kaveka Beach Club** (☎ 56-18-30), BP 13, Moorea, at the foot of Cook's Bay, is a real rough diamond. Managed by a savvy Swede named of Matts, a veteran of Tahiti, the hotel gives the impression of being well run. The setting, directly on Cook's Bay, is superb, and accommodation here represents good value.

The hotel is not overwhelmingly large (there are only 25 units), which is a plus. The bungalows are well appointed but not plush. There are water sports (including scuba diving), a white-sand beach and a good bar/restaurant. There is also a pier which is a fine place to sunbathe or swim. Rates begin at 9500 CFP for doubles in a garden bungalow or on the beach. I recommend the latter.

Pao Pao On the beach about four km from Pao Pao is *Moorea Lagoon** (☎ 56-14-68, 56-11-55), BP 11, Moorea. The atmosphere on the property, which has been completely renovated, is friendly and very Tahitian. During the holiday periods and sometimes on weekends, much of the clientele is local. There are 45 rooms and four bungalows, five hectares of gardens, a pool, bicycles, a bar/restaurant, a boutique and conference facilities. You can take advantage of a full array of water sports including an aqua six. There's also a fire dancing show every Saturday night. Rates begin at 11,000/12,000 CFP for singles/doubles.

Places to Stay – top end
Cook's Bay At the entrance to Cook's Bay and close to the airstrip is the *Bali Hai Moorea* (☎ 56-13-59), BP 415, Papeete, established by three Americans who came before the Tahiti tourist boom to run a vanilla plantation and wound up as hotel magnates. The hotel has a restaurant, two bars, a white-sand beach, water sports, Liki Tiki cruises, tennis, pool, and scuba facilities. There are 63 units; try to avoid the ones by the road because of the noise of passing autos at night. On Wednesdays there is an excellent dance review open to all. The best feature of the hotel is the landscaped plants that grow in the bathrooms and are watered by clients'

The Bali Hai Story
It is impossible to write about tourism on Moorea without mentioning the Bali Hai Boys: Jay Carliclo, Muk McCallum and Hugh Kelly. After arriving in Moorea in 1961, the three invested in a run-down vanilla plantation and inadvertently became owners of a ramshackle hotel. Their timing was impeccable. Airlines were just beginning to land in Tahiti and, when a journalist discovered their dumpy but charming hotel, success was just around the next coconut tree. Since then, the 'boys' have established hotels on Raiatea and Huahine (the latter has since closed) and have turned the original plantation into a successful experimental farm and egg-laying facility. The Bali Hai Boys are known to be free-spending good-timers. They have left their mark on the island in many ways.

The final chapter of the Bali Hai era came to a close recently when the hotels were sold to a Japanese concern.

Lumbering Hugh Kelly is fond of telling the story of the return of Moorea's missing tikis. The two stone reliefs were in an ancient religious shrine on the vanilla plantation and were left undisturbed by the three Americans. A week after Kelly showed them to a wealthy Honolulu businessman, the tikis disappeared. Kelly denied rumours that he had sold the priceless artefacts and vowed to get them back somehow. Several years passed with no trace of the relics, until a US woman approached Kelly with some startling news. She had seen the tikis at the Honolulu home of the same businessman who was the last person to see them in Moorea. Apparently this man was an avid collector of Polynesian artefacts.

Kelly decided to take the matter into his own hands. He flew to Honolulu and questioned the teenage son of the businessman about the tikis. The son insisted he knew nothing until Kelly blurted out a tear-jerking tale of a dying Tahitian woman who supposedly owned the tikis. With mock anguish, Kelly claimed the woman was shivering on her deathbed because she thought the tikis were in a cold place. The boy broke down and assured Kelly the tikis were in a warm place – on the balcony of his father's apartment. That was all the wily Kelly had to know. He confronted the businessman and threatened to spread the word to the Honolulu papers if the man didn't return the tikis. Faced with an embarrassing situation, the businessman consented. Several months later, amid pomp, press coverage from Tahiti and Hawaii, and incantations by Moorea's *tahua* (shaman), the sacred tikis were returned intact to their age-old shrine. ■

showers. A great touch. Prices start at around 8000/9500 CFP for singles/doubles.

The *Club Bali Hai** on Cook's Bay operates a time-sharing programme and occasionally rents rooms at prices starting at 9300 CFP for singles/doubles. The accommodation consists of older bungalows but they are charming.

Pao Pao The *Baie de Cook* (☎ 56-10-50) is a refurbished, classic, turn-of-the-century hotel with gingerbread trim, painted in pink and white with a green roof. The hotel is on the water's edge and has a wonderful vista. Its 76 rooms make it one of the largest single structures on the island. The rooms, done in pastels, are modern affairs, almost incongruous with the old colonial exterior. They are clean and basic. However, walking into the hotel's lobby is like walking aboard the legendary ghost ship the *Flying Dutchman*. The hotel is so empty that sometimes the receptionist is as invisible as a ghost. Given the reasonable prices – 4000/5000 CFP for singles/doubles – the hotel should be full.

Temae On a white-sand beach facing Tahiti and only two km from the airport, the *Ia Ora Moorea* (☎ 52-86-72), BP 706, Moorea, is the most luxurious and perhaps the most beautiful of the hotels on Moorea. Its famous disco, aboard an old, converted interisland schooner, unfortunately sank during a hurricane. There are three bars, two restaurants (one of them an exceptional gourmet restaurant) and all the amenities you could want such as a boutique, car rental, outrigger canoes, tennis, windsurfing, sailboats and scuba diving. A friend who stayed here commented that his money might be better spent elsewhere. That's hardly a scientific survey, but it's the best I can do. Prices begin at 22,400/24,000 CFP for singles/doubles.

Hauru The *Club Méditerranée Moorea* (☎ 56-15-00), BP 1010, Papeete, is a focal point for the young, the hip and possibly the restless. It's not everybody's cup of tea but it handily fulfils a need for people who like to choose from readily available activities – and activities is what Club Med is all about. If you didn't know, it has expanded its demographic base to include families as well as its traditional singles market. As in all Club Meds there are enough planned activities for a lifetime. However, in addition to the usual diversions there are more tours available than on any other property. For example, there are boat/snorkelling trips to the lagoons and isolated motus (islets), picnics, visits to Marlon Brando's island (Tetiaroa), bus and circle-island tours around Moorea, scuba lessons, helicopter rides, day trips to Tahiti, horse riding and deep-sea fishing, to name just a few. It also is one of two 'nightspots' on the island. Rates start at US$925 per week per person (for a shared room) which includes three meals, all the wine and beer you wish to consume and numerous activities. This does not include the US$80/130 membership fee for singles/doubles to join the 'club'. Moorea is the larger of the two French Polynesian Club Med facilities, with a capacity of 700 people.

Papetoai The 150-room *Beachcomber Parkroyal* (☎ 56-19-19) is the newest hotel on the island. This was to be Sofitel's jewel in the French Polynesian crown but it was sold to the Parkroyal organisation after management problems and considerable growing pains. The food is reportedly excellent and water sports are well provided but the hotel is by no means complete. Sand is still being brought in to create a beach where there was none and the shrubs and coconut palms planted by the landscapers haven't quite taken root. It's also obvious that the environment has been dramatically altered by the massive construction and bulldozing. It's a shame that in a period of global environmental consciousness the people bankrolling this operation appear to be unconscious or even comatose. One wonders what effect the building will have on the sensitive reef environment.

The reception area is covered by a huge canopy and the accommodation is striking – thatched-roof bungalows painted in pastels.

The whole hotel is done in pastels, giving the impression that the architect spent quite a bit of time in Miami Beach before making it to French Polynesia. Prices begin at 21,000/23,000 CFP for singles/doubles.

PLACES TO EAT

It is hard to go wrong at any restaurant in French Polynesia. The price ranges listed here for Moorea's restaurants do not include wine.

Cocotier, only one km from the Bali Hai, is my favourite restaurant. The food is tasty and moderately priced by Tahitian standards. It has nice surroundings and friendly Polynesian hospitality. What more can one ask for? Try the fish braised in soya sauce. Expect to pay around 5000 CFP for dinner for two with wine.

Bon Appetit Restaurant, Cook's Bay, serves Chinese food at 1500 to 2500 CFP. It's had mixed reviews.

Manava Restaurant, Cook's Bay, has good, basic Chinese and Tahitian food at 800 to 2000 CFP. It's another 'tourist menu' restaurant and is recommended.

Michel et Jackie, near the Bali Hai, serves French and local cuisine at 1500 to 3000 CFP. Mixed reviews on this one.

Tipanier, near Club Med, has Italian and French specialities, including pizza, at 1000 to 2500 CFP.

L'Oasis, near Club Med, has excellent seafood and French cuisine. Although it's a 'tourist menu' restaurant it's pricey (up to 4000 CFP for a meal), but among the best upmarket restaurants on the island.

Chez Pauline (☎ 56-11-26) is affiliated with the small family-run hotel of the same name in the village of Afareaitu. You must call her to reserve a place. Though I've never eaten here, I hear it's worth checking out.

Low-Budget Restaurants

Several decent, inexpensive cafes have sprung up in Moorea over the past few years and the trend is good. They include *Honu-Iti* (which means 'small turtle' in Tahitian) in Cook's Bay just on the fringes of Pao Pao. The fare includes hamburgers, sandwiches, breakfast, shakes and steaks. It's a sort of combination hot dog stand/outdoor cafe. Prices range from 500 to 1000 CFP. Also in Pao Pao is *Snack Rotui*, with the usual sandwiches, drinks and chicken. You can sit on their benches and meditate on the view of Cook's Bay. Two cokes and two sandwiches here will set you back 550 CFP.

In the evenings be sure and check out the roulette (restaurant on wheels) that parks near the wharf in Pao Pao. Not only is the food good but the outdoor ambience, on the waterfront beneath the stars, is wonderful. The fare includes chicken, chow mein and fish. Prices are in the 600 to 1000 CFP range. Another place you should not miss is *Ceasario*, a pizzeria worth walking a few miles for. Situated on the water, on the grounds of the Hibiscus Hotel, the Ceasario has an open-air design using a canopy that exploits the cooling tradewinds as natural air-conditioning. The pizza is outstanding – what you would expect from a good European eatery. Prices range from 700 to 950 CFP for the small size and 1000 to 1500 CFP for the large. Salads, good espresso, chianti and desserts are available too. Check it out.

While in the neighbourhood you might also wish to have a cup of coffee at the *Le Sylesie II* patisserie next to Carol Boutique, near the Hibiscus Hotel. Other items include breakfast, cold drinks, eggs, quiche, pizza and ice cream. Prices are in the 300 to 800 CFP range. The other patisserie near the Bali Hai in Pao Pao is also good.

ENTERTAINMENT

At Club Med there's nightly entertainment and local dances on the weekends but you must register with security before entering the property. For a more local scene try Le Tabou (☎ 56-14-68) opposite Moorea Lagoon Hotel (about four km from Pao Pao) on Saturdays. On Moorea it's best to either not expect much nightlife or bring your own.

GETTING THERE & AWAY
Air

In the mornings Air Moorea (☎ 56-10-34) flights depart every 30 minutes from Faaa Airport in Papeete. The flight time is about 10 minutes. The airport in Moorea was improved fairly recently, allowing a direct service from Moorea to the outer islands on Air Tahiti's ATR 42 aircraft. A regular service from Moorea is provided to Bora

Bora, Huahine, Manihi, Maupiti, Raiatea and Rangiroa. See the Getting Around chapter for more information.

The Air Moorea schedule is:

Depart Tahiti	Depart Moorea
6 am	6.15 am
6.30 am	6.45 am
7 am	7.15 am
7.30 am	7.45 am
8 am	8.15 am
8.30 am	8.45 am
9 am	9.15 am
10 am	10.15 am
11 am	11.15 am
noon	12.15 pm
1 pm	1.15 pm
2 pm	2.15 pm
3 pm	3.15 pm
3.30 pm	3.45 pm
4 pm	4.15 pm
4.30 pm	4.45 pm
5 pm	5.15 pm
5.30 pm	5.45 pm
6 pm	6.15 pm

There is also a helicopter service between Moorea and Faaa Airport on Tahiti Helicopter (☎ 43-34-26) and Pacific Helicopter Service (☎ 43-28-90).

Sea

At the time of writing, there are two vessels you can take from Papeete for the hour-long ride to Moorea. They dock on the quay several hundred metres up Boulevard Pomare from the tourism office, Fare Manihini (where the food vendors park at night). While on the water keep an eye open for flying fish propelling themselves off the crests of the waves and dolphins swimming up to the bow. The ferries are crammed to the scuppers with men, women, children, animals, cars, cases of Hinano beer and every other provision imaginable. Ferries include the *Tamarii Moorea II* and the *Tamarii Moorea VIII* (☎ 43-76-50), which hold 300 passengers and cost 700 CFP one way, plus 200 CFP for le truck to your accommodation.

Because of the frequency of the ferries you generally need not worry about reservations. Just go down to the dock. Upon landing at Vaiare (the administrative centre), le truck can be taken to any hotel around the island. Taxis are available too but are very costly.

The schedule for ferries is:

Depart Papeete	Depart Moorea
Monday to Thursday, and Saturday	
7 am	5.30 am
9.30 am	7 am
12.15 pm	8.30 am
1.30 pm	11.30 am
5.15 pm	3.30 am
Friday	
7 am	5.30 am
9.30 am	7 am
12.15 pm	8.30 am
1.30 pm	11 am
4 pm	2.30 pm
5.15 pm	3.30 pm
Sunday	
7 am	5.30 am
9.30 am	7.30 am
3.45 pm	2.30 pm
6 pm	5 pm
6.45 pm	5.30 pm

GETTING AROUND

My big 'beef' with Moorea is that there is no public transport, except for the regularly scheduled le trucks that coordinate with the ferries. If you land at the airport you must take a taxi, which is brutally expensive. (I paid 4000 CFP – about US$40 – for a 20-minute cab ride from the airport to Moorea Beach Club.) Evidently, many of the locals are not happy with the taxi's virtual monopoly on public transport, but the cabbies have a great deal of political clout and have made sure they hold onto a good thing. Travellers to Moorea on the cheap must get their hitch-hiking thumb out or (gasp) spend the money to rent a motor scooter or car to get around. Unfortunately for those travelling on the cheap, hitchhiking is not as easy as it once was and many low-budget visitors seldom leave the confines of the camping grounds. As a result, many travellers see only a fraction of the island. And who can blame them when it costs at least 4000 CFP per day to rent a scooter.

As on most of the outer islands, the larger hotels will supply guests with bicycles (for a price) and can arrange car rentals. Bikes can also be rented at many of the agencies.

If you really do need a taxi, calling (☎ 56-10-18) will get you one.

Car Rental

It is difficult (if not impossible) to see Moorea without a motorised vehicle (or a guided tour), so you may well find yourself in the position of renting something. Be sure and check your car or scooter for minor details like inflated tyres and brakes that work.

Independent rental agencies on the island include Danloue Rent-A-Car (☎ 56-12-58) in Temae; Arii Rent A Car (☎ 56-12-86, 56-11-03) (the local Hertz representative) with three locations around the island and Albert's Rentals (☎ 56-13-53, 56-19-28) which has cars, motorcycles and motor scooters, next to the Bali Hai in Pao Pao. One reader reported that he arranged for a rental with Albert's and the agency failed to show up at the hotel with the automobile. While it would be unfair to say this is typical of Albert (or any other rental agent) it would be fair to say that something like this would not be unheard of in French Polynesia. My dealings were with Arii Rent a Car, which has four locations on Moorea and their prices for cars, motorcycles, motor scooters and bicycles seemed representative of what is generally available on the island.

Prices for daily car rentals range from 6500 to 15,000 CFP, depending on the model. Two-wheeled vehicles are generally rented in increments of eight hours. Motorcycles (100 to 125 cc) go for 5000 CFP, motor scooters are 4000 CFP and bicycles are 900 CFP. This does not include other items such as insurance, deposit and gasoline (petrol).

AROUND THE ISLAND

I recommend staying a few days in Moorea to get the feel of the place. The visitor will immediately notice that the pace is much slower than in Tahiti and that people tend to be friendlier. The thing to do is take an around-the-island tour by renting a car or scooter, or by going with one of the many organised groups advertised by every hotel.

The following guide begins at PK 0, at the airport. In this guide we will go west, in an anti-clockwise direction.

As a common courtesy visitors should take care not to trespass on private land to take photos, whether it's someone's front yard or the Biological Research Station near Pao Pao. After all, you wouldn't want some tourist doing the same to you back home.

Temae Village –
Coco's Camping Ground (1 km)

It was here that novelist Herman Melville persuaded the chief to have the vahines perform for him the erotic Lory-Lory, a dance forbidden by the missionaries. The author came here after his release from jail in Tahiti, where he and other crew members of the *Lucy Ann* were punished for their participation in a mutiny. Temae Village is still famous for its dancing troupes that perform regularly for the island's dance revues.

To find the camping ground take the turnoff near Teavaro Beach (opposite the post office) and continue for two km until you reach Magasin Helene. The best thing about this camping ground is its proximity to a great beach. The downside is that it's shabby.

Cocotier Restaurant (3 km)

This is one of the better, moderately priced restaurants in Moorea. It is in an older white-washed home with a lovely verandah, about a 10-minute walk from the Bali Hai, on the mountain side of the road. The restaurant is petite and charming and the food is straightforward and very tasty.

Maharepa Village (3.5 km)

Maharepa Village, just before the Bali Hai Hotel, has a bush track which begins behind the Jehovah's Witnesses church that runs deep into the mountains. The beach just before the hotel offers good snorkelling.

Bali Hai Hotel (4 km)

The hotel environs include the Coconut House Restaurant, Michele & Jackie (another restaurant) and Maison Blanc. The latter is a renovated turn-of-the-century plantation house owned by one of the principals of the Bali Hai Hotel. With the vanilla boom during the latter part of the 19th and early 20th centuries, a number of homes like this were built in Moorea, but none are in such excellent shape. With a careful eye you can still see other plantation houses tucked away in the bush or along the side of the road. The style consists of clapboard construction, roofing iron and a verandah with white wooden fretwork.

Patisserie Sylesie (4.5 km)

A five-minute walk from the Bali Hai is a patisserie/outdoor cafe which has good pastries and serves breakfast and lunch. Great place for coffee, croissant and a look at a newspaper, or a nice break from the hotel scene.

Moorea Supermarket & Bank of Indo Suez (5 km)

Paraoro Village – Entrance to Cook's Bay (7 km)

Paraoro has a number of shops, car and bike rentals, and a wharf. Galerie van der Heyde, a fine art shop, is also here. The area was also one of the sites for the recent production of *Return of the Bounty*. Most of the movie scenes, however, were shot in Opunohu Bay.

Moorea Visitors' Bureau – MUST Divers (7.6 km)

Just past the beautiful (but empty) gingerbread-detailed Baie de Cook Hotel is a small dwelling wherein lies the Moorea Visitors' Bureau. They are well informed, professional and friendly. Hours are from 7.30 am to 3.30 pm daily. For information call 56-29-09. To find MUST Divers, park near the hotel

and walk along the jetty towards the shore. Their headquarters are on the jetty.

Kaveka Beach Club (7.8 km)

This is a good place to park the car and have a drink when the sun sets. The view of Cook's Bay is dramatic. Don't let the bartender talk you into buying her drinks.

Bali Hai Club & Chez Albert (8 km)

The Bali Hai Club, a sort of annexe of the original site, is also in the same general environs as a branch of the Bank of Tahiti, Bon Appetit Restaurant, a gas station and the Aimeo Boutique. On the mountain side, Chez Albert (otherwise known as Albert Family Enterprise) is an inexpensive accommodation place, one-stop rental (featuring cars and scooters) and tour agency.

Te Honu Iti Eatery (8.2 km)

You can get good and inexpensive food here. It's a cross between a fast food outlet and an outdoor cafe.

Pao Pao Village & Junction for Belvedere Lookout Road (9 km)

This village is the site of the main dock used by trading vessels. Services include a pharmacy, Chinese stores, a school, an infirmary, Bank of Polynesia, the Moorea Pearl Centre and a doctor's surgery. In the evenings it's worth a drive to see whether the roulette (an eatery on wheels) is parked on the wharf. If

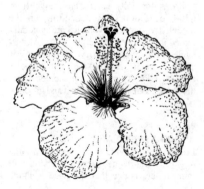

Top Left: Vanilla plant (RK)
Top Right: Stone tiki on Ua Huka (CPTM)
Bottom: Tetiaroa (Bird Island) (RK)

Top: Moorea seen from the air (TTB)
Bottom Left: Faarumai Waterfall, Tahiti (RK)
Bottom Right: Ua Huka (GH)

so, be sure and stop. The food is reasonably priced and very good. During the day Rotui Snack, frequented by locals, is also good. This is also the turn-off for the Belvedere Lookout and Pao Pao Valley. You can follow the interior road through the Pao Pao Valley to the Belvedere Lookout and the many ancient temples or marae. Halfway from the main highway to the Opunohu junction (see map) is a small boutique and botanical garden called Opuhi Plantation, owned by the 'old Tahiti hand', Alex Duprel. It's worth a visit. Pao Pao also has a small, open-air public market which is best visited early in the day.

Catholic Church (10 km)
This Catholic church has an altar inlaid with mother-of-pearl. The mural in the church features brown-skinned Polynesian versions of St Joseph, the Virgin Mary, the Archangel Gabriel and the infant Jesus. The background landscape is that of Moorea.

Richard Gump South Pacific Biological Research Station (10.9 km)
With land donated by San Francisco jewellery magnate Richard Gump, the University of California at Berkeley has established a biological research facility for terrestrial and marine life. The station consists of two buildings, a dormitory, a lab and several boats. Open to researchers from around the world, whose interests may range from insects to dolphins, the facility is definitely *not* open to the general public.

Pineapple Cannery (11 km)
Several hundred metres off the main highway (on the mountain side of the road) is a cannery which specialises in canning the island's agricultural products – pineapple, grapefruit (pamplemousse) and papaya. A local greets you and gives a well-rehearsed monologue describing the various stages of the canning process. On the grounds is a small kiosk where visitors are served shots of an excellent fruit liqueur derived from local produce. The cannery is open on week-days only, from 8 am to 4 pm. The aroma drifting out of the cannery smells exactly like someone is cooking a ham with a few slices of pineapple thrown on top. *Eaux de vie* or *liqueurs* of various types are on sale. Call 56-11-33 for more information. One more thing about the pamplemousse: it's one of the tastiest fruit juices you will ever sample and is available in litre cartons at any grocery store in French Polynesia. If you can find freshly squeezed juice at a cafe or restaurant, better yet.

Opunohu Bay (14 km)
Opunohu Bay has good snorkelling. The coral, however, is infested with crown-of-thorns starfish and there are dangerous stonefish in the vicinity, so take heed.

Robinson's Cove (17 km)
A popular yacht anchorage.

Opunohu Valley Entrance (18 km)
This road, which winds through the Opunohu Valley, is the second way to reach the interior of Moorea. The road eventually links up with the Pao Pao Valley road and comes to a dead end at the Belvedere lookout. It's worth the detour. Just prior to the road's junction on the main highway are several prawn ponds.

Papetoai (22 km)
Papetoai was formerly the seat of the Pomare I government and the scene of his conversion to Christianity. An octagonal church built by the London Missionary Society still stands here – it is the oldest European building in use in the South Pacific. (In 1811, years before Moorea's importance as a vanilla-growing region, the island was the London Missionary Society's centre for evangelical work for the entire Pacific.) The church is built on the site of the 18th-century Marae Taputaputea. All that remains of the Polynesian temple is a slim monolith outside the octagonal church. In the back of the churchyard is a solar energy panel. Also in the area are Chinese stores, a post office and a school.

Hauru (26 km)

Hauru is the community where the mammoth Club Méditeranée is located. Nearby there is a gas station, the new Moorea Beachcomber Parkroyal Hotel, two riding stables (Rupe Rupe and Tiahura Ranch), the Moorea Beach Club (hotel) and Les Tipanier. The most noticeable landmark is Le Petit Village, a horseshoe-shaped shopping promenade. The occupants include a grocery store, the Westpac bank, a doctor's office, the Ice Berg Restaurant, two jewellery shops and other amenities. Les Tipanier Hotel/Restaurant has moderately priced accommodation and good Italian food. L'Oasis, another restaurant, is expensive. This is also the beginning of a five-km stretch of sandy beach.

Camping Grounds (27 km)

A major stop for low-budget travellers to French Polynesia is Moorea's two top camping grounds, *Nelson & Josianne* and *Moorea Camping*. From the direction of Cook's Bay, Nelson & Josianne is the first camping ground you will encounter. Large and expansive, it has well-kept grounds and the best beach of the two. The achilles' heel of this establishment is its management, which at times can be a pain in the neck. Moorea Camping, a few hundred metres further down the road, is not as well appointed as Chez Nelson & Josianne but is definitely more relaxed. Facilities on both camping grounds are clean and well tended. Nearby is Moorea Village, a low-budget hotel, and Tiki Village, a quasi amusement park that purports to be a replica of a pre-Europeaon contact Tahitian village. They have regularly scheduled dance performances, feasts and (naturally) a boutique. Call them (☎ 56-10-86) for information.

Varari (28 km)

Here the 'sauvage' side of Moorea emerges, with fewer people and a foretaste of life on the outer islands of French Polynesia. It is where, until just a few years ago, the paved surface ended on the main road. There are scattered copra plantations and the feeling is more rural. Here you see snippets of the old days – women on the reef searching for seafood, washing on the line, fishing nets draped over the bushes and perhaps an old man on a bicycle cradling a fresh baguette. Varari is also the site of Marae Nuurau, a Polynesian temple used by the Marana royal family from which the Pomare dynasty originated. The marae is in a coconut grove at the mouth of a small creek and covers several hectares. The surrounding walls of the temple and the *ahu* or central platform are made of coral. Much of the structure is standing but restoration is needed.

Fare Manuia (30 km)

This consists of three fine bungalows with good access to the beach and plenty of privacy. After this point the mileage markers become scarcer.

Haapiti Village (24 km)

The village has a soccer field, Chinese store and a huge Catholic church. The church was formerly the centre of the island's Catholic mission.

Atiha Bay (20 km)

Pirogues (canoes) are set on blocks along the side of the road and nets hang from poles or ironwood trees, giving the area a pleasant, bucolic atmosphere. There is also a fine view of Tahiti. This bay has a double reef and sometimes young boys can be seen surfing from the inner reef on home-made plywood surfboards.

Auto Mechanic (19 km)

Maatea Village (14 km)

Maatea, perhaps due to its rural setting, is a close-knit, friendly village with charming homes draped in flowers. There is a Chinese store, school and movie house. Maatea is also the site of Marae Nuupere, which is on private land but is accessible from the beach. The temple is on a small coral hillock constructed directly on the shore.

Haumi Village (12 km)

Afareaitu Village (10 km)

Here you'll find Moorea's administrative centre, shops, a church, accommodation (Chez Pauline), a school and a road to an interior waterfall. Like the other Moorean communities of Papetoai, Haapiti and Maharepa, Afareaitu Village was built around the ancient temples and chiefs' dwellings of former times. There is quite a bit to see around here if you have the time to ferret it out.

Chez Pauline has a wonderful collection of prehistoric stone tikis, no doubt imbued with 'mana' to spare. There are also other artefacts such as adzes and grinding stones and several wooden relics. All have been collected from around the village. Pauline's pride are the tikis and I was told by a friend that if you offend her the easiest way to be pardoned is to ask her about the tikis.

Marae Umarea, which is the oldest (900 AD) in Moorea, is on the shore about 100 metres towards Maatea from Chez Pauline. Adjacent to it is a lovely coral garden ideal for a snorkel or a swim. At the other end of Afareaitu, just before the hospital, is an unpaved track leading to the waterfall. The four-km track crosses or passes near several ancient structures which are part of Marae Tetii as well as a few cascades. The trail gradually becomes a narrow, slippery, overgrown path for the last two km before reaching the waterfall. Recommended for stalwarts.

Vaiare Bay (5 km)

Here you will find the dock for cargo boats and the passenger cruiser *Keke III*, the *Moorea Ferry* and the *Tamarii Moorea Ferry*, which sail daily from Papeete. If you have the opportunity, watch the embarking and disembarking of passengers and loading of cargo at the dock. There is also a track which begins in Vaiare at the Chinese store just beyond the harbour and runs over the mountains to Pao Pao.

Sofitel Ia Ora Hotel
& Teavaro Beach (1 km)

The Sofitel Ia Ora Hotel offers the most luxurious accommodation on the island. You'll find excellent snorkelling nearby as well as a lovely beach called Teavaro. At the opposite end of the beach from the Ia Ora, topless bathing is considered *de rigueur*.

OPUNOHU VALLEY

The Opunohu Valley, with its reconstructed marae (temples), excellent vista and lush green meadows, is well worth taking a detour off the perimeter road for. In the time before European contact this valley was teeming with people. Now, however, it is largely deserted and is devoted to agriculture. Its population declined in the early 19th century, soon after the abandonment of the traditional religion.

Over 500 ancient structures have been recorded here, including religious and secular stone buildings and agricultural terraces. The complexity of the remains indicates a highly developed social system. The chief remnants of these buildings are six marae, reconstructed in 1967 by Y H Sinoto of the Bishop Museum in Honolulu. A council platform and two archery platforms have also been rebuilt. From the junction at Pao Pao (nine km) it is several winding km to the marae. All are an easy walk from the road.

Before reaching the marae stop at the first hill and note the pineapple plantation. Turn to the left and park. Walk across the road for a spectacular view of both Cook's and Opunohu bays.

Things to See

Marae Ahu-o-Mahine This marae has the most elaborate form and features a three-stepped ahu (platform). It was once the community marae for the Opunohu Valley and was built some time after 1780 AD. Note that it is constructed with hand-crafted, round dressed stones, similar to those of Marae Arahurahu in Paea, Tahiti.

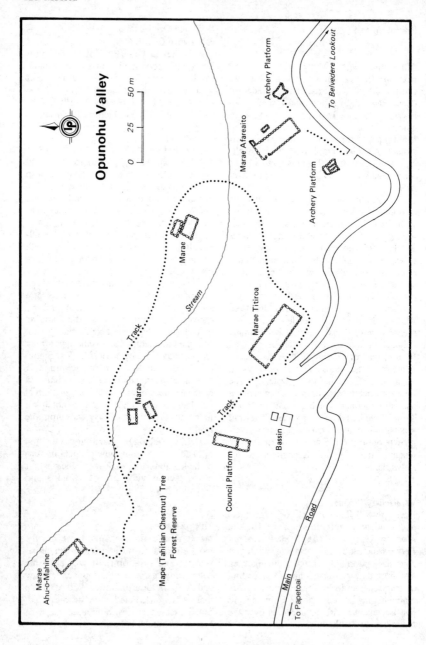

Opunohu Valley

0   25   50 m

Marae Ahu-o-Mahine

Mape (Tahitian Chestnut) Tree
Forest Reserve

Track

Stream

Marae

Marae

Marae Titiroa

Council Platform

Track

Bassin

Marae Afareaito

Archery Platform

Archery Platform

Main Road

To Papetoai

To Belvedere Lookout

Archery Platforms Archery was a sacred sport in ancient Tahiti, practised only by people of high rank – chiefs' families and warriors. As is clearly visible from the map, archery platforms have distinct crescent forms at one end. Archers perched on one knee to draw their bows and aimed for distance rather than accuracy. Of the three archery platforms in the Opunohu Valley, two have been restored. As in other parts of Polynesia, bows and arrows were not used as weapons of war. The tracks to the two archery platforms and the connecting Marae Afareaito are not easy to follow. Look for any small parting of the scrub between Marae Titiroa and the nearby parking area, and the Belvedere Lookout. The view from here is great.

Marae Afareaito Between the two restored archery platforms is Marae Afareaito, similar to Marae Titiroa further down the trail. A small ahu near one end is the principal structure of the marae, which was reserved for the gods. The upright stones near the ahu were the gods' backrests and stones in the court area marked the positions of worshippers. On the perimeter of the marae are small shrines, one attached and one detached from the main temple. Some of these independent shrines are associated with agricultural terraces and suggest that crop-fertility ceremonies were held on the structures.

Belvedere Lookout A few more km up the road is Belvedere, the finest vista of the valley. This was part of the setting for the latest film version of the *Bounty* story with Anthony Hopkins and Mel Gibson (which gave much-needed temporary employment to the locals). Continue back down the road, this time taking a left towards Opunohu Bay. On this route you will pass scenery that but for the coconut trees might belong to a Swiss valley – you'll see verdant pastures with fat, contented cattle grazing. A few more km along and you are once more on the main drag that circles the island.

Huahine

Huahine, 176 km north-west of Papeete, has a population of approximately 4500. It is actually two islands, Huahine Iti and Huahine Nui (Little Huahine and Big Huahine), which are part of the same land mass and are connected at low tide by an isthmus. (For the convenience of motorists, there is a bridge.) The island is verdant and rugged and along the coastline there are several gorgeous bays, especially Bourayne Bay and Maroe Bay, which have literally breathtaking views and, in the latter, interesting rock formations. (Be careful if going to Maroe Bay – after Faie Village the road is unpaved and has an unforgiving uphill grade that will make your trek a definite challenge. Don't even try it on a rental bike. Believe me.)

The residents have a long tradition of fierce pride and independence. According to a Tahitian proverb, 'Obstinacy is their diversion.' To this day, their cockiness is intact and their practical jokes could very well be a memorable part of the visitor's experience.

Huahine is also a landmark for surfers. Although it does not have the kind of waves that will bring people flocking from Hawaii or Australia, it does have the best surfing in French Polynesia.

ORGANISED TOURS

For tours, apart from those offered by individual hotels, both Pension Enite and Chez Lovina have set tour schedules, offering full island tours, motu picnics and archaeologically oriented excursions. Rates from both places start at 3000 CFP per person for a full island tour. Both places also offer airport/ferry 'taxi' services for 300 to 400 CFP per person. Enite also rents bikes.

Iles-Sous-Le-Vent Yacht Charters (AAFJE) (☎ 68-86-34), c/o Tourism Committee of Huahine) offers a 20-metre 'schooner' and a whole range of short and extended tours, including sunset cruises for 1800 CFP per person and day-long trips with food included for 5000 CFP. They are also open to suggestions; contact Gary Danielson.

Brian Groves (☎ 68-82-69, 42-70-60, Papeete) also offers the yacht *Tots* for similar journeys at competitive prices.

PLACES TO STAY

With the closing of the Hotel Huahine Nui, Huahine now lacks a good middle-range place to stay, though the *Hotel Bellevue* has prices near the mid-range and is excellent.

Pouvanaa

Huahine is the birthplace of Pouvanaa a Oopa, the great contemporary French Polynesian leader. Pouvanaa, a decorated WW I veteran, was the son of a Danish sailor and a Polynesian woman. In 1947 he was jailed by the French for advocating Polynesian veterans' rights, and became the spokesperson for the Tahitian independence movement. Blessed with charismatic oratorical skills and well versed in the Bible, Pouvanaa established himself as the most powerful politician in the French Polynesian Territorial Assembly. Known as Metua – 'beloved father to the Tahitians' – he lambasted the colonial system for its treatment of Polynesians as second-class citizens and fought for legislative reforms that would grant Polynesians greater autonomy.

At the zenith of his power, Pouvanaa was convicted of conspiracy in a plot to burn down Papeete and was sent to the notorious Baumette Prison in Marseilles. At the age of 64 he was sentenced to eight years of solitary confinement and banished from Polynesia for another 15 years. Ten years later he was pardoned for the crime many felt he did not commit and returned to Tahiti. Eventually he went back into politics and again served in the Territorial Assembly. He died in 1976. For an excellent account of Pouvanaa's life, Bengt Danielsson's *Moruroa Mon Amour* is recommended. ∎

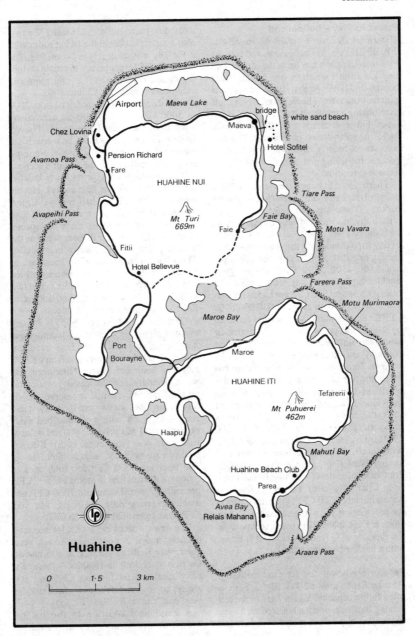

Huahine

Places to Stay – bottom end

The *Hotel Bellevue** (☎ 68-82-76, 68-81-70), BP 21, Fare, has bungalows and is in the Fitii district seven km from the airport and five km from Fare. It is one of the better bottom-end hotels on this island, though it is a bit far from town. The Bellevue is on a bluff overlooking a gorgeous bay. The hotel is not fancy but it does have all the amenities, including solar-heated hot water, restaurant, bar, steam bath(!), freshwater swimming pool, horse riding and fishing. One night's deposit is required.

There are 15 bungalows each with a double bed, bathroom , terrace and private parking. There are also eight rooms each with a double bed and single bed, private bath and balcony. The hotel offers a number of day trips throughout the island as well as fishing expeditions. The rates for one night are 3500/4500/5000 CFP for singles/doubles/triples. If you stay for two nights the rates go down by 500 CFP per room. Bungalow rates for one night are 6000/7000/8000 CFP for singles/doubles/triples and go down by 1000 CFP per room for two nights or more. The staff here are also quite friendly; contact Francois or Elaine Lefoc.

Hotel Huahine (☎ 68-82-69) in Fare has 10 rooms, a restaurant and a bar. It is adequate and simple; each room has an individual toilet and shower but you cannot lock the door. One night's deposit is required. The prices are 1700/2500/3500 CFP for singles/doubles/triples or 5000 CFP with meals. There have been rumours of special 'surfer' prices; the place, in fact, draws a lot of surfers (and those turned away from Chez Guynette). Lunch or dinner is approximately 2000 CFP; you must inform the proprietor if you plan to eat there. Excursions are available. This place seems to be the flip-side of Guynette – raucous at times, with a hardier partying attitude.

Pensions Known for its fine cooking, *Pension Enite* (☎ 68-82-37), BP 37, Fare, is often full to capacity. It is in Fare to the left leaving the dock, down a hundred metres or so, and has eight clean rooms with fans and a common bathroom with hot water. There is also a restaurant/bar and a living room with a TV. The minimum stay is two nights. The cost is 6300 CFP per person per night including three meals, or 5200 CFP for room and continental breakfast. Children get a substantial discount. Meals are priced from 2000 to 3000 CFP and can also be ordered by nonpatrons but must be reserved. Though Enite is famous for its food, be warned: the owners can be moody and the domestic scene may spill over to the visitor's scene.

The pension also provides windsurf rentals (2000 CFP for half a day), bicycle rentals (1000 CFP for half a day), airport transfers (600 CFP for a round trip), and island tours on a minibus. Enite has special 'ferry package' rates for those arriving on the biweekly ferry – Wednesday breakfast to Thursday lunch or Saturday breakfast to Sunday lunch (1½ days and one night) for 10,000 CFP (7600 CFP for children aged two to 12). Finally, those reserving rooms at Enite's must give one night's deposit.

Chez Guynette* (☎ 68-83-75) is recommended highly for the budget traveller but has become so popular with both travellers and locals (students on break, military R&R, etc) that Alain and Helene Guerineau, the warm, friendly and dedicated proprietors, urge prospective clients to reserve ahead. Situated in Fare, across from the quay, it has six rooms, each with a double bed (and perhaps a cot) and private bath, and a dorm with eight cots (communal bath). Kitchen facilities are available, as is a small library. The rates are 3000 CFP for doubles. For groups of three or four in rooms add 500 CFP per extra person. Dorms are 1000 CFP per night. If staying only one night, add 500 CFP; fans are available for 300 CFP.

The new owners have sunk a lot into renovations and it is now a very clean, very quiet, very well-run place. It is also one of the best meal deals in Huahine – there is a daily meal special for 800 CFP, and it's always copious and delicious (check out the huge chef's salad for 600 CFP, too).

A good new addition to the list of budget-minded places is *Pension Richard*

(☎ 68-82-86), BP 12, Fare, which is a simple but kind of charming place a few hundred metres left down the road from the quay (when you see the sign for Lovina's, turn left). Richard Bauwens is the gracious owner who doesn't speak a word of English but communicates admirably anyway. He offers three rooms: one has a double bed and a daybed for 3000 CFP plus 1000 CFP for a third person; one has just a double bed for 3000 CFP; the last is a four-bed setup for 1000 CFP per person. There are cooking facilities and clean common bathrooms. It's no frills but I liked it.

Chez Lovina (☎ 68-81-90, 68-88-06), BP 173, Fare, has also come out of nowhere for budget-wanderers. It's on the fringes of the 'wilds,' just past Pension Richard (can't miss it, trust me...) and has three small 'fare' for campers, each containing a double bed converting to two single beds, with mosquito nets. A kitchen and bathrooms are in a separate 'fare'. There are also three bungalows, each with a double bed and two mattresses

Archaeological Sites

Along with the very many visible marae, underground excavations have revealed that Huahine has the oldest known settlement in the Society Islands. The Vaito'otia/Fa'ahia site came to light in 1972 when a war club (similar in design to artefacts found in New Zealand) was dragged from the bottom of a pond during the construction of the Bali Hai Hotel near Fare. Archaeologist Y H Sinoto happened to be in Huahine at the time of the club's discovery and was called to the scene. Realising that it was a significant find, he coordinated subsequent excavation with the owners of the hotel. Between 1973 and 1984 Dr Sinoto unearthed the remains of an entire village, believed to have been settled between 650 and 850 AD – the oldest remains ever found in the Society Islands.

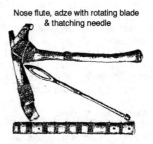
Nose flute, adze with rotating blade & thatching needle

From tool-making areas at the site, workers unearthed habitations, canoe-making areas and a chief's house as well as numerous wooden, stone and shell artefacts – adzes, fish hooks, pendants, scrapers, canoe bailers and canoe parts. Sinoto theorised that around the year 1000 AD this particular village – whose inhabitants most likely came from the Marquesas (as indicated by the style of the artefacts) – was faced with a natural catastrophe. Either a hurricane or a tsunami destroyed the village, creating a sort of Polynesian Pompeii. In all probability the villagers had to evacuate their homes quickly, leaving behind most of their possessions. This was unfortunate for the residents but a stroke of luck for future archaeologists. Many of the otherwise perishable wooden materials were buried and preserved in the mud – literally in the backyard of the future hotel.

The excavation buttresses Sinoto's theory that early Polynesian settlers came from the Marquesas to the Society Islands, eventually migrating to New Zealand. Artefacts uncovered on the Bali Hai site continue to come to the surface but Sinoto feels his work on this particular spot is '90% complete'. The inventory of artefacts leaves little doubt as to the Marquesan/Huahine/New Zealand link. Sinoto has no evidence that the area was ever resettled after the natural calamity, but it remained an important religious site. Near the entrance of the Bali Hai is the reconstructed Marae Tahuea where Tapaea, the native priest who led Captain Cook to Huahine, is thought to have prayed after his visit to the island with the English explorer.

Professor Sinoto initiated the intensive survey of Matairea Hill in 1979 with funding from Earthwatch, a nonprofit organisation in Watertown, Massachusetts. Fonds d'Entralde aux Îles de la Polynesie Francaise have also provided generous financial support. Three sessions with volunteer assistance were needed to complete the mapping of over 200 structures. In 1986, clearing, partial repairs, and test excavations were undertaken in this area. Charcoal samples were collected from test excavations to determine the dates of the occupation of this complex. The excavation revealed that the local people had raised dogs and pigs while also consuming a great deal of clams and fish. ■

on a mezzanine. Each has an equipped kitchen and bath. (They'll let you cram eight people into the bungalow.) There is also a camping area for tents.

In the 'fare', rates are 2000 / 3500 CFP for singles/doubles. Bungalows are from 3500 CFP for singles to 10,500 CFP for eight people. Camping costs 1200/2000 CFP for singles/doubles. A 5000 CFP deposit is needed for reservations. No credit cards are accepted; monthly rentals are available. There good specials in the low season. And definitely take mosquito repellent.

Tarapapa Motel (☎ 68-91-90), BP 173, Fare, is in Maeva, nine km from the airport. It has a four-roomed structure on the lagoon, and all rooms have one double bed, kitchenette and private bath. Extra cots can be added if necessary. Rates are 3500/4500/6000 CFP for singles/doubles/triples.

The place actually looks – well, tired. (The other half of the establishment is the boarded-up building across the road.) A good last resort, if you'll excuse the pun.

Places to Stay – top end

The *Bali Hai Huahine* (☎ 68-84-77, 68-82-77) was still closed as this book was being updated. Although rumours abound regarding its fate (the most reliable says that a Japanese investment group is trying to negotiate a buy), there is no way to know when it will reopen.

The top accommodation on the island is now the *Hotel Sofitel** (☎ 68-86-86, 41-04-04, Papeete; fax 68-85-25, 41-05-05), BP 38, Fare, Huahine, not far from the airport (on the tip of the same motu). The location is absolutely gorgeous – smack between two white sand beaches, a coconut grove and a pristine lagoon, with the village of Maeva directly across the bay. The views really are stunning, and the staff are playfully attentive. Car and bike rentals are available, as are any number of water activities or excursions. The restaurant is excellent and there is a swimming pool. Rates start at US$180 for garden rooms, or US$280 for spacious beach bungalows. I've heard nothing but good things about this hotel.

The *Relais Mahana* (☎ 68-81-54, fax 68-85-08) is on the southern tip of Huahine Iti in a deafeningly quiet spot with a great beach. Although closed temporarily for expansion, the Mahana should be open again by May 1992. There are to be up to 35 bungalows and rooms – on the beach and in the 'garden' – most of which can hold up to three people. Rates presently are 12,300 CFP per day for a garden bungalow and 13,800 CFP per day for a beach bungalow, though these will invariably rise. Virtually all the activities – and there are a lot of them – are free, with the exception of water-skiing. They also have a restaurant and lagoon/island tours.

The *Huahine Beach Club* (☎ 68-81-46, fax 68-85-86; 43-08-29 Papeete for reservations) is, as one letter-writer drily put it, 'now part of the chain of Tahiti hotels sharing the word 'Beach' in their name'. It certainly looks the same as all the others. Located near the village of Parea and not far from the Relais Mahana, the Beach Club offers unusually ostentatious 'traditional'-style bungalows – 16 in all, and all of course include a lengthy list of sundries offered, activities and excursions. The bungalows can accommodate up to four people and the rates are 17,000 CFP for a beach bungalow and 12,000 CFP for a garden bungalow. The bungalows are beautiful, but the beach by the Relais Mahana was nicer.

As this book was being updated more hotels were either being planned or were already under construction on Huahine. These new hotels include the 50-unit *Hotel Te Tiare No Huahine*, which is nearing completion on the south-western tip of the larger island, as well as the 26-unit *Hana Iti*, on Huahine Iti and one other property on Huahine Iti. Yes, Huahine is indeed hitting the big-time...

PLACES TO EAT

Food is available at all the hotels. The *Hotel Sofitel* has the classiest food and is the most expensive.

Snack Bar Temarara in Fare is a 'tourist menu' restaurant with a cosy cafe/bar set directly on the water. It features seafood dishes (including lobster), steak and hamburgers. The food is reasonably priced (700 to 2500 CFP) and the mix of tourists and locals provides an interesting ambience.

Along the side street around the corner from the Hotel Huahine is a new eatery, *Patisserie Tiare Tipanie*, which offers burgers or pizza for 300 CFP. They've also got ice cream.

When the copra boats come in it is always a good time to eat. Their arrival is usually accompanied by vans selling chicken, brochettes or other goodies for around 600 CFP per plate. The nearby *Enite* is also worth checking out, but reservations are necessary. If you happen to be on the far side of the island try *Relais Mahana* which is at the southernmost tip of the island near Marae Anini.

GETTING THERE & AWAY

There are air connections between Huahine and Tahiti, Bora Bora, Moorea and Raiatea. There are flights to and from Papeete two to four times daily. Most flights connect with Bora Bora and Raiatea.

The *Temehani II*, the *Taporo IV* and the *Raromatai Ferry* also sail to Huahine regularly. See the Getting Around chapter for more details.

GETTING AROUND
Car Rental

Kake Rent-a-Car (☎ 68-82-59) is on the edge of Fare towards the Bali Hai. Prices range from 3500 to 6000 CFP per four hours or 5500 to 9000 CFP for a full day, depending on the vehicle. Kake also has scooters and small Hondas available from 2200 CFP per four hours to 4000 CFP per day. Bicycles are available for 800 CFP.

Pacificar (☎ 68-81-10) also has bicycles, scooters and cars. Bikes run from 600 CFP for four hours to 1000 CFP for a full day. Scooters start at 2500 CFP for four hours. Cars are 3500/4500/5500 CFP per four/six/eight-plus hours.

Note that petrol (gasoline) can be bought at the Faremiti or Mobil stations in Fare.

FARE

The small community of Fare, which faces the waterfront, is the island's main settlement and has the usual Chinese shops, a quay to accommodate the copra boats and several pension-style hotels. Fare is almost 'wild west' in character, with its one main street shaded by huge trees and its old-fashioned clapboard stores. It is a slow-moving town in the heat of the day. An occasional auto may pass and kick up some dust or the air may be disturbed by the sounds of schoolchildren giggling or bicycle tyres gliding across the road. Occasional buses provide transport to such far-flung communities as Parea at the opposite end of the island or the village of Maeva, a 35-minute, 24-km ride from Fare. The environs of Parea are dense rainforest, and two km out of town there is a lovely golden beach. At Marae Anini itself there is another excellent beach. The roads are excellent and follow the often steep contours of the terrain, making it very worthwhile to rent a car for an around-the-island trip. For more information contact the Huahine Visitors' Bureau (☎ 68-85-69, 68-81-56) in Fare.

Activities

Horse Riding Le Petite Ferme Stable (☎ 68-82-98), BP 12, Fare, halfway between the airport and Fare, has 12 horses and able 'wranglers', Connie and Jerome Brosseron, who take group camping tours of two days or more as well as shorter rides. The cost is around 2800 CFP for two hours, 4500 CFP for four hours, 8500 CFP for day rides including a picnic. The two-day camping trips go for 13,500 CFP (including food) and day-trip mountain rides to visit the marae for 4400 CFP. The operation offers many, many more interesting opportunities.

Diving Pacific Blue Adventure (☎ 68-86-86, 68-87-21), BP 38, Fare, is near the quay in Fare and is the only dive operation in Huahine. Certification is possible and dives start at 5000 CFP. Contact Dominique Tempie, Fare.

MAEVA

In ancient times Huahine was a centre of Polynesian culture and ruled by a centralised government instead of warring tribes, as most of the other islands were. Archaeologically, Huahine is the richest island in French Polynesia and is sometimes referred to as an 'open-air museum'. In the village of Maeva alone there are 16 restored marae, the ancestral shrines of local chiefs. The stone slabs of these ancient temples jut out like phalluses on the landscape and are eerily reminiscent of the Druid ruins of Stonehenge. In the nearby lagoon, rich in crab and other seafood, are nine ancient fish traps constructed from stone, some of which have been rebuilt and are in use today.

Above Maeva village, on Matairea Hill, is the second most important temple in all of French Polynesia, as well as more recently discovered archaeological sites such as the foundations of priests' and chiefs' homes, more temples and a huge wall guarding the mountain sanctuary from sea raiders.

Opposite Maeva, just across the bridge near Marae Manunu (No 20 on map) is a monument to the Battle of Maeva in 1846. The monument, marked by seven cannons, commemorates the unequivocal French rule over Eastern Polynesia, even though constitutionally it was only a 'protectorate' until formal annexation in 1880.

Activities

Touring the Marae Grab a bus, taxi or bicycle and make your way to the Fare Pote'e, an old-style meeting house in Maeva. The 100-year-old meeting house, which had fallen into disrepair was rebuilt in 1972 by Sinoto. This is where the oceanside marae (constructed mostly in the 16th century) begins. Here the individual chiefs worshipped their ancestors at their respective temples. Heading further south down the road, you will be able to see stones piled in a 'V' shape inside the lagoon, an area particularly rich in fish, crab and other sea life. These stone structures are ancient fish weir traps, which have also been rebuilt by Dr Sinoto and work as well now as they did hundreds of years ago. Fish enter the traps by means of incoming and outgoing tides.

New Maeva Discoveries – New Trail Past Fare Pote'e and opposite the Protestant Church is one of the trail heads for the many

Mystery of Matairea Hill

The coastal flats of Maeva – where most of the reconstructed temples are located – was, according to royal tradition, subdivided by the eight royal families of Huahine for purposes of worship. That all the royal families would have their temples in the same area is extremely unusual and suggests that a large number of retainers lived nearby.

According to tradition, the second most important temple in French Polynesia, Marae Matairea-rahi, is on Matairea Hill above Maeva. Dr Y H Sinoto (the world's authority on Eastern Polynesian archaeology) of Honolulu's Bishop Museum, familiar with the temple ruins, surveyed the area and upon noting the presence of a number of stone structures, assumed he had found the remains of the retainers' homes. Upon further investigation, however, instead of retainers' residences he found 40 previously unrecorded marae and realised that the area was much more important than had previously been thought.

The survey of Matairea Hill proved significant because it uncovered for the first time marae of the Leeward Group that were of similar construction to those of the Windward Group. Although the Windward and Leeward groups were allied politically and culturally, marae found in both groups had always been of greatly different construction – an archaeological mystery. The discovery of the Matairea Hill temples provided a 'missing link' between the cultures of the Leeward Group (Huahine, Raiatea, Bora Bora and Maupiti) and the Windward Group (Tahiti, Maiao and Moorea.) The excavations indicate that marae in the Windward Group probably originated in the islands of the Leeward Group, such as Huahine, reinforcing the early cultural importance of the island. ■

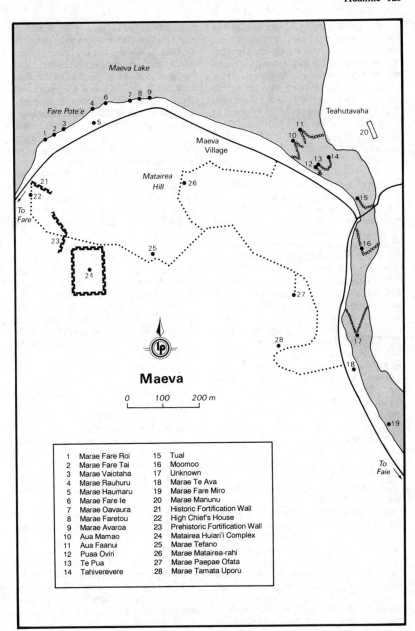

Maeva Lake

Fare Pote'e

Teahutavaha

Maeva Village

Matairea Hill

To Fare

To Faie

Maeva

0   100   200 m

1	Marae Fare Roi	15	Tual
2	Marae Fare Tai	16	Moomoo
3	Marae Vaiotaha	17	Unknown
4	Marae Rauhuru	18	Marae Te Ava
5	Marae Haumaru	19	Marae Fare Miro
6	Marae Fare Ie	20	Marae Manunu
7	Marae Oavaura	21	Historic Fortification Wall
8	Marae Faretou	22	High Chief's House
9	Marae Avaroa	23	Prehistoric Fortification Wall
10	Aua Mamao	24	Matairea Huiari'i Complex
11	Aua Faanui	25	Marae Tefano
12	Puaa Oviri	26	Marae Matairea-rahi
13	Te Pua	27	Marae Paepae Ofata
14	Tahiverevere	28	Marae Tamata Uporu

marae reconstructed by Sinoto on Matairea Hill. The trail head is not obvious; it is set behind a house so ask a local to show you. The 400-metre hike to the main section of the trail is a bit steep at the beginning. At the summit the trail opens up, and the area is covered with ferns and manioc patches. (At this point the mosquitoes begin to attack so bring some repellent along.) In former times this was a vanilla plantation and you can still see the vines spiralling up the trees and bushes.

Beginning in 1984, new excavations by Dr Sinoto revealed that Matairea Hill was occupied (according to the newly discovered cultural layers) from 1450 to 1700 AD. In his efforts to uncover the past, Sinoto has revealed a new historical trail which begins from the shore and goes to Marae Tefano (see map). The trail begins at the fortification wall (21) built in 1846 (when the French marines attacked Maeva) and up the hill adjacent to the latest Sinoto site. A few metres away is a large stone-paved area (22) which was part of a round-ended house foundation that most likely belonged to a supreme chief. Interestingly, the front terrace with the large paved area is oriented inland, facing the sacred mountain of Moua Tapu. The trail goes through the old fortification wall (23) which protected residents from invaders from Bora Bora. Just up the trail, the Matairea Huiari'i complex (24) was occupied chiefly by families who in fact occupied the entire inland slope of the Hill. Each residential unit had one or more marae. To have a density of so many chiefly families in one place was very unusual.

The most significant marae on the hill is Matairea-rahi (26), the most important temple in the Society Islands prior to the building of Taputaputea in Raiatea. Oral tradition says that when Taputaputea was to be built, stones from Matairea-rahi were transported to the building site to ensure that the new temple would retain the old temple's *mana* (power). Matairea-rahi consists of two structures: in the first, nine upright stones represent 10 districts – the 10th stone is missing. There are also stone posts that serve as intermediaries to the gods. In the rear is a raised platform (ahu), which was a throne for the gods. Below the ahu is a lower platform where sacrifices (some human) were placed. On the other structure stood a house built on posts where the images of gods were kept. The house was actually seen in 1818 by a missionary, Rev William Ellis, who saw a building perched on stilts, guarded by men day and night to protect the holy images inside. Captain Cook's painter was also supposed to have seen the temple.

Just a few hundred metres from Matairea is Marae Tefano (25), also an impressive sight. Its ahu is huge and the temple basks in the shade of a huge banyan tree, probably planted there around the time that the marae was constructed.

A km or so from Fare Pote'e, cross the small bridge and continue to your left on the motu to another very impressive temple, Marae Manunu (20). This became the marae for the community of Huahine Nui after Matairea-rahi. Next to the low offering platform is the grave of Raiti, the last high priest of Maeva. When he died in 1915 one of the huge marae slabs fell. He was buried at the marae at his request.

Marae Anini, on the southernmost tip of Huahine Iti, served this community as a worshipping place for the deities of Oro and Hiro. The last priest of the temple told Reverend Ellis in 1818 that he remembered 14 cases of human sacrifice. The principal feature of the marae is its ahu. Small platforms, or *ro'i*, were said to be for the gods Oro or Hiro. The upright stones are backrests for priests and chiefs, or memorials for deceased chiefs. A small marae was built when a royal family adopted a child of lower rank. A platform far out on the court was where the house of Oro stood. Under each post of the house a human sacrifice was rendered.

A thorough tour of the marae near Maeva will take several hours and a bit of walking so it is suggested you do it in the early morning or late afternoon. There is also a fine beach near Marae Anini.

The archaeological complex is the core of

a planned historical/ecological 'living' museum to be organised by Dr Sinoto and the French Polynesian government. Eventually, with the cooperation of the local population, scientists and the local government hope to create a master plan that will ensure the integrity and maintenance of the archaeological treasures. Ideally, Sinoto feels that agriculture can be revived by practising age-old Polynesian ecology (such as taboos against over-fishing, etc) and combining it with modern agricultural and aquacultural techniques. Sinoto would also like to rebuild the chiefs' and priests' houses near the marae and have families and caretakers occupy them on a full-time basis. The master plan would also provide recommendations as to where restaurants, hotels and commercial buildings should be built so as to protect the archaeological zone.

Raiatea & Tahaa

One hundred and ninety-two km north-west of Papeete and 40 km west of Huahine are the sister islands of Raiatea and Tahaa. The two share a common coral foundation and protected lagoon. Tahaa is three km north-west of Raiatea – roughly a 20-minute boat trip between the islands.

Legend has it that Raiatea and Tahaa were originally one island but a giant eel swallowed a young girl. Possessed by her spirit, the raging eel broke through the earth and caused the sea to flow, cutting the one island of Raiatea into two – creating Raiatea and Tahaa.

GETTING THERE & AWAY
Air
Flights with Air Tahiti from Papeete to Raiatea are available seven days a week and flying time is 45 minutes. There are also regular flights to and from Bora Bora, Huahine, Maupiti, Moorea and Rangiroa.

Sea
Raiatea and Tahaa can be reached by interisland steamer from Papeete. The *Temehani II* and the *Taporo IV* take about 19 hours. The *Raromatai Ferry* also sails regularly from Papeete. See the Getting Around chapter for more details.

Getting from Raiatea to Tahaa and back can also be exciting. Generally, you can be assured of catching a ride with one of the established 'shuttles', hitching with interisland shoppers or, in a last-ditch effort, you could ride with the schoolchildren's boat at 3 pm. The shuttle boats leave Tahaa at around 5 am and return from Uturoa at around 11 am. Most of Tahaa's communities are served. A round trip costs 800 CFP. Reservations aboard a boat are possible by calling the operator directly or by contacting the coordinator of the local OPATTI office in Tahaa (☎ 65-63-00) or Raiatea (☎ 66-23-33/34).

Otherwise, the schedule for boats is:

Patio and Hipu: Wednesday and Friday (☎ 65-63-91)
Faaaha: Tuesday, Wednesday and Friday (☎ 65-60-79)
Haamene: Tuesday, Wednesday and Friday (☎ 65-61-35)
Tapuamu and Tiva: Wednesday and Friday (☎ 65-61-18)
Poutorou: Tuesday, Wednesday and Friday (☎ 65-60-18)

GETTING AROUND
On Raiatea, taxis and le truck service to all the outlying districts are available between 5 am and 6 pm. Trucks regularly travel from one end of the island to the other two or three times per day (but then again, don't be surprised if they don't). In other words, hitchhiking is often the name of the game in Raiatea. Le truck fares range from 100 to 200 CFP.

Car rentals are available from Hotel Le Motu (☎ 66-34-06), which also offers scooters, Motu Tapu (☎ 66-33-09), a few km outside of town in the same direction as the airport, or Apetahi Location, 1.5 km from the airport, which has scooters and bikes too. Expect to pay at least 7000 CFP per day for rentals.

Raiatea

Raiatea is the largest of the Leeward Islands, with an area of 170 sq km and about 8600 inhabitants. The island is totally surrounded by a reef but has several navigable passes and the only navigable river, the Faaroa, in French Polynesia. There are no beaches on the island, but the locals will emphatically point out that the motu beaches are quite nice. Raiatea receives plenty of rainfall to irrigate its fertile soil and has a lagoon rich in sea life. Its main products are copra and

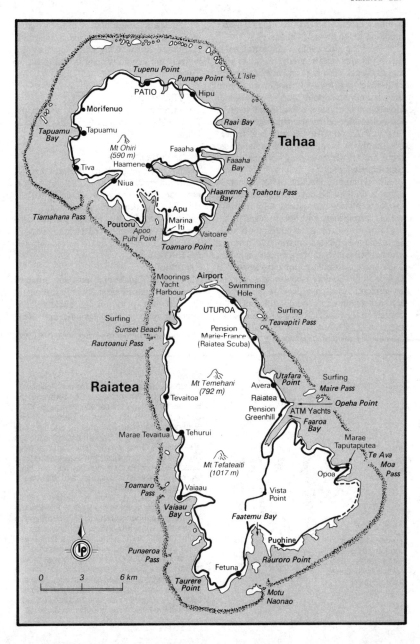

vanilla. Scientists are also developing oyster breeding in the town of Uturoa.

One of the nicest things about Raiatea is that it remains 'undiscovered' by most visitors to French Polynesia and does not have a well-developed tourist infrastructure. From the visitor's standpoint, this is very good. Hotels and pensions are few, thus Raiateans are not inundated by tourists, and are still relatively friendly. However, it is a 'major' community by French Polynesian standards: there are all the amenities – shops, rental cars, hospital, etc.

Like Huahine, Raiatea is an archaeologists's delight. Scientists have unearthed artefacts linking the island with Hawaii, which corresponds with local tradition that says Raiatea was the great jumping-off point for ancient Polynesian mariners. There are also a significant number of marae, including Taputaputea, considered the most important temple in the Society Islands and a national monument. Tevaitoa Village on the western side has a marae in good condition near the church on the headland by Point Tainuu.

Raiatea is the last bastion of fire walking in French Polynesia. Unfortunately, you'll rarely see fire walking here. Raiatean fire walkers are generally seen in Tahiti during Tiurai.

INFORMATION
For information about Raiatea, contact the Raiatea Visitors' Bureau (☎ 66-23-33/34) in Uturoa.

ORGANISED TOURS
Marie-France probably has the most popular land-tour operation. Others include Almost Paradise Tours (☎ 66-23-64) run by Kolans Bill, BP 290, Uturoa, Raiatea. Havai'i Tours (☎ 66-27-98), BP 300, Uturoa, Raiatea, also has water tours – contact Delphine Harris.

ACTIVITIES
Excursions
Most of the hotels and pensions organise excursions up the Faaroa River (traditionally the departure point for the ancient Polynesians who settled Hawaii and New

Sketched from an engraving by Betolozzi, published 1775, after a painting by Nathaniel Dance Holland

Omai
Raiatea is the home of Omai, the first Polynesian to visit Europe. When Captain Cook arrived in the Society Islands on his second voyage in 1773, Omai expressed a fervent desire to see 'Britannia'. His wish was granted and he soon became the darling of English society. Although a simpleton, Omai was friendly and charming. Dressed by his benefactors in velvet jackets, he dined in London's best homes, met the king, learned to shoot and skate, and became a favourite with the ladies.

En route back to Tahiti, he served Captain Cook as a translator in the Society Islands and Tonga. He returned to Tahiti in 1776 bearing gifts of firearms, wine, tin soldiers, kitchenware and a globe of the world. The hapless Omai was cheated out of many of his treasures by Tahitians, so Cook saw to it that he was moved to Huahine. Cook's carpenters built Omai a house there and supplied him with pigs, chickens and tools. Omai bid farewell to the crew, who had become his close friends, and held back his tears until it came time to say goodbye to Cook. ∎

Zealand). The river trip is a relatively short excursion into Faaroa Bay, a fjord-like inlet with steep, verdant cliffs on either side and up the river about a km or two into a 'heart of darkness' jungle with thick foliage. The trip lasts until the river becomes too shallow to navigate. Day trips may also include canoe rides to Raiatea's sister island of Tahaa or a trek to Mt Temehani to see the apetahi flower.

Near Uturoa is Tapioi Hill where in 1974 a television relay station was installed. The short climb to the top provides an excellent view of Raiatea and neighbouring islands.

The tumbled-down ruins of the great Marae Taputaputea are just past the village of Opoa, about 35 km from Uturoa. To get to Opoa to see the temple you can travel by road or take a motorboat ride down half the length of the lagoon to the marae site.

On the western side of Raiatea is Tevaitoa (about 15 km from Uturoa), where another temple, Marae Tainuu, is located. Continuing south along the road to Fetuna (about 45 km) you can see gorgeous landscapes for the entire length of the journey. For those wishing to drive, a road runs the 96 km circumference of the island.

At the southern end of the island just across from Fetuna Village is a large motu called Naonao, which has a nice beach and is great for picnics. The best motu is off Opeha Point, near the mouth of Faaroa Bay.

Scuba Diving

The lagoon offers excellent diving and the local scuba operator, Raiatea Scuba (☎ 66-37-10), run by Patrice Philip, BP 272, Uturoa, Raiatea, provides equipment, rentals, transport and lessons for diving enthusiasts. Aside from pelagics, soft coral and an essentially 'virgin' lagoon, the Raiatea/Tahaa area has unusual blue and purple coral. Lagoon dive sites are numerous, and many are less than 10 minutes by boat from Philip's Pension Marie-France (750 metres from the Bali Hai Hotel). For an extra charge Philip will also pick up divers from yachts or other hotels on the island. Philip has a large outrigger canoe that serves

as a dive boat and can seat up to 10 people. Rates are 5000 CFP per dive (including gear); those staying at Pension Marie-France get a special price.

Horse Riding

Kaoha Nui (☎ 66-22-46, 66-25-46), at PK 6, a ways down from Pension Marie-France, offers horseback tours for all levels of riders. Rates are 1500 CFP per hour, or 6000 CFP for a whole day. Each outing has a guide; virtually the whole island can be covered.

Flying

Raiatea even has its own aeroclub for those with the bucks to rent a plane or pilot, or both. Call Charles Higgins (☎ 66-32-44, 66-31-91), BP 20, Uturoa, Raiatea, for information.

Yacht Rental

The construction of a yacht harbour by the Moorings Ltd (☎ 66-35-93, 66-26-26), BP 165, Uturoa, Raiatea, an internationally known purveyor of 'sailing vacations', is one of the more exciting tourism developments in the Society Islands. Only five minutes from town, the yacht harbour has moorings for private vessels as well as 19 of its own 'boats' ranging in length from 11 to 15 metres.

The Moorings have two options for nautical adventurers: 'bareboating' for those who already have the skill to sail a yacht, and 'crewed' yachts in which experienced sailors are provided (at a much greater cost). In either case the Moorings people will supply all provisions from bread to booze and, if necessary, crews. Because of Raiatea's geographical position in the Society Islands, cruising to nearby Bora Bora, Huahine and Maupiti is easy. As one might imagine, cruising is not for everyone's pocketbook but for those who can afford it, it is the best way to see the islands. Prices begin at US$290 per day or US$2030 per week for an *Endeavour 37* to US$550 per day or US$3850 per week for a *Moorings 51*. You can call from the USA (☎ (800) 521-1126) for information.

ATM Yachts South Pacific (☎ 66-23-18),

BP 331, Uturoa, Raiatea, is in Faaroa Bay, directly below Pension Greenhill. The yacht club also has its own restaurant – Chez Toto. ATM has a flotilla of 25 boats of all types, including catamarans. They will provide transport from the airport and, like the Moorings, can outfit one for just about anything. ATM also provides the option of bareboating or hiring a crew; like the Moorings, too, it ain't for the budget traveller. Rates go from US$2020 per week for an *Attalia 33* to US$7880 per week for a 15-metre catamaran, including the skipper. All ATM boats have a minimum three-day hire. Contact Christophe or Barbara Zebrowski.

Danae III (☎ 66-32-95, 66-21-75, 66-35-93 or via Mahina Radio 43-79-67), is a cruising yacht also located in the harbour with the Moorings, but offering different tour selections: the 'classic' tour of the Leeward Islands, the itinerary varying with season, costing approximately US$900 for six days and five nights; extended fishing tours starting at US$875 for a three-day expedition; or, as they claim, a three-week tour 'for the health, relaxation and leisure', in which 18 days of health-oriented food and activity with everything included will run you US$1908; there is a four-person minimum. For more information contact Claude Goche, BP 251, Uturoa, Raiatea.

Other charter boats (some for fishing, all for tours) include the *Moana Vaihi* from Jean Pierre Constant (☎ 66-36-83), BP 91, Uturoa, Raiatea, and Hiro Tehahe's *Raimana II* (☎ 66-37-91), BP 845, Uturoa, Raiatea. Andre Chong (☎ 66-30-28), BP 91, Uturoa has two boats for hire. Joseph Chosoi (☎ 66-35-54, fax 66-24-77), BP 70, Uturoa, will even take you to Maupiti or Bora Bora.

UTUROA

Uturoa is the capital and main port of Raiatea and it is also the administrative centre for the Leeward Islands. It consists of one main drag flanked by two-storey cement structures interspersed with a few old-style clapboard buildings. One block from 'main street' is a quay lined with fishing boats. Uturoa is the second largest town in French Polynesia and

although it is not a metropolis it has its own electrical power station, a hospital, gendarmerie, courthouse, Chinese grocers, several small hotels, two restaurants, hardware stores, three banks, boutiques, post office, pharmacy, Air Tahiti office, schools and a barber shop. There is also a small municipal market and a plant which makes the ice used to refrigerate fish exports to Papeete.

Things to See

The market comes alive at the crack of dawn on Wednesdays, Fridays and Sundays. If you feel bored or want companionship, there are always yachts moored at the 'Moorings' yacht harbour, whose occupants are eager to trade stories and consume beer. Animal lovers may not be in attendance but for those interested there are cockfights every Sunday at 2 pm (in season, which begins in July; the arena is 200 m from Raiatea Village on the mountain side). Uturoa also hosts the annual 'Miss Raiatea Contest' in June.

Raiatea Sea Shell (☎ 66-21-35), a sort of seashell museum/collection, is at PK 10.5 in Pufao. There are 25,000 or more pieces in the exhibit, including some rare types. Admission is supposed to be free, but I'd call first.

You can even 'rent' a traditional dance troupe or a group of Polynesian musicians. For information about the dancers, contact Moeline Ihorai (☎ 66-33-21); call 66-31-49 for information about the musicians. Both start at US$150 per session and go up from there depending on time.

Places to Stay – bottom end

The *Pension Marie-France** (☎ 66-37-10, fax 66-20-94), BP 272, Uturoa, Raiatea, specialises in accommodation for divers but they do take in nondivers. The pension has relocated to 1½ km outside Uturoa (750 metres past the Bali Hai) and is ideal for those who wish to stay close to town. It is located directly on the lagoon and has a private dock for swimmers; yachts can anchor at their private jetty. Patrice Philip, the owner, is the island's only dive operator. He also leads tours to all the island's attractions, including Mount Temehani and Faaroa

River. There's also snorkelling, underwater shows, picnics on a motu, and custom tours on his large outrigger canoe. They are also video-equipped. His wife, Marie-France, is a good cook and both do their best to make the visitor feel at home.

The new place is spacious, clean and a good traveller's hangout. There is a four-bedroom house with terraces facing a swimming pool (new, for PADI instruction): two bedrooms have two single beds, and two have two double beds. These rooms are all 3600 CFP. A dormitory building houses up to seven people; the rate is 1200 CFP. There are two communal bathrooms for these rooms, with hot water. One room beside the lagoon (4500 CFP) has a double bed and a private bath (hot water); one bungalow beside the pool (4500 CFP) has a double bed. There is also a washing machine on the premises. You can cook meals yourself in the fully equipped kitchen or order them. Breakfast is 450 CFP, lunch is 1200 CFP and dinner is 1600 CFP. Business is now booming here and all lodgers are advised to reserve space by phoning the pension. Patrice will provide transfer to and from the airport (800 CFP) or pick up yachters not moored at the pension and furnish rental bicycles.

Places to Stay – middle

The *Hotel Le Motu* (☎ 66-34-06) is in the centre of town and appears to be the local 'executive's' hotel. The rooms appeared to be clean and comfortable and there is a good restaurant/bar on the premises as well as a pool hall and disco. The hotel would be recommended except for the disco and pool hall which are noisy and unacceptable for those desiring tranquillity (especially over the weekends). The hotel also provides tours, picnics, boating excursions and free transfers for guests. VISA card is accepted. The rates are 5000 CFP for singles/doubles and 6500 CFP for triples.

Places to Stay – top end

The *Bali Hai* (☎ 66-31-49) is on a lagoon five minutes from the airport, about one km from Uturoa. This is the largest and most luxurious hotel on the island and has nine over-the-water bungalows and 27 garden bungalows. There are also a pool, boutique, bar, swimming dock and all the usual excursions. Prices begin at US$110 for a single.

Places to Eat

There is one local bar in Uturoa, the *Three Stars*, which is by the *Hotel Le Motu*. Just outside town is the Bali Hai Hotel, which also has a bar and a restaurant. Other eateries include: *Le Motu* (part of the hotel with the same name), which is a 'tourist menu' place; *Jade Palace*, which has Chinese food; *Quai du Pecheurs*, which serves pizza, beer and good French food on the waterfront; *Le Gourmet* which is near the edge of town toward the Bali Hai and has meals for 3000 to 8000 CFP; and *Chez Remi*, which has excellent French and Tahitian cuisine.

There are also snack bars like the *Coconut House* and *Snack Moemoe*, which is more of an outdoor cafe serving coffee, sandwiches and beer. Both are near the waterfront. The action doesn't begin until after 10 pm on Saturday because of an important weekly event – the TV show *Dallas*.

Entertainment

The Zenith is a rollicking local disco, basically for the younger crowd, as is the Vairahi. Chez Emilliene, on the outskirts of town towards the airport, appears to be putting in a low-budget karaoke.

MT TEMEHANI

The highest point on the island is Mount Temehani (1033 metres), and it can be climbed. According to tradition one of the principal Polynesian gods, Oro, was born of this volcano. Temehani is also the home of the *tiare apetahi*, a white flower found only on this mountain. Legend has it that the blossom's five petals represent the five fingers of a young Tahitian maiden who fell in love with a Tahitian prince but was prohibited from marrying him because she was a commoner.

AROUND THE ISLAND

The newest tourist developments on Raiatea aren't really that new. However, over the last five years several places have sprung up, including: the Moorings, the largest yacht harbour outside of Papeete (see Yacht Rentals); ATM, another yacht-outing group, in Faaroa Bay; Greenhill, a low-budget pension; and Pension Marie-France, a low-budget hotel that specialises in accommodation for scuba divers. The major 'upscale' hotel in the area is the 36-unit Bali Hai (just outside Uturoa), which is small by industry standards.

Places to Stay – bottom end

One of my favourites is *Greenhill** (☎ 66-37-64), BP 598, Uturoa, Raiatea. It provides great scenery, modest prices, good food and a comfortable atmosphere. Perched on the side of a ridge overlooking Faaroa Bay, the view it affords is superb and archetypally Polynesian. It is about 12 km out of Uturoa, approximately 12 minutes by car. The pension is run by a charming, cultured French woman, Marie-Isabelle, and her equally accommodating husband Jason, who create a family-style ambience. The cooking is good and all visitors eat at a common table, making one feel like a guest at someone's home rather than at a hotel. Accommodation includes one large family villa with four bedrooms: two bedrooms have two single beds; one bedroom has one single bed; one 'apartment' has one double and one single bed. There is also a double bungalow with

two twin bedrooms, each with one double bed and private bathroom. All rooms have private bath and gorgeous views. They are also planning to build a 'honeymoon suite'.

Marie-Isabelle is an entertaining host who has lived throughout the world and is definitely an attraction in her own right. The grounds are manicured and the lodgings are clean and modest. What is most unusual at Greenhill is that all excursions and day trips are included in the tariff. Thus there are no extra charges for airport transfer, trips up the Faaroa River, round-the-island tours, snorkelling and beach trips to a nearby motu, or use of a bicycle. Whereas many hoteliers attempt to extract every franc out of the guest, here you get the feeling that the owners of Greenhill have not succumbed to one of French Polynesia's greatest sins – excessive greed. The cost of accommodation plus three meals per day is 6500 CFP. Greenhill requests that visitors make reservations at least two days prior to arrival, and a minimum two-day stay is required. Greenhill is often a weekend retreat for local government dignitaries and it's a good idea to make reservations well in advance. You must pay with cash as credit cards are not accepted.

Pension Yolande Roopinia (☎ 66-35-28) is in Avera at PK 10, next to Raiatea Village on the water. The clientele are mostly local

as Yolande does not speak English. The pension consists of one long barracks-like building with four self-contained units. Two rooms have one double bed and one single bed; two rooms have three single beds. All have kitchenettes and private baths. Frankly, it looked sort of dumpy. They have a restaurant and offer the usual excursions. The rates are 5000/6000 CFP for singles/doubles (including two meals). Airport transfer is 1000 CFP.

Places to Stay – middle

The *Sunset Beach Motel Apooiti** (☎ 66-33-47), BP 397, Uturoa, Raiatea, gets a high rating and would be ideal for families or those wishing to cook for themselves. Two km from the airport and five km from town, it has 16 very modern, comfortable self-contained bungalows in a former copra plantation adjacent to the lagoon. Kitchenette with utensils, television, free airport transfer, parking space and outrigger canoes are provided. The staff are very friendly. Fruit in season is also freely given to guests. Bungalows are set in an expansive grassy area and afford a great deal of privacy. There is even a large camping area for up to 30 tents; a large equipped kitchen and clean, communal bathrooms are available for campers. Rates are very reasonable – 5000/6000 CFP for singles/doubles, 7000/8000 CFP for triples/quadruples. Camping is 1000 CFP per day per person. Scuba diving is also available through Patrice Philip. The Apooiti does not accept credit cards but gives discounts for long stays.

The *Hotel Raiatea Village* (☎ 66-31-62, 66-33-60), BP 282, Uturoa, has six seaside bungalows and six 'garden' bungalows (all with kitchenettes). The hotel is near the Avera area, at the foot of Faaroa Bay, a 10-minute auto ride from town. The atmosphere is nice but the accommodation is overpriced, especially compared with Greenhill, one km down the road. Although on the water, swimming may not be advisable due to the presence of a particular type of algae nearby which causes extreme itching. (The owners shrugged off the danger, which made me uneasy.) Bicycle, canoe and car rentals are available. Tariffs for the 12 seaside bungalows are 5000 CFP for singles/doubles; 8000 CFP for triples/quadruples; extra beds are 1500 CFP per person. All have hot water in individual bathrooms. Three meals are available with accommodation for an additional 4000 CFP per day.

Tahaa

Tahaa is 90 sq km in area and its population numbers approximately 4000. Tahaa is not as fertile as Raiatea, doesn't have as much rainfall, is more isolated and consequently is less economically developed. Being something of a backwater, it is even more tranquil and off the beaten track. There was a time when, travelling to Tahaa, one stayed at a local's home but now there are several excellent lodgings. The island is surrounded by a reef with two passes and is served both by regularly scheduled interisland boats from Papeete and local ferry boats from Raiatea. The travelling time by boat from Raiatea is about 20 minutes.

Tahaa's agriculture is mainly in the form of subsistence farming although vanilla and copra are produced commercially. Livestock and chicken ranches are also important. Local crafts such as hand-woven hats, baskets, placemats, bedspreads, shell necklaces and wood sculpture are a cottage industry for many.

Parts of Tahaa are still only connected by a walking track but this makes for pleasant walks from Patio (the main community) to Hipu and on to Faaaha. One can also trek from Tiva to Vaitoare along a path that traverses the cliff's edge along the shoreline. One story about the island, recently substantiated, concerns the survivors of a Chilean slave ship wrecked near the village of Tiva in 1863. Before the rescue party arrived, several of the crew members disappeared. They hid in the village, married islanders and became the ancestors of Tahaa's 'Feti Panior' – the Spanish clan. To this day, their descendants live in Tiva and are renowned for their beauty.

INFORMATION

For information on the island contact the Tahaa Visitors' Bureau (☎ 65-63-00) in Patio.

ACTIVITIES

There are several tour operators on Tahaa. *Hotel Marina Iti* is definitely a place for arranging excursions, etc. Contact Philippe Robin at the hotel. Others include Stivine Ariitu at *Tivini Tours Tahaa*, (☎ 65-61-06, VHF 68), BP 184, Haamene, Tahaa. He offers a wide range of activities, both maritime and on terra firma; also, Alain and Christina Plantier of *Vanilla Tours* (☎ 65-62-46), BP 124, Haamene, Tahaa, offer four set tours, most using Marina Iti as a starting point. Andre Lemoine (☎ 65-62-56) offers guided mountain walks.

Doing it alone, there is an excellent walk from the head of Haamene Bay to the head of Hurepiti Bay over Mt Taira, which divides the island. The motus on the north-eastern coast also have the better beaches to be found. The sunsets and views of Bora Bora are stupendous from Tapuamu Bay.

PLACES TO STAY

The most interesting hotels are the *Hotel Marina Iti* (a hotel-cum-yacht mooring) and a tiny resort called *L'Ile*, which is more a collection of bungalows, on a remote motu.

Chez Pascal* (☎ 65-60-42) is in the Tapuamu district of the island a km away from the quay. It consists of one home with four clean rooms, each with a double and a single bed. There are two private baths. Cooking facilities are available and the electricity is solar powered. Activities include picnics at a nearby motu for 5000 CFP. Rooms are 4000 CFP including breakfast and dinner. Transfer from Raiatea is 3500 CFP. Write to Pascal Tameahu, Tapuamu, Tahaa.

Chez Francette* (☎ 65-63-75, ask for Martine, 9 am to 2 pm and after 6 pm), BP 142, Haamene, Tahaa, in the Tiva district, 15 minutes from the Raiatea boat dock, is a new addition and also comes highly praised. It consists of a three-bedroom concrete house, with one double and one single bed in each room. There is also a kitchen, living room and dining room. The house has a private bathroom and a large terrace overlooking the bay. A white-sand beach rounds it out. A room and full pension is 5500 CFP per person per day.

Pension Hibiscus (☎ 65-61-06) in the Haamene district is 20 minutes by boat from the quay at Uturoa. It has four 'traditional' bungalows and two new, smaller units. The four 'traditional' bungalows each have one double and one single bed, terrace and private baths, even a refrigerator; the two smaller bungalows have the same bed situation, but have outdoor bath/toilet facilities. (There have also been reports of people occasionally staying in a dormitory-style concrete barracks nearby, but the reports have not been favourable, and they've been instructed by the tourist board not to admit to having it.) Prices are 6500 CFP for one to three people in the traditional bungalows; 4500 CFP for one to three people in the smaller, family bungalows. Three meals a day cost an extra 3750 CFP. There is a small seafood restaurant on the premises, and their own 'yacht club' has free moorings and showers. Write to Mrs Teaere Aritu, BP 184, Haamene, Tahaa.

Hotel Marina Iti* (☎ 65-61-01), BP 888, Uturoa, Raiatea, is on Toamaro Point, the southernmost tip of Tahaa, 10 minutes by boat from the Raiatea Marina. It combines a marina/nautical atmosphere with four comfortable bungalows and five sailboats from 10 to 19 metres (total capacity of 30 berths in 2, 3 or 4-berth cabins). Two double bungalows have one double and one single bed, living room, terrace, and private bathroom with hot water. A garden bungalow contains one double room and one twin room, sharing a bathroom. The last bungalow has a double bed, living room, terrace, and private bath with hot water. The amenities include a bar/restaurant, electricity and transfers from the airport or dock at Raiatea.

Activities are diving, cycling, canoeing, sailing, fishing, water-skiing, windsurfing, boating trips to Bora Bora or Huahine and excursions to Raiatea's attractions. Diving rates are 5000 CFP per person per dive (including equipment). The tariff is 12,000 to 18,000 CFP per bungalow for one to three people. Three meals cost an additional 6600 CFP. An extra bed is 3000 CFP per day. Children under 12 get a 50% reduction. Marina Iti does not accept credit cards.

*L'Ile** (☎ 65-64-80 during meal hours; telex c/o Moorings 422FP), BP 119, Uturoa, an upmarket getaway run by Diego Paterlini and Francoise Burdinet, is highly recommended. Tucked away on a tiny motu off the north-eastern shore of Tahaa, it consists of 3½ hectares of land bounded by long stretches of white-sand beach. There are three bungalows – two have one double bed, the other has three single beds. All share outside communal bathrooms. Each bungalow has its own private beach and there are canoes available. Bicycles are also provided for tours of Tahaa. There is also a restaurant on the premises. Transfers to Tahaa are free but transport to Raiatea is 1000 CFP. The cost of lodging and meals is 15,500 CFP; each extra person costs 12,500 CFP. Children aged three to 12 are half-price.

Finally, *Tahaa Village* (☎ 65-61-18), BP 190, Uturoa, Raiatea, is a new addition in Tiva, three km south of Tapuamu where the boat docks. It has also gotten good reports. It offers three sparse but comfortable bungalows in the 5000 CFP range. Unfortunately, the hoped-for dormitory and camping facilities did not work out. The manager, Mr Petit, is reportedly quite hospitable and speaks excellent English.

PATIO

The capital of Tahaa is Patio, on the northern portion of the island. It has a gendarmerie, an infirmary, a post office (with radio telephone) and a school. Excursions to points of interest can be arranged with locals, including visits to spots where the mythical Polynesian hero – appropriately named Hiro – left his mark. These landmarks consist of Hiro's bowl, file, left footprint, crest and boat. The tiny islet of Hipu off the coast of Tahaa is the home of Hiro's shark. There are some strikingly beautiful bays on the island, including Haamene and Hurepiti, which a local guide will be glad to show you.

Bora Bora

Located 264 km north-west of Tahiti and just 16 km west of Tahaa lies Bora Bora. Dominated by two towering volcanic peaks and by locals who have learned a thing or two about capitalism, the island has been the subject of much publicity. Formerly a quiet retreat, it is now a mecca for US tourists, hotel entrepreneurs and, at one time, Italian film-makers. It has been the subject of a great deal of tourist development over the past few years and perhaps has reached saturation level. Bora Bora's population is about 2600.

Bora Bora is also a microcosm of the extremes that French Polynesia has to offer. No superlatives can adequately describe the spectacular beauty of its emerald-green hills and crystalline blue lagoons. At the same time, visitors may find that locals sometimes have an understandably jaded attitude towards tourists (of whom perhaps they have seen too many). The lesson has not gone unnoticed on other islands. Residents of neighbouring Maupiti shake their heads when they speak of changes on Bora Bora and vow that the same thing will not happen on their island.

Through the years, Bora Borans have learned to cope with an ebb and flow of foreigners. During WW II, 4500 US troops were stationed on the island. In 1977 the island was again occupied, this time by an army of Italian film-makers shooting Dino De Laurentiis' production of *Hurricane*. Again the economy boomed – local merchants turned a handsome profit and many of those hired by the movie-makers were riding new motorbikes or playing new cassette decks. When the Italians left, business as usual became the order of the day. Women returned to work in the hotels and men returned to their fishing boats. The islanders' flexibility is both admirable and a matter of survival.

US author James Michener has written a great deal about Bora Bora and in his epic *Hawaii* offers the theory that the island was a jumping-off point for Polynesian mariners who settled Hawaii. Michener's novel suggests that the reason for this migration was religious persecution.

INFORMATION

For information on Bora Bora, be sure and consult the Bora Bora Visitors' Bureau (☎ 67-76-36) based at the crafts centre at the Vaitape wharf.

Medical Care

Those needing medical attention on the island should call Dr Paul-Robert Thomas (☎ 67-70-92), who has been recommended by fellow travellers Jay and Robin Simke. His surgery is around the corner from the post office in Vaitape.

Useful Phone Numbers

Police Station	(☎ 67-70-58)
Hospital	(☎ 67-70-77)
Town Hall	(☎ 67-70-41)
Post Office	(☎ 67-70-74)
Visitors' Bureau	(☎ 67-76-36)

ORGANISED TOURS

Bora Bora Jeep Safari (☎ 67-70-79, 67-76-62), BP 66, Bora Bora, operated by a charming Frenchman by the name of Vincent, is a 4WD circle-island tour of Bora Bora, taking in the rugged (and seldom seen) interior of the island. This includes the most scenic WW II gun emplacement on Bora Bora and the radar station atop Popotei Ridge, which is otherwise inaccessible. This tour is one of the best things to happen to Bora Bora and should be on your 'must-do' list, especially if you are a WW II buff. The two-hour tour in a sturdy, brand new Land Rover also takes in some of the ancient marae, rusting Quonset huts, ammo dumps, the TV tower and some other great panoramas. Call Vincent and he'll pick you up at your hotel, or ask at the tour desk. The price is approximately US$40 and well worth it.

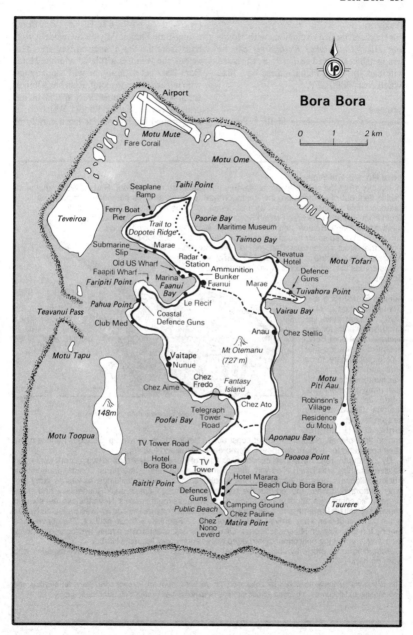

Bora Bora

Airport
Motu Mute
Fare Corail
Motu Ome

0   1   2 km

Taihi Point
Seaplane Ramp
Ferry Boat Pier
Teveiroa
Trail to Dopotei Ridge
Paorie Bay
Maritime Museum
Taimoo Bay
Submarine Slip
Marae
Old US Wharf
Faapiti Wharf
Faripiti Point
Radar Station
Ammunition Bunker
Marina
Faanui Bay
Faanui
Revatua Hotel
Motu Tofari
Defence Guns
Marae
Tuivahora Point
Le Recif
Pahua Point
Teavanui Pass
Coastal Defence Guns
Vairau Bay
Club Med
Anau
Chez Stellio
Motu Tapu
Vaitape
Nunue
Mt Otemanu
(727 m)
Chez Fredo
Fantasy Island
Chez Aime
Motu Piti Aau
148m
Chez Ato
Telegraph Tower Road
Poofai Bay
Robinson's Village
Residence du Motu
Motu Toopua
TV Tower Road
Aponapu Bay
Hotel Bora Bora
TV Tower
Paoaoa Point
Raititi Point
Hotel Marara
Beach Club Bora Bora
Defence Guns
Camping Ground
Public Beach
Chez Pauline
Taurere
Chez Nono Leverd
Matira Point

Trekking

For trekkers, guided excursions with *Mountain Hike/Mont Pahia Excursions* can be arranged by calling Christian Pons. Christian will lead you to Mt Pahia, a three-hour hike which costs 8000 CFP.

Cruises

Dean of the cruise scene is Rich Postma (☎ 67-70-79, 67-76-62), BP 66, Bora Bora, a long-time French Polynesian resident who hails from the San Francisco Bay area. His vessel, the *Vehia*, is affiliated with the Hotel Bora Bora but naturally he will take anyone who wishes to come along. Rich has a knack for making everyone feel very special on his cruises. He once took Raquel Welch for a spin around the lagoon. He has a variety of

---

Bora Bora & the War

In January 1942 the USA was still shaken by the Japanese raid on Pearl Harbor. With much of its Pacific fleet out of commission, the Pentagon had to reappraise the perimeter that could be defended until a counter-offensive against Japan could be mounted. The arc 3200 km south from Hawaii to the Free French Society Islands (now French Polynesia) and westward through Samoa and Fiji to New Zealand was believed to be defensible in those sombre, early days of the war. Bora Bora, 6400 km along the direct route from Panama to New Caledonia and Australia, was selected to be the first of a chain of refuelling bases across the South Pacific. It was code-named Bobcat.

On 8 January 1942 Admiral Ernest King and General George C Marshall approved a joint US Army-Navy plan for the occupation of Bora Bora. Bobcat became the first joint expeditionary force sent into the Pacific. It was composed of a 4000-man army garrison force, made up of the Army National Guard, a navy seaplane squadron of eight OS2U single-engine float planes, a 250-man naval construction detachment (known as 'Seabees') and a naval base command for harbour defence, waterborne services and fuel depot.

One of Bora Bora's coastal defence gun relics

By 21 January 1942 the Bobcat convoy consisting of four cargo vessels and two recently converted passenger ships was being filled with disassembled seaplanes, spare parts, bombs, ammunition, trucks, bulldozers, pontoon barge sections, landing craft and prefab buildings, as well as army and navy personnel. It was reported that the senior naval officer, Captain Jack Roudebush, had many 'unprintable comments' about the condition of the two passenger vessels. Nevertheless, the six-ship convoy set sail for Panama on 24 January. From Panama onward, the convoy was protected by five other US men-of-war. They arrived in Bora Bora on 17 February without incident. The convoy was met by the Free French Navy's schooner, *Oiseau des Îles*. Meanwhile, a navy hydrographic survey team had charted the only channel into deep water anchorage Teavanui Harbor.

According to an article by Jack Roudebush and Donald I Thomas, both US Navy captains who were on hand:

The island was virtually unspoiled by civilisation; no vehicles; no roads except coral paths for bicycles and pedestrians and coconut log bridges across streams; and no utilities except a minimal water supply...

trips including sunset cruises (US$24), deep sea fishing, or six-hour 'BBQ picnics' which include snorkelling, beachcombing and an isolated motu (US$62). He will charter the *Vehia* for US$300 to US$400 per day. His pride and joy is a new Hobie cat 21 which can take up to four passengers plus the captain for light fishing or sailing around the lagoon. The vessel is comfortable, very fast and inexpensive to charter for a couple. The price is $US60 per hour.

Another cruise company, calling itself 'Bora Bora Fun' (☎ 67-74-78), has similar day trips aboard their cat called the *Taaroa Catamaran*. The tour includes snorkelling and reef walking, or simply lounging on the beach of a motu. They are moored at the Bora Bora Beach Club. The price is 4000 CFP for

---

The only non-Polynesians on the island were Hank and Connie Hedges, a retired US couple from Illinois who had come to Bora Bora to get away from civilisation. It seemed, however, that 'civilisation' had caught up with them. Paradise was soon filled with some 4500 US servicemen, a seaplane squadron, coast and anti-aircraft defence artillery, trucks, bulldozers, tents, prefab buildings and thousands of tons of other equipment and supplies.

Though isolated, Paradise had its good points. The locals were friendly, hospitable and an 'extremely handsome lot' according to captains Roudebush and Thomas. 'The younger women were strikingly beautiful – until they smiled or spoke – nearly all had already lost their front teeth,' they continued. Elephantiasis was common among the older people and the medical and dental staff of the cruisers spent many hours ashore treating this and other ailments.

After much initial confusion the multitude of equipment was sorted and unloaded. The main problem was off-loading the pontoon bridges to ferry the cargo ashore. Naturally, the 'jewellery' (fittings) to string the pontoons together had been inadvertently stowed deep in the holds, making the pontoons useless without them. Eventually the ingenious Americans welded a few pontoon barges together and managed to ferry enough cargo out of the hold to get at the jewellery.

The Seabees eventually figured out where to put their seaplanes, bombs, etc and improvised shelters for engines, radio shops, photo labs and all the other wonders of war. In addition, an aviation machinist's mate who had been a well-digger in civilian life made sure that the seaplane base had the first freshwater showers on the island.

The face of Bora Bora quickly changed. Army camps and artillery sites sprang up throughout the island and, according to Roudebush and Thomas, 'the din created by heavy trucks and bulldozers shattered its tranquillity, to the delight of the young natives who had never seen these mechanical monsters'. All footpaths and bridges had been destroyed by the vehicles and the Seabees set about construction of heavy duty *American* roads.

The isolation sought by the retired US couple, the Hedges, was gone forever. But life went on. Hank Hedges, a retired civil engineer, assisted in building the waterworks and his wife Connie became mother to 4500 servicemen.

As part of the island's defence, the seven-inch guns were painstakingly unloaded and hauled up the hills. Three of the four original batteries can still be seen today as can the remains of many of the other military paraphernalia. The guns were never fired in anger – the Battle of Midway eliminated any threat of hostility. In any case, they were of little military value – their range hardly went beyond the outer reef.

The fuel depot in Faanui Bay was completed in June 1942 and a signal station on Bora Bora's highest peak, Otemanu, was installed. The US signalmen never failed to be amazed at the capability of the 'kibitzing natives' to spot ships in the distance and describe their features long before they were visible to the lookouts, who had binoculars.

By 1943, the Seabees had constructed an airstrip on the northern side of the island as a staging base for use by aircraft being ferried to the forward areas. This now serves as Bora Bora's commercial airport. This was not the only legacy of the Americans. By the time the island was handed back to the French in June 1946, the local stock had been invigorated with the addition of several dozen children fathered by Americans.

Most of the information in this section was furnished by a fine article in the March 1986 issue of *Shipmate*, by Captain Jack Roudebush USN (Ret) & Captain Donald I Thomas USN (Ret). ■

a 3½-hour tour. Charters can also be arranged. Call Mr Pierre English for more information.

A local Tahitian, Johnny Tinorua, also takes people out on his 14-passenger outrigger speed canoe for day trips, which include a BBQ on a motu and snorkelling. His tours are recommended and leave daily at 9.30 am. The cost is around 4000 CFP per person.

Those interested in a luxury yacht would do well to check out the *Epicurien II*, a 19-metre sloop with a teak interior and all the accoutrements of the good life. The vessel, which comes with crew, can be chartered for day trips. For more information contact the Marara Hotel or your tour desk.

ACTIVITIES
Diving
There are two dive operators on the island: Erwin Christian, whose headquarters, Moana Adventure Tours (☎ 67-70-33), is next to the Hotel Bora Bora; and Claude Sibani, who runs a nautical centre called the Calypso Club (☎ 67-74-64) near the Matira Beach Hotel. Christian, an internationally known photographer, has an exclusive arrangement as a dive operator with the Hotel Bora Bora and can be reached through them. The rates are 6000 CFP for a lagoon dive and 7000 CFP outside the reef. The cost for a resort dive is 6000 CFP.

Claude Sibani's shop not only provides services to divers but has water-skiing, parasailing, outrigger tours, jet skis, motorboat rental, Hobie cats, windsurfing, glass-bottomed boat tours, pedal cars, underwater still cameras and videos, and a snack bar. Claude takes divers out from all the hotels (except the Bora Bora) and charges 5500 CFP for a resort dive or to see the manta rays inside the lagoon and 6500 CFP outside the reef.

Snorkelling
Alas, snorkelling is not particularly good along the shore of Bora Bora except for the area around Bora Bora Hotel. The reason I was given is that the island has been over-fished. To get any decent snorkelling in

elsewhere, you must go out to the reef or motus on a boat. The waters around the Hotel Bora Bora are full of fish because the hotel has established an underwater 'park' where fishing is strictly forbidden. The hotel grounds are not generally open to the public but with permission it's OK to snorkel.

Fishing
Sport fishing is quite good just outside Bora Bora's reef, where you can hook blue marlin, yellowfin tuna, sailfish, wahoo and mahimahi as well as bottom fish such as snapper and grouper.

Perhaps the premier charter boat skipper on Bora is Keith 'Taaroa' Olson, a strapping native of the San Francisco Bay area. Keith tuned into the Tahitian way of life while visiting French Polynesia with his parents in the '60s, dropped out of US society and has made Bora Bora his home for the past two decades. His vessel, the *Te Aratai II* is an eight-metre Farallon and he charges 35,000 CFP for five hours (booze included) or 45,000 CFP for a full day (nine hours). Keith speaks fluent Tahitian and is also well versed in the local culture. He's a good source of information about French Polynesia and has seen it all. He is amenable to shorter trips for neophytes who don't want to spend five hours at sea. He can be reached at home (☎ 67-71-96) or at Bloody Mary's (☎ 67-72-86). Write to him at BP 91, Vaitape, Bora Bora.

Shark Feeding
This is another one of those 'no-miss' activities in Bora Bora. Reportedly originated by the Hotel Marara, feeding the sharks is a common activity run by all the hotels. Someone takes you, snorkel and flippers in hand, to part of the lagoon that is roped off. Your guide stands in the roped-off section throwing bait in the water while a dozen or so black tip reef sharks get into their patented feeding frenzy. The audience stands a safe distance away.

Feeding the Fish
If you think you've done everything there is

to do on the island, feeding the fish should be given consideration. To do this, grab a stale loaf of French bread and walk out on the dock at the Hotel Bora Bora. Casting your bread anywhere will result in a feeding frenzy that will roil the waters. Bring the kids and your children will never stop talking about it. Incidentally, the hotel is also the largest 'brown noddy' bird rookery on the island.

PLACES TO STAY

Bora Bora has some excellent mid-range and top-end places to stay. One note of caution: if camping, you should take care not to use the facilities at other hotels, even if you are just going in to use the bathroom – management frowns upon it.

Places to Stay – bottom end

Vaitape The *Hotel Royal Bora Bora* (☎ 67-71-54) in the main community of Vaitape has been called by one reader the 'Fawlty Towers' of French Polynesia. Without getting too far into the idiosyncrasies of management I would have to say the reader struck the nail on its proverbial head. It has eight rather musty bungalows with two single beds or a double bed (including bathroom) and three rooms with two single beds (common bathroom). There is also a deserted restaurant/bar on the premises. None of the reports I've heard have been terribly complementary. One couple (who coined the 'Fawlty Towers' moniker) found it amusing to stay there, in a perverse kind of way. The best thing you can say about the Royal Bora Bora is that the prices are reasonable. Room rates begin at 1500 CFP per person for the first day, 1000 CFP for the second day, 900 CFP for day three and 800 CFP for day four.

Chez Ato et Sylvain* (☎ 67-77-27) is the closest thing to Shangri-La that exists in Bora Bora – at least from the perspective of altitude. The property lies in the shadow of Mt Otemanu, on a verdant hillside about ½ km from the main road and about two km from Vaitape (just before entering Paofai Bay). Chez Ato is an Eden-like setting, splashed with fruit, flora and nursed to

impeccable sublimity by its owner, Ato. A sturdily built Bora Boran, Ato is a gracious host who will ply you with the abundant fruit that grows on his estate. The quarters are hexagonal, with an open courtyard that consists mostly of a pond, with a huge boulder in it. There are five spartan rooms with plenty of light, two communal showers and one toilet. The cost is 2000 CFP per person. If you want to see the top of 727-metre high Mt Otemanu, Ato will guide you there for 5000 CFP. Ato's place takes up about a square mile of mountainside and is often cooled by the trade winds. Check it out.

Chez Fredo (☎ 67-70-31), 500 metres from the dock in Vaitape, has two bungalows with one double bed and two single beds plus private bath and kitchen. There is also one bungalow with one bedroom, bath and kitchen. The bungalow costs 5000 CFP for singles/doubles and 1000 CFP per extra person. Chez Fredo would be recommended except for the reports that it gets a bit noisy, with a multitude of children running around the place. The minimum stay is two days. Speak to Mme Doom at Bora Bora Burgers in Vaitape.

Chez Aime is the oldest dorm-style accommodation in Bora Bora and it looks it. There are five rooms with two to three bunks per room. The communal (outdoor) baths and toilets are OK. The kitchen is also acceptable but in general the place is run-down. The cost is 1000 CFP per person.

Le Recif (☎ 63-73-87) also doubles as a disco on weekends but at the back of the property is a pleasant garden with three bungalows. Two of the lodgings can take three people and a larger unit can handle up to six. One of the units has a kitchen. The place is clean and adequate but rather run-down. If you stay over the weekend you had better like loud rock. The cost is 4000 CFP for singles/doubles plus 1000 CFP per extra person.

Motu Tane *Fare Corail** (☎ 67-74-50) is a house constructed of white coral and belonging to the French explorer Emile Victor. On Motu Tane, five minutes by boat from the

Bora Bora Airport, it is comparatively isolated and has a great white-sand beach and excellent swimming conditions. The house consists of a living room, bedroom, dining room, kitchen, terrace and bath. Activities include outrigger canoeing and visits to Vaitape, and round-trip transfer is provided. Rates are 12,000 CFP for doubles. A 20% deposit is mandatory for reservations and a three-day minimum stay is required.

Matira *Chez Nono Leverd** (☎ 67-71-38, 67-74-27), BP 12, Vaitape, Bora Bora, on Matira Beach is perhaps the nicest mid-range accommodation on the island. Not only are the units well appointed, but they are within spitting distance of the best beach in the Society Islands. There's also a view of Maupiti.

The property has three units: a house with six rooms (that can be rented out individually) with shared kitchen and bath; a twin Polynesian-style bungalow unit each with a bedroom and bathroom; and a large bungalow with double bed and two singles, kitchen and bathroom. The house has a large sitting room with TV, kitchen and communal bathroom. Food is available on request, as are excursions. Rooms in the 'big' house cost 3000/5000 CFP for singles/doubles and 2000 CFP for an extra person. The twin bungalow is 6000 CFP for singles/doubles. The private bungalow rents for 12,000 CFP for singles/doubles, plus 2000 CFP per extra person. The facilities are clean and the atmosphere is great. Bicycles are also available for rent. Breakfast costs 600 CFP; dinner is 1800 CFP and must be reserved a day in advance.

Chez Robert & Tina (☎ 67-72-92) is on Matira beach just down the road from Chez Nono Leverd. Robert has two units: a house with three bedrooms with double beds, living room, kitchen, terrace and common bath; and a second house with five bedrooms, kitchen and bath. Both places are clean but rather spartan. In a word, 'adequate' or, as the French would say, 'correct'. The kitchen facilities are provided but you must buy sugar, salt and condiments from the store. Round-trip transfers from the dock are provided and circle-island tours via outrigger or picnics on the beach are available. Robert's lagoon tours are have been recommended. The rates are 3000/6000 CFP for singles/doubles and 2500 CFP for each extra person.

Nunue *Chez Rosina* (☎ 76-70-91), BP 51, Nunue, Bora Bora, five km from Vaitape, in Paofai Bay, has two rooms with double beds – two with private bathrooms and two with common bathrooms. The rates are 5500/9000 CFP for singles/doubles. Guests share cooking facilities with the owners. Excursions are available.

Camping *Chez Pauline** (☎ 67-72-16), BP 215, Vaitape, Bora Bora, lies in the Matira Point area, just prior to the Marara Hotel, and is one of two camping grounds in Bora Bora. The locale is gorgeous – a white-sand beach shaded by lovely coconut palms. The main disadvantage is that it's almost 10 km from town – a long walk to the corner store for groceries. Still, the minor inconvenience is worth it. Amenities include a quality shower/bathing area and among the best kitchen facilities (which include three sinks, several gas burners and two refrigerators) of any camping ground in French Polynesia. A nice touch is the several picnic tables facing the sea covered with 'palapa'-style thatched roofs that make a nice common eating and reading area. The main camping area is a small strip of grass along the sea, shaded by coconut trees which double as clotheslines. The disadvantage is its small size.

Aside from the camping area there are seven small bungalows with two cots, each priced at 3500 CFP for singles/doubles. An extra person can be squeezed in for another 2500 CFP. The bungalows are as good as any other private lodging you'll find on the island. There are also two larger 'fares' with double beds, kitchenette and private bath for 9000 CFP. Camping rates are 1000 CFP per camper (BYO equipment). There is also a clean dorm unit with bunks for 10 people, for

Top: Octagonal Church – the oldest European building in French Polynesia (RK)
Bottom: Faaroa Bay seen from Pension Greenhill, Raiatea (RK)

Top: Tie-dyed pareus, Bora Bora (RK)
Bottom: Aponapu Bay, Bora Bora (RK)

1500 CFP. Round-trip transfer to the boat dock is included. Transport is available on a daily basis for shopping trips.

Pauline, who watches over her property with a definite air of authority, is friendly and professional. She is also a successful Tahitian entrepreneur. At the time of writing, she was building 10 bungalows on the other side of the road (to accommodate singles or doubles), with kitchenettes, to be rented for 9000 CFP. Pauline's camping ground is more expensive than others but she works hard at providing a good, clean environment for backpackers.

*Chez Stellio** (☎ 67-71-32) in the village of Anau is approximately six km further down the road from Chez Pauline. Though Chez Stellio is on the water it lacks a beach and abuts a seawall. The communal kitchen is more than adequate, with two stoves, two fridges, several sinks, tile floor and a large preparation table. The facilities are clean and acceptable. There is a dorm unit which sleeps ten as well as a house with five rooms and cooking facilities. Two rooms in the home have double beds and the three rooms have two singles each. There is also a fairly large camping area. Prices are 800 CFP for camping, 1300 CFP for the dorm and 4000 CFP for the rooms. Aside from accommodation, Stellio provides round-the-island tours for 2800 CFP, shark-feeding expeditions, reef walks and snorkelling trips to view giant clams. Prices for longer stays are negotiable. Transport to town is free coming in but 300 CFP on the way back home. Stellio, however, provides round-trip transport to and from the dock. All in all it's a bit rough around the edges and a bit far from town but a satisfactory place to stay.

Bora Bora Beach Club (☎ 67-71-16), BP 252, Nunue, Bora Bora, gets an 'A' for friendly employees. It is a fairly new hotel, with basic amenities like the other beach clubs in the chain. One of the best things about it is its location on Matira Beach, the best beach on the island. The BBC has 36 rooms with refrigerator, ceiling fan and private terrace. The walls are thin enough to make you hope you don't get a newly wed

couple as neighbours. Free activities include windsurfing, canoe paddling and volleyball. There is also a restaurant, bar, windsurfing, pool and excursions. Rates begin at 11,000/13,000 CFP for singles/doubles.

Places to Stay – middle

Matira Eight km from the village of Vaitape near the finest beach on the island is *Hotel Matira* (☎ 67-70-51), BP 31, Vaitape, Bora Bora. It has 28 bungalows, some with kitchenettes. There is a good, moderately priced Chinese restaurant on the premises. The restaurant prices range from 1000 to 2000 CFP and the menu includes chop suey, seafood, fish and lobster. Room prices begin at 9000/10,500 CFP for singles/doubles without kitchenette and 9900/12,600 CFP with kitchenette. The cabins are nice but like many things on this island are way overpriced. Transfer to Vaitape is not included.

Vaitape Three km from town on Fare Piti point is the *Yacht Club de Bora Bora** (☎ 67-70-69, 67-71-34), BP 17, Vaitape, Bora Bora, which has one of the best moderately priced restaurants on the island, as well as some excellent accommodation. If you can imagine what a restaurant in Tahiti should look like, it might resemble the Yacht Club. The bar is rough-hewn hardwood with ample decking, a great deal of which is over the water. Let's call it an 'aqua-deck'. Part of the aqua-deck has been cut away to expose the reef below. This open area has been turned into an 'aqua-pen' where all manner of creatures – turtles, surgeon fish, sharks and the like – swim about.

There are six bungalows – three over the water and three in the garden. All are painted turquoise and sport thatched roofs. They are well appointed, with hardwood floors, four-posted beds with mosquito nets, batten-style windows and step-down bathrooms. The views are great. The Yacht Club also has French Polynesia's only floating bungalows, which are actually catamaran units. They are equipped with kitchenette, bathroom and solar electricity and accommodate four people. The price for a garden bungalow is

9000 CFP, an over-the-water bungalow is 10,000 CFP and a floating bungalow is 20,000 CFP. There are moorings for 17 yachts as well as laundry and bathing facilities for yachties. Other amenities include water sport activities and boat rentals. The in-house restaurant, which specialises in seafood, is one of the best – if not the best – on the island. Meals range from 1500 to 3700 CFP.

If you happen to be at the tourist office in Vaitape ask the manager Sylvain if his property *Sylvain' Pool Parlor* is up and running. At the time of writing, it was still under preparation. Not only will visitors be able to shoot pool, but the charming Sylvain will have bungalows for rent in the 10,000 to 12,000 CFP range. Sylvain is an enjoyable guy who makes a good host.

Despite the not-so-original name, *Fantasy Island** (☎ 67-76-88, 42-54-16) looked like a nominal winner, if you're in the market for a self-contained unit with plenty of room. Constructed on the former set for de Laurentiis' *Hurricane*, it consists of two large bungalows, one with room for four and the other for six. Both have private bath (with hot water), kitchen, sofabeds and fans. The environs are pleasant, with a pond and well-tended gardens about 1½ km from Vaitape. The larger bungalow has two bedrooms, each with a double bed. The smaller unit has one bedroom with double bed.

Fantasy Island is easy to find: just look for what appears to be an old colonial mansion on the way to Matira from Vaitape. The smaller bungalow is priced at 10,000 CFP for doubles and 12,000 CFP for four people. The two-bedroom unit goes for 15,000 CFP for four people and 17,000 CFP for six.

Faanui *Bora Bora Bungalows* (67-71-33) is in Faanui, near the half-completed Hyatt Hotel. There are 11 bungalows on the mountain side and three over the water. Each bungalow has two bedrooms, a living room, dining room, bathroom and terrace. They will accommodate five people. I have been told this place is good for long-term rentals but frankly the area seems rather eerie and deserted. Prices begin at 12,000 CFP for a garden bungalow and 15,000 CFP for an over-the-water bungalow. Monthly rentals begin at 140,000 CFP.

Anau *Revatua Club** (☎ 67-71-67), BP 159, Anau, Bora Bora, is set far away from the teeming crowds, on the eastern side of Bora Bora, 16 km from Vaitape. Where several years ago there was nothing, there is now a chartreuse, colonial-style bar/restaurant with a terrace on the water that belongs in a Bogart movie. The atmosphere is definitely barefoot, local and French, which I found comfortable. Chez Christian, the hotel restaurant, serves 'Marseille-style' cuisine and is among the best on the island. The bar, which serves excellent *tapas* (snacks), is friendly and a good spot to meet locals – sometimes not the easiest thing to do in this country. The only possible fault is that the 16 rooms are a little spartan for the price. Revatua is ideal for people who want to feel isolated. There is excellent snorkelling close by and, I'm sure, the only glass-bottomed double canoe with stereo. Prices begin at 8426 CFP for a unit which will accommodate three adults and one child. Add an extra 4100 CFP for breakfast and dinner. Tours are also available.

Piti Aau *Residence du Motu* (☎ 67-74-01/02) may be the real fantasy island accommodation on Bora Bora. On the eastern side of the island on a small motu, Piti Aau, it lies on the reef's outer edge where the ocean meets the lagoon. Needless to say, the view is fabulous. There are four units amidst a grove of coconut palms and papaya trees. The 'villa' (which sleeps six) has three bedrooms with two double beds, three bathrooms, a kitchen and a living room with a view of the lagoon. The 'grand fare' (which sleeps eight) has two bedrooms with two double beds, two bathrooms, a kitchen and a living room. There are also two small fares (sleeping a maximum of six) each with three rooms, and each room contains a double bed, bath and kitchen. They're quite nice looking, but after 6 pm electricity is only temporarily available. The list of activities reads like a phone book; most are included in the tariff. Rates are 25,000 CFP for the villa, 20,000 CFP for the grand fare and 15,000 CFP for the two smaller bungalows. Contact Josy Muller at the phone numbers above, or Robert Malbete at BP 249, Bora Bora.

North of Residence du Motu is *Robinson's Village* (☎ 67-74-28), BP 161, Bora Bora, which seems a bit more diverse, since you can rent anything from a rounded, 'Robinson (Crusoe?)-style' bungalow/hut to, if it turns your crank, an anchored sailboat (with tender). There are few hangups of avarice here – you can cook for yourself, there's a grocery store nearby and they have a snack bar. They offer free snorkelling and windsurfing; activities at cost include a sunset cruise, scuba diving, excursions, deep-sea fishing, and island cruises by pirogue, bikes, scooters or cars. On-the-spot rentals include motorboats, bikes, scooters and cars. Rates are surprisingly low – bungalows are 3000/4500 CFP for singles/doubles. The sailboat with tender goes for 15,000 CFP per day. Breakfast and dinner are 1800 CFP. The lagoon crossing is 500 CFP by day and 1000 CFP by night. (To get to RV wharf, catch the VAIHO truck from Vaitape upon arrival from Bora Bora's airport ferry to Anau (400 to 500 CFP). The person to contact is Algame Sarl.

Places to Stay – top end
Vaitape The *Club Med* (☎ 67-72-57) – a Club Med village – is 1½ km from Vaitape. It is much smaller and more intimate than Club Med on Moorea. It has a bar, restaurant, nightclub, snorkelling, windsurfing, volleyball, outrigger canoe rides, visits to a neighbouring motu, excursions, and all the usual Club Med activities. Other than 'Le Recif' it is the only 'social scene' on Bora Bora and is open to outsiders for dinner or dancing. There is room for 80 guests in bungalows constructed on pilings over the water. All fares have sundecks over the lagoon, ceiling fans, oversized twin beds, and bathroom. Prices start at US$1100 per person per week (for shared accommodation), all meals, booze and activities included. Anyone considering Club Med should contact them directly, as many packages are available.

Nunue *Hotel Bora Bora* (☎ 67-70-28) has perhaps the best location on the island, with terrific views and a good beach. It was recently purchased by an Indonesian businessman but has retained the same management. Years ago it was named by *Andrew Harper's Hideaway Report* as the 'Island Resort of the Year'. Whether it has maintained that status is debatable. The hotel is still primarily an American destination.

The feeling at Hotel Bora Bora is very 'country club' – quiet, reserved. There are 80 bungalows (including 15 over the water), a conference room, a good restaurant, two bars, a boutique, scuba facilities, snorkelling, shark-feeding expeditions, canoes, tennis, a white-sand beach and bicycles. In the early evening, huge manta rays glide gracefully to the pier under the lights and the fish can be fed off the dock. Management, to their credit, have created a nature preserve around both the hotel grounds and the waters surrounding the property, which is rigorously maintained. Car rentals are available at the hotel.

Charter cruises are available on American expat Rich Postma's sleek vessel, the *Vehia*. Rich, a veteran skipper who is savvy to Tahiti's ways, has taken out numerous celebrities but treats everyone like they are someone special. His presence at the Hotel Bora Bora is a huge plus. The hotel is six km from the main village of Vaitape in Nunue, Bora Bora. Prices begin at 27,300 CFP for singles/doubles and go all the way up to 47,250 CFP for the top of the line over-the-water bungalow.

Matira *Hotel Marara** (☎ 67-70-46), BP 6, Bora Bora was originally constructed by Italian film producer Dino De Laurentiis to house his staff during the production of *Hurricane*. Although the movie bombed, the hotel was a better investment. Located on Matira Beach, it has 64 bungalows, a good restaurant, bar, boutique, an excellent array of water sport activities, tennis, jeep tours, car rentals, windsurfing, deep-sea fishing, a disco, bicycles, glass-bottomed boat trips and sunset cruises. One of the hotel staff told me they invented 'shark feeding' which is now a regular item at most of the resorts. About 60% of the clientele are North American and the rest are European or South American, thus providing an 'international' flavour.

If the Hotel Bora Bora is a 'country club', Marara is more of a 'resort'. The atmosphere is more relaxed, the staff are friendly and the prices are much less than those at the Bora Bora – although they are not 'cheap' by any means. The Marara also has an excellent Tahitian dance review – perhaps the best on the island. It can be seen daily at 8 pm and admission is free. Although I recommend the Marara, mostly because of the ambience, the rooms are in need of refurbishing, something I was told is in the offing. Rates begin at 23,400/25,400 CFP for singles/doubles.

Bora Bora Moana Beach Hotel is still the newest luxury accommodation on Bora Bora. It is smaller and more intimate than the Hotel Bora Bora. Some people prefer it to any other hotel on the island. It is adjacent to the Hotel Matira, just a few metres down the road from the Hotel Bora Bora. It is also the most expensive hotel in French Polynesia, so you would expect the Bora Bora Moana to live up to its claim. It is managed by the same organisation that has enjoyed tremendous success with the Beachcomber in Tahiti, so you can justifiably expect high standards. The hotel's 30 over-the-water bungalows are the lap of luxury. The touches include woven pandanus mats and tapa cloth on the walls, rattan furniture and glass coffee tables that enable one to peer directly into the lagoon below. There is also a direct international dialling service from each room, room service from 6 am to 9 pm and transport by speedboat directly from the airport to the individual bungalow. Activities include the usual water sports, sunset cruises and the like. The food is *nouvelle*, and the chef is imported from the Bel Air in Los Angeles. There are 10 beach bungalows and 30 over-the-water bungalows. Beach bungalows cost 36,800 CFP for doubles and over-the-water bungalows are 49,800 CFP.

PLACES TO EAT

In addition to the hotels, there are several good restaurants on the island. Perhaps the best is the *Bora Bora Yacht Club*, which is a favourite of locals. Expect to pay 750 CFP for an espresso, 250 CFP for a soft drink, 400 CFP for a beer, 650 CFP for a salad or appetiser and 1500 to 3700 CFP for a meal. If you add a bottle of wine, dinner will easily run in the 10,000 CFP range for two. Fortunately, by the time you pay the bill the ambience will have put you in a relaxed mood.

If you want to treat yourself try *Chez Christian* at the Revatua Hotel, on the far side of the island, which has first-class 'Marseille-style' seafood and French cooking. If you make a reservation, they will pick you up from any hotel on the island. Prices are in the 2000 to 4000 CFP range and worth it. There is a good bar scene during the day and nice tapas (snacks).

Bloody Mary's near the Hotel Bora Bora is an institution on the island. The patron chooses his or her own fish and the chef slaps it on the grill. The fish couldn't be fresher, but it is pricey – 2500 CFP (for barbequed chicken or T-bone steak) to 4500 CFP for barbequed lobster dinner. Appetisers range from 800 to 1000 CFP. The ambience is quite nice – sand floor, thatched roof and coconut tree stumps for chairs. It's a hangout for Americans and a favourite of celebrities, as witnessed by the names of the rich and famous Americans who have dined there, such as John Denver, Mac Davis, Judge Rheinhold, Willie Nelson and others.

The biggest change in the eatery department has been the sprouting up of decent, low-end eateries, especially near the Matira area, where there is a major camping ground and a number of hotels. Among the new hamburger stands is *Kaina Snacks*, a 12-minute walk from Chez Pauline going towards Vaitape. Run by an enterprising local, it is literally a stand with a small counter and a gravel floor. Patrons sit comfortably on coconut stump stools and have a wide selection of Tahitian and Western-style fast foods such as hamburgers, cheeseburgers, fishburgers, steaks with fries, ice cream, beer and soft drinks. Prices range from 600 to 900 CFP – very reasonable by Tahitian standards. The atmosphere is good too.

If you continue towards Vaitape for another half a km or so you will find *Ben's Place*, a lean-to, open-air cafe with a wider and more expensive range of food than Kaina Snacks. There is also a picnic table to sit on. Ben Teraitepo is an engaging native Bora Boran who cut his teeth working in California. He and his USA-born wife, Robin, like shooting the breeze, particularly with Americans, for whom they seem to have an affinity. Ben offers pizza for 950 CFP, lasagna or steak for 1500 CFP (including salad and fries) and tuna steak and fries for 2200 CFP. This is the kind of eatery that may be too expensive for the average backpacker but a nice alternative to the very expensive hotel cuisine. Bens' Place is open Wednesdays to Mondays from 11 am to 8 pm.

Down the road towards Vaitape is *Snack Matira*, about 200 metres before the Hotel Bora Bora, opposite Chez Helene (a boutique). It has basic fare in the 300 to 750 CFP range, including hamburgers, pizza, chicken and soft drinks. Another place to check out is *Table du Mandarin* (☎ 67-72-04) (opposite the boutique Musee Rosine Temarui). The structure resembles a bamboo 'nipa hut' in the Philippines and specialises in Vietnamese food. The fare is very good, reasonably priced (a bit more expensive than Ben's) and well worth a visit.

In the same general neighbourhood, *Restaurant Matira* near Matira Point serves basic Chinese fare – no frills – for 1000 to 2000 CFP. The food is OK and the restaurant overlooks the water, which makes for a pleasant environment.

One place not to miss, especially if you are staying near Vaitape, is the *Restaurant Vaitape*, which is more an inexpensive cafe that doubles as the island's only bakery. It's terrific for breakfast and is open on Sundays.

It features the usual – coffee, croissants, buns and other pastries. You can find it in the centre of town, across from the Bank of Polynesia and the post office. Check it out. Other inexpensive eateries in town are *Mama Chou's*, *Snack Tiare* and *Bora Bora Burgers*.

ENTERTAINMENT

Taking into account Bora Bora's small size, it has more hangouts than you might expect. On a Friday evening begin the circuit by hitting Bloody Mary's for a beer or two. More than likely there will be an informal Tahitian combo strumming away on guitars and ukuleles. Next stop is the Club Med variety show, always good for a few chuckles. Following this it is disco time. Assuming your appetite for nightlife is insatiable (as is the case with most Tahitians), next on the

agenda is Le Recif, Bora Bora's only after-hours club. It is a Tahitian-style disco – crowded, noisy, dark, smoke-filled and loaded with drunks.

After the disco closes it's time to pile into the car, drive around to the other side of the island and (beer in hand) watch the sun come up. By this time you will undoubtedly have worked up an appetite so, like your Tahitian hosts, you can breakfast on poisson cru (raw fish marinated in lemon juice), which is delicious and will give you the strength to carry on until the following night.

GETTING THERE & AWAY
There are flights to Bora Bora from Papeete four to six times daily and once daily from Moorea. The flight time is about 50 minutes. There is an air service to Bora Bora from Raiatea, Huahine, Manihi, Maupiti and Rangiroa. See the Getting Around chapter for more details. There is a free shuttle service run by the airport from the small motu where the airport is and from the main dock in Vaitape. Bora Bora is accessible from Papeete via the interisland vessels *Taporo IV*, the *Temehani II* and the *Raromatai Ferry*. The journey takes a full day.

GETTING AROUND
All major hotels can arrange car rentals; if you are not staying at a large hotel, auto rentals can be made through Bora Bora Rent-A-Car (☎ 67-70-03), south of Vaitape; Maeva Rent-A-Car (☎ 67-76-78) in Vaitape; Mautara Rent-A-Car (☎ 67-73-16) in Vaitape and Bora Bora Tours (% 67-70-28) at the Hotel Bora Bora.

Most of the larger hotels provide bicycles for their patrons and Bora Bora is small enough to make this type of transport sufficient. Expect to pay around 5500 CFP for four hours and 6500 CFP for eight hours not including gas and insurance. Scooters are available at Bora Bora Rent-A-Car and Maeva Rent-A-Car. Rentals will set you back 3500 CFP for four hours and 4000 CFP for eight hours.

Bicycles can be rented at Bora Bora Rent-A-Car, Mautara Rent-A-Car and Maeva Rent-A-Car. Least expensive is Mautara, which charges 800 CFP for eight hours and 1000 CFP for 24 hours.

AROUND THE ISLAND
Bora Bora is about 32 km in circumference and the best way to see it is from a bicycle seat. Bikes can be rented from many places and some hotels lend them to visitors as part of the tariff. Depending on what form of conveyance you use, the round-the-island tour can take from 90 minutes to several hours. The tour starts from the Hotel Bora Bora and goes anti-clockwise around the island.

Martine's Creations (0.5 km)
Martine's small boutique began as a roadside stand and is now a 'chic' shop selling black pearls, tie-dyed T-shirts and air-brushed T-shirts that are of her own creation. It's a good place to start looking for souvenirs and cheaper than hotel gift shops. It is one of many boutiques and family-run crafts stands, an important cottage industry on the island.

Restaurant & Hotel Matira (1 km)
A good basic Chinese cafe serving moderately priced food. The same proprietor has over-priced bungalows with kitchen facilities.

Coastal Defence Guns (1.1 km)
Less than 100 metres past the Matira Restaurant (on the hillside) are the most accessible coastal defence guns. The trail begins opposite cabin no 18 on the Matira property. It is best to ask the proprietor of the restaurant whether you can see the site, because the track begins on his land. It takes about five to 10 minutes to hike the trail, depending on what kind of shape you are in. Just be glad you weren't one of the 400 GIs who literally dragged the 13,636-kg gun up that hill. Even with the aid of blocks and tackle, it couldn't have been an easy task. For those wondering, the whole gun assembly weighed approximately 31,800 kg. Note that the weight of

each piece of the gun assembly is stamped upon it. Ironically, the seven-inch guns only had a range of about 16 km and even the military deemed this largely ineffective. Note the graffiti inscribed on the cement: 'Battleing (sic) Battery B-276C'.

Matira Point (2 km)

Here you'll find the best beach on the island and the greatest concentration of hotels. It's easy to miss the public beach, which is accessed via the small road on the point. To get there turn down the point at the Moana Hotel sign. There are several *palapas* (mushroom-like canopies), a facility to change clothing in, and plenty of room on the beach.

Continuing down the point are two accommodation places: Chez Nono Leverd, which is recommended, and Chez Robert et Tina. If you are in the market for a good quality pareu (sarong), look for a small vendor called Chez Helene opposite Snack Matira. Helene is friendly and has competitive prices – you can expect to pay around 1000 CFP. Her stall is also set up so that you can see her making the pareus.

Chez Pauline Camping Ground (2.2 km)

This is not the largest, but is without a doubt the most beautiful, camping ground in French Polynesia. It consists of a small grassy strip of land shaded by coconut trees, adjacent to the beach.

Hotel Marara (3 km)

This hotel caters mostly for European and South American clientele. It was built in 1977 by film maker Dino De Laurentiis to house his movie crew during the filming of *Hurricane* (which was a dreadful bomb).

Anau Village/Chez Stellio Camping Ground (8 km)

Anau is the most typically Polynesian of the villages on Bora Bora. The village has churches, a school, a general store and rambling, tin-roofed homes with well-kept gardens. It's not a terribly friendly place. However, Chez Stellio, a camping ground in the village is anything but unfriendly. It doesn't have the beach and the number of places that Chez Pauline has, but it's worth considering.

Mt Otemanu & Otemanu Cave (8.5 km)

At this juncture you are in the shadow of Mt Otemanu, highest point on the island. Near the summit but not easily accessible is the cave, formerly a burial area. On its walls, graffiti proclaims that 'Kilroy was here'. Do not attempt to climb to the cave – the ascent is steep and dangerous.

Marae Taharuu (12 km)

Marae Taharuu, on Tuivahora Point, is a tall, natural obelisk which appears to still be used by non-Christian Tahitians. To get there stop at the top of the hill (the only hill!) and park your vehicle. Take the well-trodden path descending towards the shore and follow it for about 100 metres. At the summit of the path you'll see the obelisk, a black thumb-like boulder jutting from the earth. Note that several smaller stones have been placed in a pattern at the foot of the shrine, and take care not to disturb them. This point also affords an excellent view. It's possible to hike all the way down to the shore if you desire.

Marae Aehua-tai & Coastal Defence Guns – Tuivahora Point (12.2 km)

After hiking back to the main road do not speed down. The road may be rutted and ultimately unhealthy for you. Descending from the hill to the beach below is a path to Marae Aehua-tai, an ancient Polynesian temple, and one of several on Bora Bora. The next several km past the temple are virtually uninhabited, sprinkled only with a few houses and several banana groves, coconut palms and taro patches. Tuivahora Point is also the locale for the most spectacular gun emplacement on the island. To get there take the first right at the bottom of the hill (past Marae Aehua-tai), which is a rutted jeep track that follows the beach. Continue along this lonely road past a concrete platform that looks like a foundation for a home. Carry on to the second platform down the road a few metres more and stop. At this point park your bike and backtrack a few metres. Note a jeep track that goes straight up the hill. Follow it and voilà, you have arrived. There's a great view here and easy access to the site.

Revatua Club & Chez Christian Restaurant (12.8 km)

One of Bora's newer hotels, this is a chartreuse-green, colonial-looking structure right on the water and in the middle of nowhere. It's a great place to stop for refreshments and by now you will need something to quench your thirst. Chez Christian is one of the better restaurants on the island, with great seafood and French cuisine. Just a few metres past the hotel is a small stand selling souvenirs and drinking nuts (coconuts).

Taimoo Bay (13.5 km)

There's great swimming here and clear water for snorkelling. Another km down the road you will see the many holes that land crabs call home. If you have the courage grab them from behind, place in a sack and cook them up for a splendid meal.

Taihi Point (16 km)

This is the northernmost point of the island and the beginning of a track that will take you to an old radar installation constructed by the US forces on the top of Popotei Ridge. The hike is long and arduous – better to take a jeep. Look for the minuscule 'Maritime Museum' not too far from here. It is run by Betrand Derasse, an architect who has constructed a number of ship models.

Bora Bora Bungalows (17 km)

The 'bungalows' perched on stilts on the hillside are condos, and some are owned by Jack Nicholson and Marlon Brando. Don't look too hard though; chances are the stars will be enjoying other tax write-offs than these. Adjacent to the bungalows was the site of a Hyatt Hotel. However, the developer ran out of money and the half-completed hotel now slowly deteriorates in the tropical sun.

It will still be deteriorating when you get there.

Ferry Boat Pier & Seaplane Ramp (18 km)

The pier still used today was another product of Yankee engineering. Just prior to that is a concrete ramp that slopes gently under the water of the lagoon and was used as a seaplane base.

Marae Fare-Opu & Submarine Slip (19 km)

This temple is just along the side of the road. Look for turtle petroglyphs on some of the slabs. Turtles were sacred to the ancient Polynesians, and were only consumed by chiefs and priests. Adjacent to the marae is a large concrete slip reaching into the lagoon where, most likely, children will be swimming. This was built to accommodate submarines but has seen more action as a swimming hole. A few metres from the sub slip are the remnants of a pier where the seaplanes used to tie up. The pier could accommodate up to 12 OS2U single-engine float seaplanes.

Faanui Bay & Village (20 km)

This is the section of the island where most of the 6000 US servicemen were stationed during operation Bobcat in WW II. Faanui Bay was chosen by the US Navy as the most strategic place for a base – protected on all sides by land and directly opposite a motu. Thus, the base could be seen only from the air. The bay had to be extensively dredged to accommodate submarines and other vessels, and to this day remains severely environmentally damaged. Visible in the area are pilings from a dock, the water for seaplanes, and several Quonset huts (corrugated steel huts of semi-circular shape) nestled in the bushes along the roadside. Also visible is a massive ammunition bunker on the hillside. At this point look for a dirt road inland. You can hike to the other side of the island from here and the view is terrific. The trail ends in

Anau Village. It's not recommended for bicycles.

Marae Tianapa (20.5 km)

This fairly large temple has two small petroglyphs and was associated with Mt Pahia, the 700-metre peak that towers over Vaitape. It is in a field close to the base of the nearby mountain.

Marae Marotetini (21 km)

A five-minute walk from the road, the marae lies on the shore behind a small coconut grove. According to the old religion, the marae is associated with Mt Otemanu and was the most important temple on Bora Bora. It was restored in 1968 by Dr Y H Sinoto. It was used in the old days by a religious sect entertaining the local population. Near the marae are two tombs built for the Bora Bora royal family during the last century.

Stories of those who purposefully or inadvertently defile the old shrines and suffer the consequences abound in French Polynesia. According to one story, in 1973 a labourer working near Marae Marotetini discovered a rusted biscuit tin containing what were believed to be the charred remnants of the clothing of the last queen of Bora Bora. The

tin was accidentally destroyed and not long afterwards (despite the efforts of modern medicine) the worker died of a mysterious malady.

According to author Milas Hinshaw's account of the incident in *Bora Bora E*, after the worker's death his body 'turned black – resembling a corpse that had been consumed by fire'. Hinshaw and his son claim to have been cursed by this same marae when they picked up several human bones there and took them home as souvenirs. Not until five years later, after returning the bones to their resting place, did the author's spate of bad luck stop. Why it took him five years to figure this out, I do not know.

Faanui Power Station (21 km)

In the village of Faanui, this steam generator is powered by coconut husks. Several hundred metres past the station is a sturdy freight dock built by the US Seabees during the war. It is still used as the major freight unloading facility on Bora Bora. If your map

Faanui Power Station

indicates a track across the mountains to Anau and Vairau Bay, this is incorrect. There is a track from Faanui to the water catchment tank near a waterfall. The route to the waterfall is obscured by deep brush so, if you go looking for it, make sure you can get back.

Le Recif (21.5 km)
Le Recif is the island's only after-hours haunt – weekends are the best. The music is loud and the crowd is raucous. It's a very 'local' scene, with plenty of beer consumed and occasional fights.

Yacht Club (22 km)
This is a watering hole and hotel serving very good food.

Coastal Defence Guns (23.4 km)
About 50 metres prior to Club Med is a marked path leading up the hill to another battery of Mark II coastal defence guns. These guns protected Teavanui Pass directly below, which is the island's only access to the ocean. It's a 10 to 15-minute walk up a steep hill.

Club Med (23.5 km)
The Club Med scene at Bora Bora is much smaller than the one on Moorea. It is one of the few night spots on the island and it is open to the public.

Vaitape Village (25-26 km)
This is Bora Bora's major community. There is a plethora of shops and boutiques, including Magasin Roger (a general store), Establissements Loussan (with the best selection of meat and produce), Chin Lee (the largest market on the island) and a gas (petrol) station. There are also banks, schools, a gendarmerie, the Air Tahiti bureau (across from the mayor's office), a post office (which boasts a new microwave installation for international calls), a commercial centre which has a doctor's/dentist's surgery, bank, and Bora Bora Rent-A-Car. There are also several inexpensive pensions. Several eateries are recommended in the Places to Eat section, but the best place for breakfast is the island's only bakery, Restaurant Vaitape, opposite the post office and Bank of Polynesia.

The newest structure is the Centre Artisanal de Bora Bora, which also houses a tourist office directly on the wharf. Say hello to the very capable manager, Sylvain. It's a good place to window-shop. Near the pier is a granite slab monument to Alan Gerbault, who sailed his yacht the *Firecrest* around the world from 1923 to 1929.

Governor's Mansion (27 km)
The weathered grey building that looks like a grand turn-of-the-century home is actually a facade. It's part of a movie set built by Di Laurentiis for his bomb, *Hurricane*, and is meant to be a replica of the governor's mansion in American Samoa. Part of the mansion is now the Fantasy Island Resort.

Chez Ato (28 km)
Look for a road going half a km up the mountainside to Chez Ato, a delightful accommodation place in the shadow of Mt Otemanu.

Remnants of Tautu's Museum/Overland Road to Telegraph Tower (29 km)
A collection of anchors, a Mark II coastal defence gun, the carcasses of army vehicles and other objects strewn around make up what was informally known as Tautu's Museum. Tautu is a large Tahitian who likes large things. He used to live in the A-frame behind the collection which made up his front yard. Tautu's aim was to convert a couple of defunct interisland ships into a floating bar/museum some day. To no-one's surprise, it didn't quite happen. At this point look for a mountain road opposite the soccer field and the gymnasium. Following it will take you to a telegraph tower and eventually to the opposite side of the island. Atop the crest of the steep hill is a magnificent panoramic view of Vaitape and a motu, Piti Auu, on the opposite side. This same direction

affords vistas of Raiatea and Tahaa. It's not recommended for bicycles.

TV Tower & Lookout (29.7 km)

Keep your eye out for a road that begins next to a double-columned telephone pole and park your bike. Stay to the left and don't wander into someone's front yard (which will be on your right). A steep five-minute walk up the hill will reward you with one of the best views on the entire island. Don't climb the TV tower, or you will get into trouble.

Bloody Mary's (30 km)

This place is a Bora Bora institution. Outside is a huge carved double-boomed canoe with one boom longer than the other, for tacking against the wind. There is also a huge slab of wood where the names of celebrities who have hallowed Bloody Mary's (à la Jimmy Buffet, Ringo Starr, etc) are carved. The fabled bar/restaurant is under fairly new management and the food is still good. Gone are the rooms to stay, though. Although very expensive it's a great place to hang out, sip on a beer and meet the local US crowd.

Moana Arts (31.5 km)

This is a fine shop run by the famous Tahitian photographer Erwin Christian. There is a great selection of cards, posters and fashions.

Hotel Bora Bora (32 km)

The hotel is expensive, and popular with free-spending Americans.

Maupiti

Despite its gradually increasing popularity with travellers, Maupiti remains an unexploited gem of French Polynesia. It is the smallest (25 sq km) and the most isolated of the Leewards. It lies 37 km west of Bora Bora and has a population of about 1000. In two hours or less, you can hike the nine-km road that circles the island without seeing another human being. A 30-minute walk from the main village is the snow-white, crescent-shaped Tereia Beach on the edge of a turquoise lagoon.

Maupiti is surrounded by small coral islets (motus) on the fringing reef and there is one archaeological site on nearby Motu Pae'ao. Maupitans have a disarming friendliness that matches the pristine beauty of their island. They are perhaps the most hospitable islanders in the Society Islands. Maupiti also seems to be an island of children (and dogs) – Kid Lilliput. Here, unlike some other islands, the children (and there are a lot of them) might still take your hand in the streets with a smile and a 'Bonjour!'

You will find that the hotels provide transport for day trips to some of the nearby motus. The airport is on Motu Tuanai and transport is provided to Vai'ea Village. There is no deluxe accommodation on Maupiti; the visitor must either stay in a pension-style arrangement or lodge with a family. Activities are also usually left to the individual, though a personal favourite is to wander down to the front of the dock at 'noonish' for the daily spirited *boule* (bocce, or bowls) contests. As one travel writer, James Kay (no relation to the author), described Maupiti:

There are no hotels, just a few no-star rated boarding houses, no rental cars, bikes or motor scooters, no taxis or buses, no bars or restaurants, no bank, no credit cards, and nothing in the way of planned activities. I mean nothing.

Maupitans have adopted a 'no hotel' policy to preserve the island as it is. They have had several offers to build modern hotels, which the village elders have refused – Bora Bora's hotels are just a few km away. There is, however, a post office (by the dock), but banking is still done whenever the bank representative sails into town for a couple of days.

On Maupiti, as in many isolated communities, the residents have the curious habit of burning their lanterns all night. If you ask why, they may or may not tell you that the reason is to keep the tupa'pau (ghosts) away. If we are to believe the inhabitants, Maupiti is a haven for every type of ghost, spirit and supernatural creature imaginable. There is even a semiannual beach party strictly for ghosts; every so often someone from the village passes the beach while these exclusive affairs happen to be going on. Maupitans say that from the empty beach – once the site of a village – the sounds of musical instruments and laughter are quite audible.

PLACES TO STAY

Travellers to Maupiti should note that the places to stay in the main village, Vai'ea, have had some serious water shortages. Consequently, water consumption is restricted by the community. This is not so for the hotels on the motus.

Chez Floriette* (☎ 67-80-85), BP 43, Vai'ea, Maupiti, is in Vai'ea Village, to the left and not far down from the boat dock. It's a three-room house and each room has a double bed. There is also a bungalow with one double and one single mattress, but beware the marathon basketball games directly outside the window. All share communal baths with cold water, and Floriette assures me that there are no problems with her water. Floriette is an irrepressibly cheery, engaging host who runs a clean, quiet place and speaks better English than she thinks.

Activities include motu picnic excursions and long walks. The price is 5500 CFP per person including three meals, or 4000 CFP with breakfast and dinner, and the tariff includes airport transport.

Chez Mareta (☎ 67-80-25) is directly next door to Chez Floriette. There are four rooms with double beds and the upstairs appears to be in the process of expansion for more. Guests can also choose a single mattress in the cosy 'loft' room, which is a wonderful place to listen to the church choir practising next door in the evenings. There is also a 'salon', terrace, kitchenette and common bath. Activities include trips to the motus, picnics and the like. The rates are 4000 CFP per person including all meals, 3000 CFP with breakfast and dinner, or 1000 CFP for a room only. The address is BP 1, Vai'ea, Maupiti.

*Hotel Avira** (you may also hear it as *Chez/Pension Edna*) (☎ 67-80-26), BP 2, Vai'ea, Maupiti, 15 minutes by boat from the airport on isolated Motu Hu'apiti, is the top accommodation on the island. The food is great, as is the beach and the owners are very hospitable. There are eight bungalows in all. Three are on the beach; two have one room with a double and single bed and a bath; the other is a family unit with one double bed and three singles, plus bath. There are five 'garden bungalows' with communal bath. Three have a double bed, one has two singles, and the other has one double and one single bed. Swimming on the beach is exceptional. There is also a restaurant/bar, washing machine, fishing trips and tours of Maupiti, and the tap water is potable. Day trips can be easily organised. The rates are about 7500 CFP per person including all meals for the beach bungalows and 6500 CFP for the garden bungalows. Airport transfer is 2000 CFP. Write to Mme Edna Terai for reservations.

*Fare Pae'ao** (☎ 67-81-01), BP 33, Maupiti, is another top-rated place on a motu with a great beach and swimming, 15 minutes from the airport and the 'big' island.

The food is very good, as is the hospitality. It consists of one home with two bedrooms, each with a double bed, and another room with a double and two cots. There is also a kitchen, bathroom and large terrace on the premises. Activities include windsurfing, snorkelling, beachcombing, fishing and other water sports. The cost is 6000 CFP including food. The tap water is potable on the motu and solar electricity is available. Children under 12 get a 50% discount. Airport transfer is 1000 CFP per person. Write to Jeannine Tavaearii.

Pension Huranui (☎ 67-81-07) is 300 metres north of the boat dock, on the left side (look for the bluish house with white latticework along the porch side). It is a three-bedroom house, and each room consists of a double bed. There is also a living room, a large terrace and two communal bathrooms with cold water. The rate is 6000 CFP for 'pension complete' (three meals per day are provided). Transfers to/from the airport are 1000 CFP. Contact Mr and Mrs Hura Temataru, Farauru District, Maupiti.

Pension Eri (☎ 67-81-29 between 12 and 1 pm and after 6 pm), one km from the boat dock, is new. It consists of a house with four rooms, each containing a double bed. It also has a salon, kitchen, terrace with a 'motu view', and communal baths with cold water. Eri's also offers airport transfers, motu picnics and auto tours of the island. The rate

with meals is 5000 CFP. The postal address is Vai'ea, Maupiti.

Pension Tamati (☎ 67-80-10), 600 metres from the dock, is also new. It is a large building with nine rooms – five have doubles and four have singles. All have private baths with cold water and none offer any frills. The rates are 4600 CFP per person for room and all meals, and 2000 CFP for room and breakfast. Children under 12 are half price. Contact Mr Ferdinand Tapuhiro, Vai'ea, Maupiti.

At the time of writing, *Pension Papahari* was being renovated out of the old *Sunset Beach* on Motu Tiapaa, ostensibly because the name was 'too American'. No detailed information is available, but the price should be in the 6000 CFP range. There is not yet a telephone, but for information, contact Vilna Tuheiava (☎ 67-80-60). She also happens to be the sister of Floriette of *Chez Floriette*.

GETTING THERE & AWAY

Flights are available two or three times a week, depending on season, from Bora Bora, Raiatea, Papeete and Huahine. The flight time is 30 minutes from Raiatea and 20 minutes from Bora Bora. Unlike Bora Bora, transfer from the airport to the 'big' island is not included; it will cost you 400 CFP.

Maupiti is regularly served by the *Taporo I* from Raiatea. See the Getting Around chapter for more details.

The Tuamotus
&
The Marquesas

The Tuamotus

The Tuamotus, also called Paumotu, meaning 'low or dangerous archipelago', comprise one upthrust coral island, a dozen fairly large atolls and countless small atolls and reefs. The coral island, Makatea, is one of the Pacific's three phosphate islands. The 78 islands are scattered over 15° of longitude and 10° of latitude immediately east of the Society Islands. With the exception of Makatea, the islands are extremely low, with an elevation not exceeding two to three metres above sea level. The Tuamotus conform to the pattern of the coral atoll. Some are complete, unbroken circles of land, while others are a necklace of islands with intervening spaces of deep channels, shallow water or bare coral rock. Fakareva and Rangiroa are good examples of large atoll islands with navigable passes into their interior lagoons.

Apart from a cultured pearl industry established over the past 25 years on several of the islands, the economy is based on copra. Harvesting copra is tedious, back-breaking work that involves splitting ripe coconuts with a machete, drying them in the sun, plucking the meat out and drying the meat once more in an area protected from land crabs – usually in overhead racks. The atolls are divided into family parcels so that each clan has sufficient land from which to harvest a crop. Thanks to generous subsidies from the Tahitian government, the price of copra is kept artificially high to make certain the islanders will be able to make a worthwhile income. After the copra is harvested, it is placed in burlap bags, weighed and recorded in the Chinese shopkeeper's ledger. The shopkeeper usually acts as an intermediary by giving credit at the shop in exchange for the crop, which is eventually shipped to Papeete via the copra boats.

As in all the islands of French Polynesia, the trading schooners are the most important link with the outside world. When a boat arrives, the entire village flocks to watch copra being loaded and staples from the mainland being unloaded. On board there may be a store run by the supercargo, that sells staples and luxury items such as cigarettes, hard liquor, chocolate and coffee.

If you have a desert island fantasy, the Tuamotus are the place to live it out. Be prepared to live on quantities of fish, rice, corned beef, stale French bread, *ipo* (a Tuamotan dumpling) and perhaps some turtle. The actual settlements consist of little more than a church, Chinese store, pier, water tower or cistern and several rows of clapboard or fired-limestone homes with tin roofs. In the evening the major pastime is playing guitar or, for the older folks, listening to Radio Tahiti, which broadcasts news, music and messages to the outer islands. For the young people, time is spent cooking, fishing, harvesting copra and planning liaisons with girl or boyfriends.

The Tuamotus have an eerie ambience not found on other high islands. You notice it several days after arriving. There is something elementally different about an atoll, something you feel but which is hard to articulate. Perhaps it is because you are forced to look inward. There are no caves to hide in, no mountains to climb, no valleys to explore and nowhere to escape. You become aware that you are on an insignificant speck of coral in the middle of an immense ocean. You feel stripped of all the familiar trappings of civilisation, with nothing to fall back on. Despite the monotonous sound of lapping waves on the coral reef, the rustle of ceaseless trade winds through palm fronds and the mercilessly brilliant sun, the primal beauty of an atoll casts an unforgettable spell.

Accommodation – Rules of Thumb

Many of the accommodation places in the Tuamotus discount their tariffs by 500 CFP per person per day for people staying more than three days. Thus, a single costing 1500 CFP goes down to 1000 CFP after three days, a double costing 5000 CFP goes down to 4000 CFP, etc.

Virtually all the accommodation places on the outer islands offer a *pension complete* plan, which means visitors can pay an extra 1500 to 2500 CFP for three meals a day. This is usually advisable on the smaller islands. After all, even with cooking facilities, it so much easier to have your meals prepared for you. Generally there are no fast-food restaurants on remote coral atolls, so there's not much choice.

Almost all the pensions offer free visits to a motu (an outer island) where visitors can swim, picnic and perhaps snorkel. Often visitors are dropped off by a small boat while the owner of the pension is on the way to work, perhaps to a civil service job in the main village. Be sure and bring your sun block, a hat and good book.

Finally, given the extreme isolation of these islands, it's not a bad idea to write before you drop in. A letter addressed to the pension, c/o the village, with the name of the island, will get there. Generally, the population of the villages is several hundred people at the most. The postman will not have to ring twice.

GETTING THERE & AWAY
Air transport via Air Tahiti (☎ 42-24-44 for reservations, 42-70-00 for accommodation) is available to all the islands listed in this chapter unless otherwise noted. Special air passes are available on Air Tahiti for the Leeward/Windward and Tuamotu Groups. See the Getting Around chapter for more details on transport to these islands via inter-island vessel.

RANGIROA
Rangiroa is the largest atoll in the Tuamotus (the lagoon has an area of about 1020 sq km) and is the second-largest atoll in the world. Located 322 km north-west of Papeete, it measures 68 km in length and 23 km in width. This huge atoll has miles of empty white-sand beaches and silent groves of coconut palms. Rangiroa atoll is so wide that it is impossible when standing on one side of

the lagoon to see the opposite shore. A highly recommended activity is to hire a boat and play Robinson Crusoe for a day. Rangiroa's lagoon has an exceptional variety and quantity of marine life. Fish of every size and description, including sharks, manta rays, jack, surgeon fish, mullet, pompano, parrot fish, grouper, puffer fish, butterfly fish, trumpet fish and eels, live in its waters. Some of the local hotels specialise in diving, snorkelling and glass-bottomed boat excursions. From the port it is possible to see local divers spear fish and then feed the unfortunate, wriggling creatures to the nearest shark. Rangiroa's major drawback is that, like Bora Bora, it is a prime example of what happens to an island inundated by tourists – the locals can be indifferent to guests. The population is about 1500 and local crafts include making shell hats and necklaces.

Information
For information on the island contact the Rangiroa Visitors' Bureau (☎ 96-04-60) in Avatoru.

Organised Tours
A rather amazing activity in Rangiroa is 'shooting the pass', which is a free-for-all, mile-long current rush through the reef passes with mask, snorkel and fins. Those without a hyperactive type-T personality can choose to view the spectacle from a glass-bottomed boat. Otherwise, any number of local operators are available for independent or group excursions for sailing the interior of the lagoon, fishing trips (deep sea or otherwise), visiting the 'Blue Lagoon' or bird sanctuary on Motu Paio, or searching for dolphins frolicking in the strong currents at Site Ohutu in the late afternoon.

A few operators are: Tane Tamaehu (☎ 96-04-68, Rangiroa), who offers tours with a glass-bottomed boat; Pierre Francois Amar (☎ 96-04-13; fax 200), BP 69, Avatoru, Rangiroa, who has a catamaran and a lengthy list of offerings; Tixier Tevaea (☎ 96-04-50) with an eight-metre vessel and offering many excursions; Jacques Nuytten ('Jack's Rent-a-Boat') (☎ 96-04-69), BP 61,

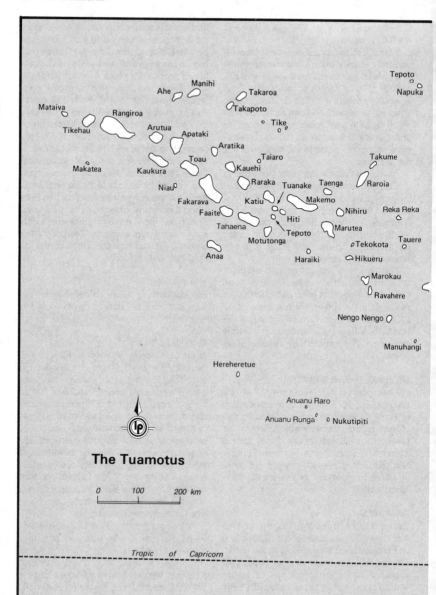

The Tuamotus

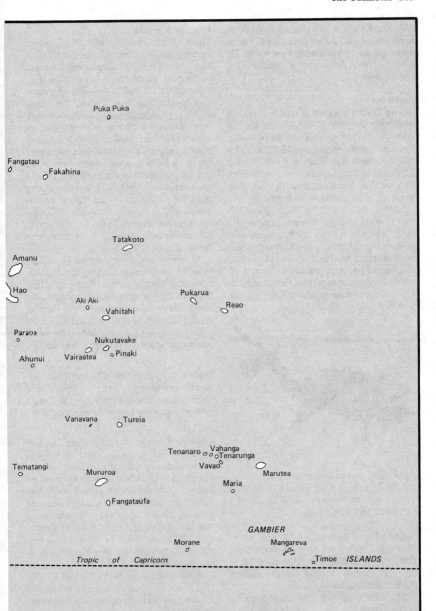

Puka Puka

Fangatau
Fakahina

Tatakoto

Amanu

Hao

Aki Aki
Vahitahi

Pukarua
Reao

Paraoa

Nukutavake
Ahunui   Vairaatea   Pinaki

Vanavana   Tureia

Tenanaro   Vahanga
Tenarunga
Vavao
Tematangi   Mururoa   Marutea
Maria

Fangataufa

GAMBIER
Morane   Mangareva
Tropic   of   Capricorn   Timoe ISLANDS

Avatoru, Rangiroa, offering all-day excursions aboard his 10-metre vessel; and Punua Tamaehu (of 'Chez Punua') (☎ 96-04-73) with another potpourri of possibilities aboard boats.

Activities

Diving Diving is a main attraction for many of Rangiroa's visitors – sharks are the big attraction in the lagoon. There are two main operators on the island, the Hotel Kia Ora and the Manta Ray Club (☎ 96-04-80), BP 55, Avatoru, both of which are run by Yves Lefevre. The programme at the Kia Ora, however, is for guests of the hotel only.

Lefevre's tariffs at the Manta Ray Club start at 4000 CFP per dive including equipment. He also teaches. Both programmes dive the lagoon, the passes and the open sea; night dives are also possible. The Manta Ray programme is very popular right now. It would be prudent to contact the Manta Ray Club ahead of time regarding lodgings and particulars.

Cycling If you just want to cycle around, Carole Plovier at *Chez Carole* in Avatoru Village will rent you a bicycle – 500 CFP for half a day, 900 CFP all day.

Getting There & Away

There are flights every day of the week from Papeete – the flight time is 70 minutes. There are also flights to Bora Bora, Huahine, Manihi, Moorea and Raiatea.

The most comfortable interisland schooner to Rangiroa is the *Aranui*, but others are available on an irregular basis.

Avatoru & Tiputa

There are two main villages on the island: Avatoru (on the same islet as the Kia Ora Hotel) and Tiputa, directly on the other side of the pass. Each village has pension-style accommodation and is one-fifth as expensive as the Kia Ora. Tiputa, the major administrative community, has a town hall, post office, gendarmerie, infirmary, primary school and boarding school. You'll see many trees, stately walkways and even manicured lawns – a rarity in islands where fresh water and soil are precious commodities. Once a prosperous community with revenue coming from the pearl/shell trade, Tiputa lost its gleam and economic life with the widespread use of plastics. In the island's heyday soil was actually brought in by those who could afford it.

Avatoru is near the airport and has offices of the civil aviation and fishing departments, schools, a hospital and another post office. Many of the homes in both villages are constructed from solid, limestone-fired material much like concrete in texture and durability. Their whitewash has long since worn away, leaving ancient, weather-beaten surfaces.

Places to Stay – bottom end Note that prices on many of the pensions are 'approximate' and always subject to change – or perhaps the whim of the proprietor.

Avatoru Accommodation at *Chez Glorine** (☎ 96-03-58) is highly rated as bargain accommodation and has good food and hospitality. It is five km from the airport on the lagoon. There are six bungalows in all: four have any number of combinations of doubles, singles and bunks; the remaining two have two single beds. All have private baths. Rates are 5500 CFP per day including meals. Excursions are available. There is also a restaurant/bar with a TV.

Pension Raira Lagon* (☎ 96-04-23, 96-03-23) has also garnered kudos. It's beside the sea, one km from the airport (near Hotel La Bouteille a la Mer). Four traditional-style bungalows are offered: three bungalows

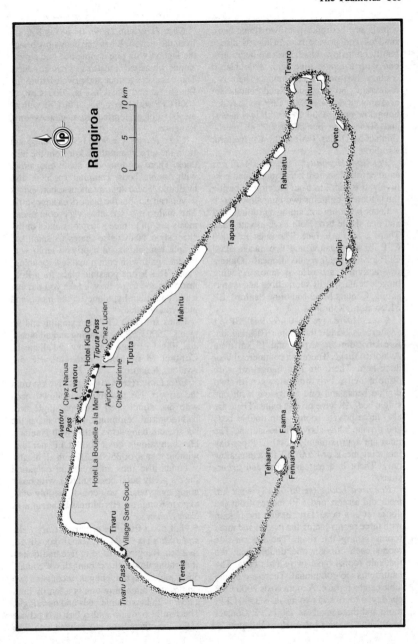

Rangiroa

0   5   10 km

Tevaro
Vahituri
Ovete
Rahuiatu
Tapuaa
Otepipi
Mahitu
Chez Lucien
Tiputa
Tiputa Pass
Hotel Kia Ora
Avatoru
Chez Nanua
Avatoru Pass
Hotel La Boutielle a la Mer
Airport
Chez Glorinne
Faama
Tehaare
Fenuaroa
Tivaru
Village Sans Souci
Tivaru Pass
Tereia

contain one bedroom with two single beds, sundeck and private bath. There is also a family bungalow which has two bedrooms, one with a single, one with a double. It contains two private bathrooms. There is a restaurant and excursions and rentals are available. Rates are 3000 CFP per day for bungalow only, 4500 CFP with two meals, and 5000 for a bungalow and all meals. Contact M Didier Tehina, BP 42, Avatoru, Rangiroa.

*Pension Herenui** (☎ 96-04-71) is another establishment being mentioned positively. It is four km from the airport, beside the lagoon. It contains two bungalows, each with one bedroom containing one double bed and one single bed. Both have private bath. There is also a terrace. The rates are 4000 CFP for a bungalow and two meals, 5000 CFP for a bungalow and all meals. Quite a few activities are offered here, including bicycle rentals, drift snorkelling and waterskiing. Contact Mme Victorine Sanford, BP 31, Avatoru, Rangiroa.

Chez Marie (☎ 96-03-92/94), BP 51 Avatoru, is beside the Tiputa Pass lagoon, five km from the airport and 13 km from Avatoru Village. There is a commercial boat dock here. There are four bungalows with double beds, two bungalows with two double beds, and one bungalow with one single bed. All have private baths. There are also three private rooms with double beds and private baths above the restaurant. The rates are approximately 5500 CFP per day including meals or 1200 CFP for a bungalow only. There is a restaurant/bar and excursions.

Rangiroa Lodge (☎ 96-02-13) is six km from the airport and 350 metres from the docks. It is a new 'fare' beside the lagoon with three rooms facing the lagoon and three rooms facing the road. The lagoon-side rooms each contain one double bed; the roadside rooms have two single beds. The bathrooms are communal. There are picnic tables and a terrace. A room costs 2000 CFP per day; a room and two meals is 3500 CFP; room and three meals is 4500 CFP. Contact M or Mme Jacques Ly, Avatoru Village.

Chez Henriette (☎ 96-04-68) is 8½ km from the airport. It has one bungalow beside the lagoon with one double bed and a mezzanine where extra mattresses can be added. There is also a terrace and private bathroom. Bungalow and breakfast is 2000 CFP, or 4000 CFP with two meals, 5000 CFP with all meals. Contact Henriette Kamaehu, Avatoru, Rangiroa.

Chez Nanua (☎ 96-03-88) is three km from the airport and three km from the boat dock. There are four very small bungalows with double beds; camping space is also available. These digs are about as bare-bones as you can get, but the place does have spirit. The bathrooms are also very communal; meals are quite nice – copious and family-cheer style. Nanua also shares six small and simple bungalows on a private motu with Punua, again with communal (eye-opening) baths. This is one possible place for a Robinson Crusoe trip – they'll take you out and leave you, literally, alone on the motu, and pick you up later.

Rates are 1000 CFP for camping and no meals, 2500 CFP for camping and all meals, and 3000 CFP for a bungalow and all meals. Contact M or Mme Tamaehu, BP 54, Avatoru, Rangiroa.

Chez Punua (☎ 96-04-73) is five km from the airport. He has four bungalows, each with one double bed and one single bed; bathrooms are communal. He also shares the six spartan bungalows listed with Nanua's. His bungalows cost 2000 CFP per day without meals, or 3500 CFP with all meals.

Punua also runs an excursion operation (he's a pretty good boat builder), with boats going everywhere you could possibly wish to go in Rangiroa. His address is the same as *Chez Nanua's*.

Half a km from the airport is *Chez Felix and Judith* (☎ 96-04-41, Rangiroa), BP 18, Avatoru, Rangiroa, offering five traditional-style bungalows: three bungalows contain one double bed; one bungalow contains two singles; the remaining one is a family bungalow with two double beds and one single. The family bungalow also has two private baths; the others have one private bath. The rates are 5000 CFP for bungalow and all meals.

Chez Mata (☎ 96-03-78/91) is between the airport and Avatoru, beside the ocean. There are two new concrete bungalows, each with one double bed and an individual bathroom. They are also planning a restaurant. The cost is 5000 CFP for a bungalow and all meals. Contact Mme Mata Putoa, BP 33, Avatoru, Rangiroa.

Tiputa The *Chez Lucien* (☎ 96-03-55) is 500 metres from the boat dock. It has three Polynesian-style bungalows: one family bungalow has two bedrooms (each with one double bed) and three double mattresses on a mezzanine, a living room, terrace and private bath; the other two contain one room (each with two double beds), two single beds on a mezzanine, and a private bath. Rates are 5000 CFP per person with all meals; a 5000 CFP deposit is required for reservation. Contact M and Mme Lucien and Esther Pe'a, BP 69, Tiputa, Rangiroa.

Pension Estall (☎ 96-04-16, 96-03-16) is 500 metres from the boat dock, between the ocean and the lagoon. There are three traditional bungalows, each containing one room with one double and one single bed and a private bath. There is also a large, three-bedroom concrete house accommodating up to 12 people. The rate for a bungalow and all meals is 5000 CFP per person. Contact M or Mme Estall, BP 13 Tiputa, Rangiroa.

Places to Stay – middle The *Village Sans Souci** (☎ 42-48-33, Papeete) c/o Sara Nantz, BP 22, Avatoru, is an hour's boat ride from Avatoru on a tiny motu. Travellers have found this resort to be the best in its class in Rangiroa. There are 13 bungalows, each with a double bed, and a seafood restaurant. Visitors are provided with sheets but they don't have a maid service. Showers and toilets are in a separate building. The tariff includes breakfast, lunch, dinner and round-trip transport from the hotel to the airport. Activities include fishing, scuba diving and snorkelling, and lots of long, private walks. (A four-plus hour trek to Avatoru has been

done and sounds fascinating.) The rates for three nights are 30,500/50,000 CFP for singles/doubles. Rates for one week are 56,500/102,000 CFP for singles/doubles. The rate for children eight years and under is 3200 CFP per day. A deposit of 10,000 CFP is necessary for a reservation.

One km from the airport, on a beach facing the lagoon, is *La Bouteille a la Mer* (☎ 96-03-34, 43-99-30 in Papeete; fax 96-02-90), BP 17, Avatoru. It has 11 double/triple bungalows, a bungalow for five people, a restaurant and a bar. Activities include snorkelling, fishing, sailing, diving, windsurfing, water-skiing and excursions to islets. Daily hotel rates are approximately 13,000/20,500/28,500 CFP for singles/doubles/triples with all meals included.

Rangiroa Village (☎ 96-03-83), BP 8, Avatoru, is one km from Avatoru. There are nine bungalows, as well as a restaurant/bar, a great beach, snorkelling, outrigger canoes, bicycles and windsurfing. Rates are approximately 10,000/15,500/20,000 CFP for singles/doubles/triples with all meals included.

Pension Tereva (☎ 96 02-87, 96-03-11) consists of only one bungalow but it has a special Italian touch. Loana Sanford, the owner, speaks Italian and serves her Italian meals on fine china and real silver. The bungalow is in the centre of Avatoru, 500 metres from the boat dock. Prices are 8000/12,000 CFP per day for singles/doubles and 14,000 CFP for four people with two meals per day.

Places to Stay – top end The *Kia Ora Rangiroa** (☎ 96-03-84; fax 96-04-93) is the nicest hotel on this beautifully forlorn atoll and the best in the Tuamotus. A short drive from the airport, it has 30 bungalows, five suites, a restaurant and a bar. There are excellent facilities for diving, which is the main attraction. Complementary activities include snorkelling, windsurfing, sailing and fishing. Diving facilities at the Kia Ora are first class and the equipment is well maintained. Rates begin at approximately US$250 for singles. The postal address for reservations is BP 4607, Papeete.

MANIHI

Manihi is 520 km north-east of Papeete. I found Manihi's 300 inhabitants to be much friendlier than those of Rangiroa, the only other atoll in the Tuamotus with a hotel. The presence of the hotel (called Kaina Village) and a cultured pearl industry have made the island a comparatively prosperous community. In the Tuamotus, prosperity means owning Mercury outboards, Sony tape decks and clothing without holes. Islanders embrace their improved standard of living, as they know what it is like to do without. The old outhouses built on stilts over the water's edge serve as graphic reminders of the way life was not too long ago.

Manihi's villagers take pride in their limestone and clapboard homes, which are lined along two main 'streets' of sand. Most homes have attractive front and back yards arranged with shells, shrubs and flowers. They are either fenced in or surrounded by curbs to discourage the bands of scrawny, marauding dogs that always populate Polynesian villages. There is one main concrete dock, a flagpole and a village square where old people gossip under the shade of a huge tree.

The island's 15-year-old cultured pearl industry provides the bread and butter for the island. Throughout the lagoon are rows of stakes resembling barbecue spits. From these hang metal rods to which growing oysters are wired. They produce lustrous 'black pearls' with a silver sheen unique to French Polynesia. Every year, Japanese specialists are flown into Manihi to implant tiny spheres of Mississippi River mussel shell in the black pearl oysters collected from the lagoon by local divers. After three years the oysters are harvested. Out of every 100 oysters, only seven will eventually yield commercially usable pearls.

Organised Tours

Kaina Village gives an excellent tour of the pearl facilities, located in an unobtrusive shack nearby on the village waterfront. The tour includes a boat ride in the lagoon, where a diver is sent to retrieve an oyster. The 'ripe' oyster is opened and the pearl is extracted and passed around the boat for inspection by the guests. There are no free samples; prices for a 'cheap' string of pearls start at around US$750 and go up exponentially from there. A more affordable souvenir is the 'demi-pearl', a sort of pearl on the half-shell. It is actually a hemisphere of plastic that has been glued to the inside of a live oyster and, over the course of a year, has become overlaid with mother-of-pearl. These cost about US$25 each.

Activities

Diving Kaina Village (☎ 42-75-53, Tahiti) has a diving operation run by Coco Chaze. Rates are 3500 CFP for dives inside the lagoon and 5000 CFP outside the reef.

Places to Stay – bottom end

The *Chez Marguerite Fareea** (☎ 96-43-03) is rated as the best budget accommodation on the island. She has five bungalows, each with one room containing one double and one single bed and private bath. The pension is on a motu. Electricity is available from 6 am to noon and 6 to 10 pm. Activities such as picnics on the motus and fishing are extra. Rates are 5500 CFP per person, including meals. Airport transfer is provided; please advise as to date of arrival and flight number. Write to Ilot Topiheiri, Manihi, Tuamotu.

Chez Teiva also requests that when making reservations you give your arrival date and flight. They offer one house which has three rooms (with single and double beds), private bath, and kitchen. There are also four fares, each with double and single beds, kitchen and communal bath. Rates are 4500 CFP per person including meals. Write to Mme Puahea, Turipaoa, Manihi, Tuamotu.

Chez Faura Pitori (☎ 42-95-39, Tahiti) provides accommodation on a motu with a great beach. There are three bungalows, each with two single beds and a common bath. Rates are approximately 5000 CFP per person. Call the above number for reservations.

Manahune Village (☎ 96-42-28) is in Turipoa Village, 2½ km from the airport by boat. There is a wooden building with four rooms, each with a double bed, and a communal bath. The rates are 6000 CFP with all meals, 4500 CFP with breakfast and dinner only. Write to M Georges Matitai, BP 1347, Papeete, Tahiti.

Le Keshi (☎ 96-43-13) is closer to a middle-range hotel, since there's a restaurant on the premises, linen is available and, of course, the price is higher. It's on a motu 20 minutes by boat from the airport, on the edge of the lagoon. There are five bungalows (two facing the lagoon) with one double bed, mosquito netting, private bath (cold water) and – get this – tiled floors and wood panelling! A single bed may also be added to the room. Rates are 5000 CFP for the bungalow only, 6000 CFP for a bungalow and two meals or 7000 CFP for 'pension complete'. Children under 12 are half-price. Contact M Raymond Vergnes, Motu Taugaraufara, Manihi.

Places to Stay – top end
Set on a white-sand beach, Kaina Village (☎ 42-75-53, Tahiti), BP 2460, Papeete, is a smaller-scale operation than Kia Ora and boasts bungalows constructed over the lagoon's shore that have self-contained waste treatment systems. There are 16 bungalows and two suites, a bar, a restaurant and excellent snorkelling/diving.

Although the hotel is isolated from the village, it is more accessible to guests than are the villages in Rangiroa, and visitors are apt to have more contact with locals. A visit to a nearby black pearl 'farm' and the local Paumotu Village are also attractions. Spearfishing is good in the lagoon, and the villagers have an easy time catching dinner in their fish trap. Kaina Village once inspired a popular song on the Tahitian hit parade called, appropriately enough, Kaina Village in Manihi. Prices begin at approximately 16,000/23,000 CFP for singles/doubles.

Entertainment
Entertainment in Manihi consists of Sunday soccer games, shooting pool, the local version of bocce, and catching sharks off the pier. The last one is done at night with a handline attached to a giant hook baited with a chunk of moray eel. When the participants land a shark, they slash its spinal cord with a machete and extract the shark's jaw for a souvenir. Near the pier is a pool filled with harmless nurse sharks with which village boys like to wrestle for the tourists' cameras.

Getting There & Away
There are flights from Papeete four times a week. The flight time (including a stopover in Rangiroa) is two hours and 15 minutes. Flights to Manihi are also available to and from Rangiroa, Huahine, Bora Bora, Moorea and Raiatea.

There are several interisland vessels sailing to Manihi regularly from Papeete.

AHE
Ahe, the most popular of the Tuamotus with the yachting community, can only be reached by launch from neighbouring Manihi. Ahe does not reap the benefits of any tourist trade or commercial pearl industry; consequently it is isolated and poor. On Manihi, most residents have modern cisterns, sleep on beds and wash their dishes under a freshwater tap. On Ahe, a cistern is apt to be a rusty oil drum, the kids may sleep on a mat on the ground, and the dishes are likely to be done in the waters of the lagoon. Items that some Westerners would consider rubbish – tin cans, glass bottles and plastic bags – are all used and re-used. What Ahe lacks in comfort, however, is made up for in the kindness of the inhabitants. The axiom about 'the poorer a people, the more generous' certainly holds true on this island. There are no locked doors, and a visitor is always offered what little the family has.

Ahe's inhabitants make their living by harvesting copra and selling fish to a refrigerated storage boat that makes a regular stop on its way to Tahiti. The island was originally settled by people from Manihi and there is a friendly rivalry between the two communities. There is one small but comfortable pension for visitors.

On Ahe, you learn to appreciate life's simple pleasures. I spent a memorable evening there with some locals. Sitting outside the home of a man whose wife was expecting a baby at any moment, we sang, passed around a battered guitar and slugged away at a bottle of Algerian red wine. The expectant father disappeared inside between songs to comfort his wife. The brilliant moon that loomed over us added to the tension in the air. The baby was not born that evening, so our vigil continued through the next night. We traded ghost stories and passed around a bottle of cheap Caribbean rum. Finally, the father announced the birth of a girl and the entire village was invited to the man's one-room shack for a *fête*. Inside, the single bed where the mother held the newborn child was partitioned off by a blanket. A few jackets and a spearfishing gun hung by nails tacked to the clapboard wall, and several men sat on rough-hewn chairs drinking beer by the light of a kerosene lamp. Throughout the party, three children slept soundly on floor mats in a corner of the shack.

Getting There & Away
There is no air service to Ahe but there is a daily skiff from Manihi.

MORUROA, FANGATAUFA, HAO & THE OUTER LIMITS
The Moruroa and Fangataufa atolls are not open to visitors but are well known as nuclear testing sites. Testing began (above ground) in 1966 but was moved underground in 1975 and restricted to Moruroa. Total tests exceed 160 to date, including neutron tests, and the publicly acknowledged hydrogen series. Although the base at Hao was built to provide logistic assistance for the military, it is also an airfield used by civilian (Air Tahiti) flights, and visitors to some Tuamotu destinations may find themselves landing there.

All the other islands listed in this section – Anaa, Arutua, Takapoto, Kaukura, Takaroa, Tikehau, Mataiva, Raroia and Fakarava – are strictly civilian islands and are also served by Air Tahiti.

RAROIA
It was on Raroia's reef that Thor Heyerdahl's raft *Kon-Tiki* was wrecked in 1947 and his crew of five other Scandinavians (including author Bengt Danielsson) were washed ashore. They were en route to Mangareva in the Gambier Islands to test Heyerdahl's theory (based on an Inca legend) that it was possible to sail from South America to Polynesia. Instead, the intrepid adventurers had drifted off course to Raroia.

TAKAPOTO
Located 624 km north-east of Papeete, there are about 465 people living on this forlorn atoll. Most dwell in the community of Fakatopatere, which is about one km from the airport. Only 16 km long, Takapoto has beautiful white-sand beaches and a thriving cultured pearl industry. What it doesn't have is a pass into the lagoon, but villagers get around this by landing whaleboats near the reef. It is said that when inhabitants of the island return by boat a double rainbow appears over the island. With all the pearls in the lagoon, there is no need to look for a pot of gold. Over the past few years several small pensions have sprouted up on this distant atoll.

Transport within the atoll is easy because many of the villagers work daily on copra plantations on the opposite side of the lagoon from the village. Transport by air is also frequent: there are flights from Papeete twice a week with connections to Kaukura and Apataki.

Places to Stay
All four pensions listed here provide transport to and from the airport, and electricity from 7 am to 10 pm. They are one km or less from the airport, in the village of Fakatopatere. In addition, they will all discount their tariffs by 500 CFP per person per day for guests staying more than three days.

Chez Lea Teahu (☎ 98-65-56) has one large home with two bedrooms, each with a double bed, and a small dorm with two doubles and two single beds. The owner provides transport to and from the airport.

Visits to a nearby motu are also offered. The tariff is 5000 CFP per person for 'pension complete'.

Chez Emile Taraihau (☎ 98-65-25) consists of one bungalow with a double bed, outside bath, kitchenette and terrace. The price is 1500/2500 CFP for singles/doubles for the first three days.

Chez Cathy Ruamotu (☎ 98-65-68) has one house with two bedrooms, each with a double bed, living room, fully equipped kitchen and common bathroom. The price is 1500/2500 CFP for singles/doubles (room only) or 3000/5000 CFP for 'pension complete'. Trips to remote motus are available.

Chez Terai Mahaeahea (☎ 98-65-54) consists of one house with one bedroom with double bed, and another room with a double and a single. The room-only price is the usual 1500/2500 CFP for singles/doubles, or 3000/5000 CFP for 'pension complete'.

TAKAROA

Takaroa is separated from Takapoto by only eight km of ocean. With a length of 24 km and a width of eight km at its widest point, the atoll is oblong, resembling a giant protozoan. It is home to about 400 people and is one of the few remaining atolls with marae. The pass here is three metres deep and anchorages are good in all parts of the lagoon.

Places to Stay

All the accommodation on Takaroa is in or near the village of Teavaroa, which is two km from the airport. All units have electricity, and round-trip transfers to and from the airport are provided. As in most of the pensions on the outer islands, after the third day the price drops by 500 CFP per person.

Chez Eugenie Ennemoser (☎ 98-22-36/40) consists of one home with two bedrooms with a double bed each, and a bungalow with two doubles. The home has a living room and fully equipped kitchen. The outside bath is communal. The Ennemosers (who hail from Germany) provide trips to the motu and other excursions, which are supplementary. The price is 3000/5000 CFP for singles/doubles with meals, or 1500/2500 CFP without meals.

Chez Bertha Alvarez (☎ 98-22-62/79) has one house with three rooms, each with a double bed. There is also a kitchen and a communal bath. Bertha's prices are 3000/5000 CFP for singles/doubles with meals, or 1500/2500 CFP without.

Chez Moeata Puaroo (☎ 98-22-73) has a house near the beach with two bedrooms, each with a double bed, living room, fully equipped kitchen and communal bath. The Puaroos offer visits to the motus and other excursions. The price is 3000/5000 CFP for singles/doubles for 'pension complete', or 1500/2500 CFP for rooms only.

Chez Hiriata Tehina (☎ 98-22-34/57) also has a house with three rooms, each with a double bed, living room, kitchen and common bath. There is also a white-sand beach nearby. Prices are 3000/5000 CFP for singles/doubles for 'pension complete', or 1500/2500 CFP sans food. The usual visits to the motu are also provided.

Chez Vahinerii Temanaha (☎ 98-22-46), located near a beach, has one home with two rooms, each with a double bed. There is also a kitchen, living room and communal bath. Visits to the motu are provided, as are other excursions on demand. The tariff is 4000/8000 CFP for singles/doubles including three meals, or 2000/4000 CFP without food.

FAKARAVA

Fakarava has an unusual rectangular shape and, measuring 60 km by 25 km, is the second-largest atoll in French Polynesia. (Rangiroa is the largest.) Rotoava village, located near Ngaure pass (which is one km wide) is home to most of the atoll's 248 inhabitants. There is also a small settlement in Tetamanu Village. The island is approximately 400 km north-east of Tahiti.

Places to Stay

The *Tetamanu Village* (☎ 43-64-15, 43-55-29, Tahiti), BP 9364, Motu Uta, Tahiti, is a three-hour boat ride from the airport to the interior of Fakarava's lagoon. There are four small bungalows on the lagoon, each with two singles. There are also two common baths. However, the attraction here is not the bungalows but rather the *Sea Bell*, an 18-metre vessel with four cabins that will take the intrepid traveller on a seven-day fishing, swimming, snorkelling and eating trip in the waters of the lagoon. The trip costs 68,000 CFP for adults and 34,000 CFP for children. The owner/operator, Sunny Richmond, provides return transport to and from Fakarava's airport. Call the above phone numbers and ask for Jean-Pierre.

Te Purotu, run by Mme Ruita Maire, is in the village of Rotoava, four km from the airport. She has one house with two bedrooms, each with a double bed and private bath. She offers excursions to the motu with a picnic. The price, including all meals is 5000 CFP. Transfers are 500 CFP per person. Mme Maire asks that visitors make reservations before they show up. Write to Mme Maire c/o Rotoava Village, Fakarava, French Polynesia.

ANAA

Anaa was the first atoll I ever visited and it made an indelible impression upon me. Located 437 km east of Tahiti, it is an oval-shaped island comprising 11 islets enclosing a shallow lagoon. There is no pass through the coral reef, but landing is easy on the lee side, where the reef slopes up to the shore. Once the most populous atoll in the entire Tuamotu Group, it is now a quiet backwater which sees few visitors and numbers about 500 inhabitants. Tuuhora is the most important of the five villages.

Anaa is the model of the prototypical, sun and wind-scarred atoll described at the beginning of this chapter. My experience on the atoll came from a week-long stay at the Yaplo residence, a family of Chinese and Paumotu ancestry.

During my sojourn on the island, among the activities I participated in was a turtle hunt. To get there, many hours were spent paddling a canoe far into the lagoon. We did find a turtle but an unnamed greenhorn spooked the creature into the depths with his flippers before the prey was even close to being turtle soup. Fortunately my hosts graciously hid their disappointment. Needless to say, the ride back home was memorable for its silence. If Tevea Yaplo reads this I'm sure he will remember. Anaa, by the way, was seriously damaged by a cyclone several years ago and the entire village has since been rebuilt.

Places to Stay

The *Pension Te Hoa Nui* (☎ 98-32-32) operated by the Gatata family, has two bungalows, each with two single beds. There is also a living room and bathroom in each unit. A room with three meals is 3000/5000 CFP for singles/doubles, or 1500/2500 CFP without food. As usual, the price drops by 500 CFP per person per day after three days' stay.

KAUKURA

Kaukura, 325 km north-east of Tahiti, is oval-shaped and 40 km long. The lagoon is shallow, with a narrow pass. The population numbers around 300, all of whom live in the village of Raitahiti.

Places to Stay

The *Chez Claire Parker* consists of two houses. Each house has three rooms, with a double bed in each room. There is one common bath. Mme Parker's home is in the village of Raitahiti, about two km from the airport, near a beach. She provides excursions to a distant motu for 7000 CFP for the use of the boat, which holds up to eight people. The cost is 4500 CFP per person, including three meals. Write to Mme Parker c/o Village de Raitahiti, Kaukura.

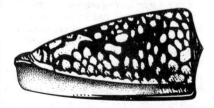

ARUTUA

Like Anaa, nearly all the housing on Arutua was seriously damaged or destroyed in 1983, when a cyclone ravaged the atoll. Most of the nearly 300 inhabitants live in the village of Rautini. The island is almost circular, with a diameter of 29 km and there is a pass through the reef to allow small vessels in. Arutua has unusually abundant fish, which have been preserved through a system of 'fish parks' and pearl farms. The island is also known as the home of some of the best musicians in the Tuamotus.

All accommodation on Arutua is in or near the village of Rautini, which happens to be close to a dock serving the airport. There is no private phone service to this island so all communication must be by mail.

Places to Stay

The *Pension Mairava* consists of one house with communal bath and six rooms, each with a double bed. An extra bunk can be added to rooms if needed. Activities include fishing and visits to the pearl farm in the lagoon. The price is 5000 CFP per person for 'pension complete'. Write to the Charles family, c/o Rautini Village, Arutua, French Polynesia for reservations.

Pension Pikui consists of a house in the village with communal bath and three rooms – two with double beds and one with three singles. The proprietors, the Tuteina family, also have a house on Motu Mutukiore, with two bedrooms with a double bed in each. Round-trip transfers to the motu cost 1000 CFP. Activities include picnics, trolling in the lagoon or fishing off the reef for lobsters. The cost for these excursions varies according to how much gasoline is consumed by the boats. The price is 4000 CFP per person for 'pension complete'.

Pension Tapu, operated by Jean and Estelle Tapu, has four bungalows – two with one double bed each and two with one single bed each. There are two communal bathrooms and one kitchen. Activities include fishing, visits to the Tapu family pearl farm and a visit to an underwater fish reserve. The

price per person is 5000 CFP for 'pension complete' or 3000 CFP for room only.

TIKEHAU

With a diameter of 26 km and a near-circular shape, Tikehau resembles Arutua. When Jacques Cousteau's research group made a study of the Tuamotus in 1987, they found Tikehau's lagoon to contain among the largest quantity of fish in the entire archipelago. The fish are maintained, as in Arutua, through a number of 'fish parks'. The island has just over 300 inhabitants.

All accommodation on Tikehau, except for the Tikehau Village, is in the village of Tuterahera, two km from the airport. The Tikehau Village is in the village of Tematie, only 300 metres from the airport.

Places to Stay

The *Tikehau Village* (☎ 96-22-57/86) is large by Tuamotu standards, encompassing five bungalows – two with double beds and two with two single beds each. Each of these units has a private bath. The fifth bungalow has a double bed with no bath. There are excursions to a motu, an underwater fish reserve, as well as an automobile tour of the island and visits to the village. The price is 5000 CFP per person with three meals. Call Agence Pacific Travel (☎ 42-93-85) in Papeete for reservations.

Chez Natua (☎ 96-22-34) consists of one house with four rooms with a double bed in each, and a room with two bunks. There is also a communal kitchen and bath. Excursions include visits to the underwater reserve and picnics on the motu for 2000 CFP per person. The price is 3500 CFP for 'pension complete.'

Chez Maxime (☎ 96-22-38) is a house with four bedrooms, each with a double bed and communal bath. Excursions to the underwater reserve are also available for 2000 CFP per person. The price is 3500 CFP for 'pension complete.'

Chez Habanita (☎ 96-22-48) is a home with three bedrooms, each with double bed. There is also a kitchen and common bath. Activities include tours of the island and –

you guessed it – picnics for 2000 CFP per person and visits to the underwater 'fish park'. The price is 4000 CFP for 'pension complete' or 2000 CFP without food.

Chez Faahei (☎ 96-22-33) consists of a home with two bedrooms, each with a double bed. A communal bath is also available. Unlike most pensions, round-trip transfers to the airport cost 1000 CFP. A visit to the fish reserve costs 10,000 CFP for a vessel – minimum two persons and maximum six. The price for 'pension complete' is 3500 CFP per day.

Chez Verona is a house with three rooms, two with a double bed each, and one with two double beds and a single, and a communal bath. A number of excursions are provided, including fishing trips, picnics, snorkelling and boat rental for up to a week. For 10,000 CFP they will provide a boat for a combined picnic/visit to the park. The tariff is 3500 CFP for 'pension complete'.

Chez Isadore et Nini is a home with three rooms, each with a double bed, and a communal bath. There are the usual activities including the well-known visit to the park for 2000 CFP per person. The price is 3500 CFP for 'pension complete.'

MATAIVA

There is one lone pension on Mataiva.

Places to Stay

The *Te Fare Taina* (☎ 96-32-47) is the only show in town. Located 300 metres from the airport in the village of Teavaava, the Fare Taina has two bungalows on the beach, each with a double bed and a terrace overlooking the lagoon. There is one communal bath. Perhaps the most attractive feature of this pension is the beautiful white-sand beach. The Tepehu family provides – you guessed it – picnic excursions to a motu for 2000 CFP per person. The tariff is 5000 CFP, including meals.

The Marquesas

Jutting vertically from the ocean floor 1250 km north-east of Tahiti, the emerald-green Marquesas Islands form the most spectacular and remote archipelago in French Polynesia.

Called by Marquesans 'Te Henua' – the Land of Men – the islands are divided into two subgroups: the Windward Group in the south-east, comprising Hiva Oa, Tahuata, Fatu Hiva and the smaller islets of Motane, Fatu Uku and Thomasset; and the Leeward Group 110 km to the north-west, comprising Ua Pou, Nuku Hiva and Ua Huka.

Because of their proximity to the doldrums of the equator where the south-east trade winds begin to wane, the islands have always been in a sort of backwater of the Pacific, and even in this day of air travel they remain isolated. Lacking reefs, volcanic in origin and geologically young, they rise like spires from the sea with their jagged and precipitous profiles. There are no coastal plains, and valleys are deep, trench-like and lush. The climate in the Marquesas is, on average, hotter and wetter than that of the rest of French Polynesia. The mean temperature is 28°C.

The islands' main product is oranges, which were exported to California, New

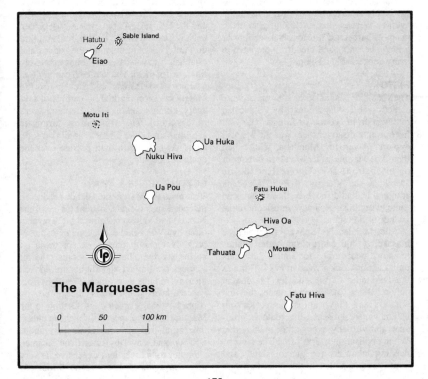

Zealand and Australia in the 19th century. Marquesans depended more on breadfruit and food cultivated from the land than on food from the sea, which was less accessible to them because of the lack of reefs. They were a warlike lot who practised human sacrifice and, unlike their Tahitian cousins, were cannibals.

The Marquesans were most famous for their skill as tattoo artists and carvers of wood and stone. Local artisans are famous for woodcarvings and hand-crafted ukuleles. Today they still carve statues and bowls but skilled artisans are few. The remains of their temples and imposing stone tikis still stand.

Perhaps the most maddening thing about these islands is a tiny, ubiquitous creature called the no-no, a nasty gnat whose bite causes an itching welt.

The culinary spectrum in the Marquesas invariably includes a few things outside the average Western diet, including goat meat, heaps of barbecued lobster (ever see lobster leftover before?), and breadfruit prepared in every conceivable fashion.

HISTORY

The six major islands of the Marquesas were settled over 2000 years ago by Polynesian mariners from Samoa or Tonga. The first European to discover them was the Spanish explorer Alvaro de Mendana, who called them Las Marquesas de Mendoza in honour of his patron, Don Garcia Hurtado de Mendoza, the Viceroy of Peru. Mendana assumed he had discovered these islands en route to establishing a new Jerusalem in the Islands of Solomon.

After Mendana's discovery (in which he massacred 200 Marquesans) the islands remained undisturbed for almost 200 years until Captain Cook arrived in 1774. This was the beginning of the end for Marquesan culture. After Cook's appearance, the first whalers and slave ships came, leaving behind venereal disease, tuberculosis, influenza and virtually every other malady that White civilisation had to offer. The slavers, needing labourers for guano islands and South American plantations, picked up their

unfortunate victims with promises of a better life, and sold them to the highest bidder. The sum of these tragic events destroyed the Marquesan people. When Cook first visited the islands, the population numbered about 50,000. Fifty years later it was down to about 5000 and fell to 1200 before the population started to increase again. Today it stands at about 8000.

The first missionaries arrived on the scene in 1798 and in the following half-century different evangelistic sects zealously competed for the souls of the Marquesans. During this period of intense missionary activity the US writer Herman Melville jumped ship from a whaler and eventually wrote *Typee* based on his experiences in the Marquesas. His autobiographical account about the effects of changes made by missionaries on the indigenous population created a storm of controversy in the USA and the UK. In 1842 the French, just beaten to New Zealand by the British, sent Admiral du Petit-Thours to colonise the islands and establish a naval base but found relatively little use for them. The late 19th century was a time of darkness and death for the Marquesan race, marked by periods of savagery, killings and, as Greg Denning states in his book *The Marquesas*, 'orgiastic cannibalism'. The French administration could do little more than preside over the death of a people.

GETTING THERE & AWAY

Visitors to the Marquesas Islands need to be independent travellers, patient (as in all the islands) and able to rough it a bit. Travel is often by 4WD vehicle, boat and even horseback. Not many tourists except those on yachts see the Marquesas because the air services are limited and flights are booked up to six months in advance. The flight from Papeete takes seven hours; the journey by copra boat takes seven days. Getting to the Marquesas from Papeete is not cheap either; the round-trip air fare costs just under US$800 and travel by interisland steamer, although sometimes less expensive, is very time-consuming. For this reason, the islands

Top: Marae Aehua-tai, Bora Bora (RK)
Bottom: Camping ground, Bora Bora (RK)

Top: Young Marquesan (RK)
Bottom Left: Wearing tiare apetahi (crown of flowers) (GH)
Bottom Right: Making copra, Bora Bora (RK)

are among the least physically adulterated in French Polynesia. This will undoubtedly change in the near future, however – tourist authorities are already planning to expand the airport facilities to accommodate jets.

Air

Aside from interisland vessels such as the *Taporo V*, the *Tamarii Tuamotu*, the *Kahoa Nui* and the newly refitted *Aranui*, Air Tahiti has a regularly scheduled service two days a week from Papeete to Nuku Hiva for 36,700 CFP. From Nuku Hiva, which is in effect a hub for the other islands in the archipelago, there are flights to Hiva Oa, Ua Huka and Ua Pou. Air fares within the Marquesas range from 4900 to 8400 CFP. The other islands are only accessible by boat. Flights are also possible late in the week from the Marquesas to Rangiroa, Manihi and Napuka, with fares ranging from 24,150 to 27,300 CFP.

Sea

The *Aranui*, a modern interisland freighter which has been converted to take passengers, is the most comfortable (and probably the best) way to see the Marquesas. It also stops in several of the Tuamotu Islands (including

---

The *Aranui* Experience

Travelling aboard the *Aranui* is a dichotomous experience – it's a real live sweaty freighter with a luxury liner complex. Passengers padding around the condensed but thoroughly comfortable living area are a pleasantly surprised hodgepodge of adventurers, would-be adventurers, wanderlusters, in-transit locals and the inevitable majority of the simply curious. Its activities are a night-and-day gamut of whirlwind movement or sedentary splendour. Mountaintops to reef-floors, horseback to the back of dusty 4WDs, it's always thoroughly different.

With this wonderfully appealing skew to the unusual, what the *Aranui* does best is eschew the ostentatious and garish extravagances of antiseptic cruise ships and, thankfully, avoid the clique-ish nature of tour travel. The *Aranui* simply offers the subtly captivating Marquesas Islands and the chance to be among them. It does this with a grin.

As all cruise ships should be, but usually aren't, its chief draw is the speed with which passengers' pretences are shed and a genuinely warm camaraderie develops. The itinerary, too, is a wholly democratic process (you often don't know what's on for tomorrow until you vote at dinner, if you even know which island you're aiming for next) and there are always more than enough islands to choose from. The excursions ashore vary from frenetic, bouncy cross-island 4WD jaunts to brow-popping jungle and road treks on foot. Destinations include quiet coves where you can snorkel, picnic on absolutely deserted ribbons of virgin sand or explore pools of primeval, icy water fed by towering waterfalls.

The minute you leave the *Aranui* the day is chock-full of Marquesan immersion and sensory overload. The experience begins by clambering down the side of the ship like a D-day soldier into the bulging arms of a Marquesan stevedore in the bouncing whaleboat for the often wet and wild ride ashore. After the day's activities, it's back aboard the ship in the often extended stretches of interisland cruising. Despite the vastly scaled-down nature of the ship (compared with conventional cruise vessels) there's always something to do if you grow tired. If nothing else, how could you possibly grow weary of watching the smooth-limbed acrobatic crew load and unload cargo like skilled, riotous looters? Then there's the modest lounge and library, and the assortment of impromptu chess matches with the captain and crew around the bar while listening to the revelry of every evening's Tahitian hootenanny. Polynesians must come out of the womb dancing and plunking the ukulele.

But the true essence of the trip is to be found during the more common and amazingly intense periods of introspective solitude under the highest of midnight skies and grinning moons.

You can drink with Gauguin's ghost or simply stand and feel the thick warm night breeze blowing across your body. Or you can watch the dolphins shooting the pass with the ship as it enters the cradled shoulders of another comfortable Marquesan bay and know a bit more clearly what it is that the 'Land of Men' possesses.

This is what the *Aranui*, with its 'just enough' simple comforts, offers best. ■

Tom Huhti

Manihi and Takapoto). Cruises last for 16 days and take in Ua Pou, Nuku Hiva, Hiva Oa, Tahuata, Fatu Hiva and Ua Huka in the Marquesas. The cabins on the 80-metre vessel have been completely refurbished for 'tourists' and even a small dining room and bar have been installed. Despite the upgrading for 'tourists' and the excellent food, this vessel has no pretensions about being a luxury cruise boat. It is a working freighter and stops at every island, loading and unloading cargo like clockwork. Prices, which include food and land tours, start at US$1390 for deck passage and range from US$2730 to US$3740 for cabins. For those who have the means and enjoy travelling on interisland vessels, the *Aranui* is the ticket.

The alternative to the *Aranui* is the irregularly scheduled boats, which may not be as 'user friendly' and may entail trips of up to 25 days at sea.

Over the years the most consistent visitors to the Marquesas have been US yachts, which often make the Marquesas part of their itinerary because the islands are the first landfall en route to Tahiti from the US west coast. For further information in the USA call (415) 541-0674 in San Francisco.

GETTING AROUND

It is not necessary to plead with yachters for a ride from island to island, should you wind up in the Marquesas (though it remains a possibility). Options include waiting for a ride aboard the *Taporo V* or the *Aranui* or other freighters whenever they show up, or taking the new interisland ferry – the *Kaoha Nui* – which departs from Taiohae, Nuku Hiva, once a month on its four-day voyage. (The schedule is always open to change, remember.) The itinerary includes Vaipaee, Hakahau, Atuona, Vaitahu, Omoa, Hanavave and Nuku a Taha. Prices between each destination generally range from 1000 to 2300 CFP. In Taiohae, Nuku Hiva, contact Philippe Tepea (☎ 92-04-63, 92-03-96).

Note that the maps of most of the islands depict 'roads', but these are often walking paths or rutted jeep trails at best. However, the lack of tar-sealed roads should not be a

major concern. The traveller will most likely not be doing much driving in the Marquesas Islands.

NUKU HIVA

Nuku Hiva is the most important island in the Marquesas – it is the economic and governmental centre of the archipelago. The island is set for a 'friendly invasion' by the French military sometime soon, which will dramatically build up the island's infrastructure, including a round-the-island paved road and a major docking facility.

Nuku Hiva is also dramatically beautiful, with three major bays along the southern coast and equally breathtaking inlets on the northern coast. There are numerous remains of life before European contact, such as *paepae*, the stone foundations on which the Marquesans constructed their homes; *akua*, fortifications; and *mea'ae*, temples. The ruins testify to the once large population that the island supported. Nuku Hiva is 340 sq km in area and has a population of about 2100. It is 112 km north of Hiva Oa and 37 km west of Ua Huka.

Organised Tours

Boat Boat tours are available from a number of people including Laurent Falchetto (☎ 92-03-07), Lucien Lirzin (☎ 92-03-51) and Pierre Teikitohe (☎ 92-04-90, 92-03-72), who also does fishing expeditions. Philippe Batallard of Charter Mana Iti (☎ 92-73-90, fax 92-73-44; in Tahiti, contact Reve Tahitien Travel, (☎ 41-05-24) has a 19-metre boat and offers complete boat/land package tours.

Rates range from 8000 to 10,000 CFP for half-hour trips to Taipivai or the Hakaui waterfall, to 17,000 to 25,000 CFP for rides to the Nuku Ataha Airport or to Hatiheu. Visitors should note that the major points of interest on the island are accessible, but only with the proper transport and, most of the time, with the aid of a guide.

Boat excursions from Hatiheu can be made to various bays and valleys including Aakapa, Anaho, Taiohae and Pua. Fares range from 5000 to 20,000 CFP. Round-trip transport to the airport is also available for 19,000 CFP. Fishing trips cost 8000 CFP and horse rides to ancient temples and tikis are 2000 CFP per person. The address is c/o Yvonne Katupa.

Car Cars (with driver) are available for excursions around the island from Joseph Puhetini (☎ 92-03-47), Joseph Tamarii (☎ 92-03-48, 92-02-95) or Didier Benatar (☎ 92-04-91, fax 92-03-67). Rates range from 1500 CFP for a tour of the village to 15,000 CFP for 2½-hour trips to Toovi Plateau or to Hatiheu. There is generally an eight-person maximum. Cars without drivers are available from Pierre Teikitohe (☎ 92-04-90, 92-03-72) and rates are from 10,000 CFP per day for an older Toyota 4WD.

Didier Benatar also runs Excursion Safari Marquises, which is a well-run and comprehensive tour company. He speaks flawless English and knows virtually everything about the island, and thus is an excellent guide. He offers short guided tours or even week-long journeys with everything included. He is currently attempting to set up tours between islands in the Marquesas. His address is BP 82, Taiohae; in Tahiti, reservations can be made through Reve Tahitien Travel (☎ 41-05-24). He is highly recommended.

Other tour operators include Georges Taupotini at Pua Excursions Nuku Hiva (☎ 92-02-94, 92-04-18), BP 99, Taiohae; and Philippe Batallard of Charter Mana Iti (see boat tours, on previous page).

Activities
Horse Riding Louis and Sabine Teikiteetini (☎ 92-03-01, leave a message), have a variety of rides out of Taiohae, most in the day-long range, for 5000 to 6000 CFP. They also rent short-term: 1500 CFP per hour or

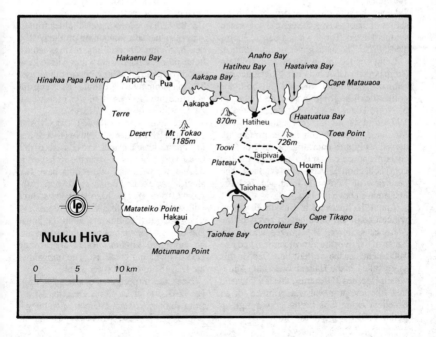

2500 CFP per half-day. Make sure you have raincoat, trousers, tennis shoes, insect repellent and warm clothing. Rates do not include food and lodging. Write to BP 171, Taiohae, Nuku Hiva for more information. Horses can also be obtained from Raymond Gendron and Roo Rootauhine in the village.

Getting Around

To/From the Airport A few km inland from the northern part of the west coast is the Nuku a Taha Airport – the most important in the Marquesas. To reach the main settlement of Taiohae you must take a 15-minute bus ride to the coast and then catch a boat from the coast almost halfway round the island. The boat ride lasts about an hour and 45 minutes.

Air Tahiti can be reached in Taiohae (☎ 92-03-41) or at the airport (☎ 92-01-45).

Taiohae

Taiohae, the administrative centre, is on the shores of Taiohae Bay, the central bay on the southern coast. The town has banks, shops, a post office and other government facilities.

Long visited by whalers and soldiers (from both the USA and France), Taiohae has remnants of an old fort and jail built for political exiles. There is also the Cathedral of Notre Dame, which was constructed in 1974 and is the largest church in the Marquesas. The church has magnificently carved sculptures adorning the interior. The Bishop's house contains a small (but still a gem) collection of Marquesan artefacts. The best view of Taiohae is from Muake Pass, 863 metres above the bay.

About 10 km west is Hakaui Bay, into which one of the three largest rivers of the Marquesas flows. The gorges above the banks of the river are almost vertical and rise 1000 metres on the western side. Deep in this same valley is the Hakaui Waterfall, Ahuii, which cascades 350 metres; this is a fantastic trek (the icy, primeval waters make for an excellent swim; look for the graves high up in the bluffs a few km into the walk).

Information General tourism information can be found in the Public Works Building, in front of the pier at Taiohae Bay. Ask for Debora Kimitete (☎ 92-03-72) or write to BP 38, Taiohae, Nuku Hiva, Marquesas. Maps are occasionally available – but only very occasionally. Kovivi's Restaurant also has tourist information.

Places to Stay *Hotel Moana Nui* (☎ 92-03-30; fax 92-00-02), c/o Felicite Kautai, BP 9, Taiohae, is one km from the dock and has four rooms with one large bed each, and three more rooms each with two small beds. Bathrooms are private and the cost including breakfast is US$30. Lunch or dinner is US$25.

The *Keikahahui Inn** (☎ and fax 92-03-82), c/o Frank Corser, BP 21, Taiohae, Nuku Hiva, is two km from the wharf and has three Polynesian-style bungalows with a view of the bay. Each bungalow has a large and a small bed, shower (hot water), bathroom and verandah. The cost including breakfast is US$85/125/165 for singles/doubles/triples. Activities include sunbathing on the nearby beach, diving, snorkelling, hiking, tennis, horse riding, village tours with visits to local wood sculptors and excursions to other bays. The inn is run by a US couple and is considered the premier resort in the Marquesas. And yes, they do accept VISA here.

Chez Fetu* (☎ 92-03-66), c/o Cyprien Peterano, BP 22, Taiohae, Nuku Hiva, is just 500 metres from the dock and consists of one house with four rooms – two rooms have one double bed each and two rooms have two singles each. The rooms share two bathrooms. There are also four bungalows, three with one room, the other with two rooms. All have individual bathrooms. Both the house and the bungalows have a living room and an equipped kitchen. Rates are around US$20 including breakfast. The bungalows are US$450 to US$500 per month.

Near the airport is the *Moetai Village* (☎ 92-04-91) at La Terre Deserte, 32 km from Taiohae Village. There are five bungalows, four with three twin beds and bath, one with four twins. The rates including breakfast are US$25/35/45 for singles/ doubles/ triples. Each extra person costs US$10. Meals are US$18 for lunch or dinner.

Places to Eat *Kovivi's Restaurant* is about 500 metres from the Taiohae Bay pier. Lunch is US$10 to US$15, dinner up to US$30. It has tourist information but is closed on Saturday mornings and Sundays. With reservations, you can also eat at *Keikahanui Inn* or *Moana Nui*. *Snack Pakiu*, about 500 metres from the market on the waterfront street of Taiohae Bay, has meals in the US$8 range. *Snack Celine*, near the Catholic Mission 1½ km from the dock, has daily specials from 800 CFP or meals in the 2000 CFP range. There are also food trucks on the main waterfront drag in Taiohae, with dishes from 800 CFP.

Toovi Plateau

The central portion of the island is dominated by the fertile Toovi Plateau. The plateau is rich in flora and fauna and the government has an agricultural station which tests potential crops and tree-planting projects. The Muake Pass also overlooks Taiohae Bay from the plateau.

The Coast

The west coast is high, rocky and dry; the eastern side of the island is a formidable line of sheer cliffs. Tucked away in the Taipivai Valley, just west of the coast, are many old temples, or paepae, and large tikis. It is perhaps the most beautiful valley in the Marquesas and was where Herman Melville sojourned in 1842 after deserting his whaler.

The northern bays, accessible by boat and in some cases by 4WD vehicle, are also spectacular and some have beaches. Many Marquesans (and this author) regard Anaho Bay as the best bay by far in the Marquesas – the snorkelling is stunning. The stretch of coast between this bay and Pua, 15 km from the airport, is amazing. (The Pua area itself is still often regarded as *tabu* by the locals.)

The landscape sloping down from the plateau is volcanic and almost lunar in texture. The village of Hatiheu, on Hatiheu Bay, provides accommodation, horse riding and boating excursions in the area. (There are some good petroglyphs around; on a lucky day, one of the many friendly archaeologists working in the area might give you a fascinating lecture on how much we really don't know about the Marquesas.) Note the statue of the Virgin Mary atop the bluffs overlooking Hatiheu.

Places to Stay In Hatihue, *Chez Yvonne** (☎ 92-02-97) is about an hour's boat ride (25 km) from the airport of Nuku a Taha and is two hours by road from Taiohae. The accommodation consists of three bungalows – all doubles – but no hot water. Rates including breakfast are 1800 CFP per person. Yvonne's has a good restaurant and the place also comes highly recommended by the locals.

Pension Clarisse Omatai is 29 km by mountain road from Taiohae Village. There are two bungalows with facilities in each for two people and private bath (no hot water). Activities include boat trips, horse riding and hikes to visit tikis. Rates are approximately 1500 CFP.

In Anaho, at the time of writing *Pension Anaho* (☎ 92-01-46) was temporarily closed for remodelling. It has five sparse but comfortable bungalows right on the beach at Anaho Bay. Upon reopening, the prices should be in the 2000 CFP range. Contact Rose-Marie Foucaud, Anaho, Nuku Hiva.

UA HUKA

Ua Huka is 1448 km north-east of Papeete. It is around 80 sq km in area, with a population of about 500. Ua Huka is believed to have the oldest archaeological sites in the Marquesas and scientists postulate that it was the dispersal point for settlement of the archipelago. It was never popular with early traders due to the lack of sandalwood and protected anchorage, but today its tiny airstrip is serviced once a week for connections to other Marquesas Islands and Tahiti. On Ua Huka numerous wild horses and goats run free and sometimes pilots must be wary of horses grazing near the runway.

The island's main attractions are the ruins in the Hane Valley, which are ancient tikis believed to be some type of peace offering between warring groups, the view from the high plateau, and excursions to Vaikivi Valley and bird islands near Invisible Bay on the southern coast. All the lazy, friendly villages (Hane, Hokatu, Vaipaee and Haavai) are on the southern coast and have accommodation. Vaipaee also has an interesting archaeological museum a ways inland from the boat landing. The island is famous for its woodcarvers, and offshore lobster and fish are plentiful. The highest point is Mt Hitikau at 855 metres. For an eye-popping sight be around when the *Aranui* snakes its way into lovely little Vaipaee Bay and turns completely around, with literally inches to spare.

Air Tahiti can be reached at 92-60-13 during the week.

Organised Tours
Car In Vaipaee, Marcel Paro (☎ 92-60-24) offers guided tours in his Toyota 4WD for around US$100 and up. Contact Joseph Lichtle (☎ 92-60-72) in Haavai Village; he offers a good number of excursions, both land and sea (see Haavai, in the Places to Stay section).

Boat Georges Brown (☎ 92-60-17, evenings) and Joseph Lichtle also rent out boats with drivers. Lichtle offers many destinations. Eugene Fournier (☎ 92-60-04) also rents out a boat with a guide, weather permitting.

Places to Stay
Vaipaee *Chez Tati Laura* (☎ 92-60-22) is a house with three rooms, each with double bed, electricity, communal kitchen and bathroom with hot water. Daily costs are 3500 CFP per person with meals or 1200 CFP without meals. Breakfast is 300 CFP, lunch or dinner 1000 CFP.

Chez Alexis Scallamera (☎ 92-60-19) is a four-room house, each room with one double and one single bed, sharing two communal bathrooms. A room is dirt-cheap at 1000 CFP without meals, or 3000 CFP with meals.

Hane *Auberge Hitikau** (☎ 92-60-68) is seven km from the airport and consists of a duplex home with four rooms, each with double bed. There is a communal bath, a restaurant/bar and excellent excursions to the valleys and to Bird Island, a bird sanctuary. The Hane Valley tikis are a humid 45-minute uphill climb through some at times thick forest. Rates are 2000/3000 CFP for single/doubles for room only, or 5500 CFP per person with meals. Breakfast is 500 CFP and lunch or dinner is 1500 CFP. This is recommended accommodation. Contact Celine Fournier, Hane.

Hokatu *Chez Maurice et Delphine** (☎ 92-60-55) is seven km from the airport and offers a house with three rooms, each with a double bed. There is an equipped kitchen and two bathrooms with hot water, a salon with sofas, and a terrace with a great mountain and ocean view. Rates are 1500 CFP for room only, or 3500 CFP with meals.

Ua Huka

0   5   10 km

Haavai *Chez Joseph Lichtle* (☎ 92-60-72) is close to a nice white-sand beach with good swimming, five km from the nearest settlement. He has a small archaeological display with many Marquesan artefacts. The owner is the only person living in the valley and has a farm with fresh vegetables, fruit, cattle, pigs, chickens and ducks. He has two bungalows, each with double bed, private bathroom, electricity and a terrace with a good ocean view. In addition there are two houses, each with three rooms (double beds), common kitchens and bathrooms. The daily cost including meals is 4500 CFP per person. Horse riding is available for 1500 CFP per day and there are excursions to Bird Island, which is just offshore.

Getting Around

Boat Paul Teatiu (☎ 92-60-54) offers inter-island transport to Nuku Hiva or Ua Pou – starting at US$400 for a maximum of seven passengers.

Horse This is the best way to get around the island. Joseph Lichtle rents out horses, as do Alexis Fournier (☎ 92-60-05), and Georges Brown (☎ 92-60-17, evenings), who charges 2500 CFP for half a day and 5000 CFP for a whole day.

HIVA OA

Hiva Oa is 1433 km north-east of Papeete and perhaps is best known as the burial place of the painter Paul Gauguin. The island was

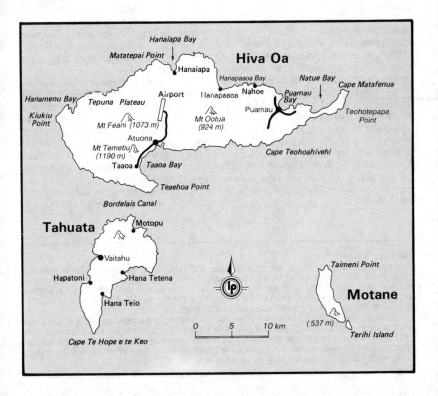

originally named Sunday Island by Mendana when he discovered it on a Sunday in 1595. Almost 300 years later, Robert Louis Stevenson said of the island, 'I thought it the loveliest, and by far the most ominous spot on earth'. To this day it still retains the paradox of wild beauty and sombre bearing. Very little of the island's 320 sq km is flat, but an airport has been laboriously constructed on a ridge above Atuona. The highest point on the island is Mt Temetiu, at 1190 metres.

Things to Buy

Those interested in purchasing sculptures or precious woods from Marquesan forests such as tou, sandalwood and miro (rosewood) can contact Guy Huhina in Puamau. To buy woven baskets contact Germaine Timuamoea in Hanapaaoa. In Atuona see Jeanine Moreau.

Getting Around

Car Rental David's Rent-a-Car (☎ 92-72-87) is approximately 300 metres beyond the cluster of buildings including the post office in Atuona. There are two 4WDs available for hire – without drivers! – for 8500 CFP per journey, with air-con and unlimited mileage, or 7000 CFP without air-con.

Romeo Ciantar (☎ 92-74-55), outside Atuona about a third of the way to Taaoa, has a wider selection of Suzuki Samurais and double-cabin 4WDs beginning at 4000 CFP per trip plus 35 CFP per km. Here you can be your own driver. The place is even building a snack-bar.

Boat Ozanne Rohi (☎ 92-73-43, 92-74-65, ask for Marie-Louise) in Atuona has trips around the island for US$200 and up, or interisland transfers for lots of money.

Atuona

The main settlement of Atuona, the second largest town in the Marquesas, has the only safe bay on Hiva Oa, created by the flooding of a tremendous crater. Towering 1190 metres above this is Mt Temetiu. The largest building in town is the boarding school for girls, run by the sisters of St Joseph of Cluny. There are also three stores, a hospital and dentist's office, two banks, two restaurants and a variety of accommodation possibilities with the locals.

The population of Atuona is about 1700, only a vestige of the large population the island once had. Many homes are built on the foundations of paepae. At one time there were many large tikis on the island but most of those that were within easy reach of the town have now been scattered to museums all over the world.

Near Gauguin's grave is the tomb of French singer Jacques Brel, who also spent his last years on Hiva Oa and died in 1978. (For more information on Gauguin see the Tahiti chapter.) There is a large archaeological reconstruction of a village in Upeke Valley, halfway between Atuona and Taaoa – take your mosquito repellent and get ready to suck humidity.

Air Tahiti can be reached in Atuona (☎ 92-73-41) or at the airport (☎ 92-72-31).

Gauguin's Death

Atuona's most famous resident was Paul Gauguin, who came to the island in 1902 from Tahiti and died here in 1903. He is buried on a hill that overlooks the village. On his tomb is a replica of his ceramic work, Oviri, which translates from Marquesan as 'the savage' and symbolises the goddess of death, mourning and destruction. Nothing remains of the home he built – his 'Maison du Jouir' (House of Pleasure). Only the well where he drew his water still exists.

In Atuona, Gauguin learned from the locals how to carve wood, but found no peace on the island. He was constantly at odds with the local gendarme and priest, who looked on with displeasure at his drinking orgies with the natives. Meanwhile, the humid, sweltering climate intensified the suffering caused by the venereal disease he had contracted in Paris years before. When he died, the villagers wept, while the gendarme and the priest sighed in relief. ■

Places to Stay The *Atuona Commune Bungalows* (☎ 92-73-37, fax 92-74-95), Maire d'Atuona, BP 18, Village of Atuona, Hiva Oa, has three small bungalows, each with double bed, shower, bathroom, electricity, refrigerator and hot plate. In addition there are two larger double bungalows, each with two rooms, two double beds, shower, bathroom, gas stove and verandah. Daily rates for the small bungalows are approximately US$18/22 for single/doubles and for the larger bungalows are US$15/19. Meals are not included in the price.

Saucort's Bungalow (☎ 92-73-33) consists of one large bungalow with double bed, dining room, kitchen, bathroom and electricity. The cost is approximately US$30 without meals.

Temetiu Village (☎ 92-73-02), BP 52, Hiva Oa, is one km from Atuona and has three bungalows – one with a single bed, one with a double bed, and the third with two rooms of three singles each. All have private bath. There is a restaurant/bar on the premises, specialising in lobster and...goat. A room with breakfast is 3000 CFP. Dinner is 1500 CFP.

Hotel Maire* (☎ 92-74-550), BP 75, Hiva Oa, is in the 'wilds', near the base of the hills between Atuona and Taaoa, not far from the ocean. Two bungalows are presently available; another four are anticipated. The two bungalows each have one double, kitchenette, private bath, a salon with another single bed, and a terrace. The rates are 5500/6500 CFP for doubles/triples with all meals.

Chez Andre Teissier (☎ 92-73-51), BP 34, Hiva Oa, is near Atuona. It comprises a two-storey building with six double rooms sharing three communal baths with hot water, a salon and a large terrace with an ocean view. A room is 3500 CFP; meals are an extra 2100 CFP.

Places to Eat *Restaurant/Bar Bonna* has 'local' fare, as does *Restaurant Hoa Nui*, which has a good reputation and meals starting at 1000 CFP. *Snack Atuona* is across the street from the post office and has meals for between US$8 and US$12. *Snack Maire* has

dishes for 200 to 1000 CFP. *Snack MakeMake* specialises in Chinese food.

Around the Coast
On the north-east coast near the village of Puamau are the largest stone sculptures in the Marquesas, considered to be archaeological links to the tikis on Easter Island and those of Necker Island near Hawaii. They are a sweaty 30-minute walk inland from the small Puamau dock, and nearby is the final resting place of Tehau Moena, a last queen in the Marquesas, who was, oddly enough, buried here with her bike. Accommodation is available in Puamau and overland excursions can be made to the tikis from the main community of Atuona. Hanaiapa Village is another of those subtly eye-catching little Marquesan hamlets.

Places to Stay In Puamau, *Chez Bernard Heitaa* (☎ 92-72-27) has a house with two rooms with double beds, electricity, common bathroom and kitchen. Daily rates are approximately US$30 per person with meals or US$15 without meals. Lunch or dinner is US$15 per meal. Mr Heitaa also has excursions to the famous tikis of Puamau by land rover.

TAHUATA
Only 55 sq km in area, Tahuata is south of the Bordelais Canal opposite Hiva Oa. It is popular mainly with visiting yachts because the island is accessible only by boat.

A small church, post office, clinic, store and handful of dwellings are all that make up the main village of Vaitahu and serve the 550 inhabitants. There are archaeological sites here and petroglyphs in the Hanatahua Valley, which can be reached by the *Tamanu*, a boat that sails from Vaitahu, or via horseback from Hapatoni. Hapatoni is a picturesque and friendly village by the sea, and is only 15 minutes by boat from Vaitahu. The seafront road in Hapatoni is made almost entirely from ancient paved stones. The road is shaded by tamanu trees, which are often used in wood carving. There are also monuments to the 1842 battle between the French and the Marquesans. All the villages have local wood sculptors selling their wares; in Vaitahu see Edwin Fii or Sebastien Barsinas (aka Kehu).

The highest point on the island is the summit of Tumu Maea Ufu, at 472 metres. The northern side of the island has some nice white-sand beaches.

Places to Stay & Eat
The *Chez Naani Barsinas* (☎ 92-92-26) is a house with four rooms: two have a double and a single bed, two have two singles. The daily cost including meals is 3500 CFP per person, or 1500 CFP for room only. This is also the local restaurant.

Getting Around
Boat There is a regular (twice-weekly, Thursday and Friday) boat service from Atuona (in Hiva Oa) to Tahuata. Before leaving Atuona it is advisable to notify the Mayor of Tahuata of your arrival 24 hours in advance: Commune de Tahuata (☎ 92-92-19/20). The communal boat that operates between the two islands holds a maximum of 15 passengers and departs from the Atuona quay for the one-hour voyage. The round trip costs about 3000 CFP; renting this same boat costs 15,000 CFP.

Nicolas Barsinas is in Vaitahu Village on Tahuata and also takes passengers between the two islands; he can take four to six passengers. The round-trip price is 8800 CFP. He also offers tours of Tahuata island for 10,000 CFP.

Other local boat operators on Tahuata include Victor Teikipupuni, Vaitahu (☎ 92-92-25); Celestin Teikipupuni, Vaitahu (☎ 92-92-13); and Louis Timau, Vaitahu.

Motorised outriggers (without drivers) are available from Tehoho Burns in Vaitahu; he will also give short tours of the bays for 3000 CFP per boat.

For yachtees, fuel can be purchased in 750 ml bottles for approximately 3000 to 3500 CFP. In Vaitahu see Henriette Putatoutaki, Marie-Therese Vaki or Namauefitu Timau; in Hapatoni see Titioutu Teikipupuni.

Car Rental/Horse There are no official rental opportunities for either cars or horses; asking a local will probably bring results, however.

FATU HIVA
The 80-sq km island of Fatu Hiva was once famous for its tattoo artists and an islander's body might be tattooed completely by the time they died. Unfortunately this great art went with them to the grave. Today Fatu Hiva is the only island in the Marquesas where tapa cloth, produced from the bark of mulberry or breadfruit trees, is regularly made. (It's not too expensive, either.) Local artisans also carve wooden tikis and manufacture *monoi*, a perfumed coconut oil with fragrances derived from tiare blossoms and sandalwood.

Fatu Hiva is famous for its own variety of monoi, called *umu hei*, blended with seven herbs, sandalwood, tiare Tahiti, *pitate* (a small, fragrant white flower) and ylang ylang flower. The fragrant oil is used as perfume, for massages, to ward off mosquitoes or to seduce a lover.

There are two principal valleys – Hanavave and Omoa – on the western coast and each have several paepae. Hanavave Village, located on the Bay of Virgins, is particularly lovely, and a wonderful trek (for those in better shape) is the serpentine wander here from Omoa – 17 km of verdant splendour, dizzying views, and even the majestic waterfall visible from the path deep inside Vaieenui Valley. Take water and give yourself four or more hours for the journey (a couple of days if you go into the valley, because you'll fall in love with it and stay, I guarantee you; note the intriguing 'hole' in the top of the bluffs). Nature has blessed Fatu Hiva with more rain than any other island in the Marquesas, giving it a land and seascape that a Tahitian described to me as 'shockingly beautiful'.

The population of the island is about 500. The highest point on Fatu Hiva is Mt Touaouoho, at 960 metres. Activities include horse riding, wild pig hunting and visits to the archaeological sites in Omoa and

Hanavave. Contact the mairie (town hall) for further information.

Thor Heyerdahl (of *Kon-Tiki* fame) spent most of 1936 on Fatu Hiva and wrote a book of the same name about his time here.

History

Fatu Hiva was the first island to be discovered by Europeans, who wasted no time in showing their true colours. Don Alvaro Mendana's visit of 21 July 1595 ended in a bloody massacre of 200 Marquesans shortly after meeting them. Apparently the Marquesans had come aboard the Spaniard's boat and perhaps became too bold for the Europeans' sensibilities. The 'natives' were warned with a few shots and when they fled the Spanish followed, murdering all they could find. As a 'gift' the Spanish left behind three large crucifixes and carved the date in a tree. The first meeting was a fitting preamble to the horrors of venereal disease, rum, kidnapping and all the other delights of civilisation which were to be bestowed on the lucky Marquesans in future years.

Although lacking good anchorages the island was popular with whalers in the mid-19th century. This was due to the fact that it was well away from the authorities' eyes and visitors could debauch and raise hell without interference.

Places to Stay

Nearly every accommodation place on Fatu Hiva (as in nearly all of the Marquesas) is very spartan – in short, don't expect a lot of creature comforts.

Omoa *Chez Joseph Tetuanui* (☎ 92-80-09) is a house with two rooms and an equipped kitchen, and charges 1500 CFP without meals. He offers tours in his 4WD.

Chez Lionel Cantois (☎ 92-80-04/05) is a four-person bungalow with a kitchenette and private bathroom. Rates without meals are 1000 CFP or 25,000 CFP per month. He also hires out himself and his land rover for tours for 7000 CFP.

Both the *Chez Marie Claire Ehueiana* (☎ 92-80-16) and the *Chez Cecile Gilmore*

(☎ 92-80-54) are houses with two rooms with double beds and common baths. Marie charges 1500 CFP without meals or 35,000 CFP per month. Cecile offers a room and all meals for 3500 CFP, or 2000 CFP for the room alone.

Chez Norma Ropati (☎ 92-80-13) offers four rooms in a house, each with a double bed and common bath. Rates are 4000 CFP with all meals, 1500 CFP without meals, or 30,000 CFP per month.

Hanavave *Chez Veronique Kamia* (☎ 92-80-56) is a house with two rooms for 2000 CFP with meals or 35,000 CFP per month. *Chez Jacques Tevenino* has just one room at a cost of 1500 CFP. Nearby are orange, grapefruit and banana trees, and coffee plants. Tapa cloth and sandalwood oil processing can be observed by visitors. *Chez Tutai*

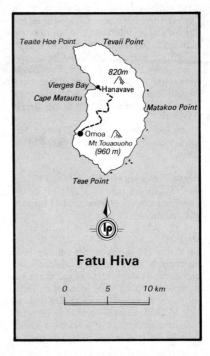

Fatu Hiva

Koheinui has a room in the family home for 1000 CFP without meals. Ahutoui Tevenino may also have lodgings, if necessary.

Places to Eat
In Omoa, *Chez Mme Vaea Ropati* has breakfast for 500 CFP and lunch or dinner for 1000 CFP. *Chez Mme Bernadette Cantois* is a snack place offering dishes for 500 to 700 CFP.

Getting Around
The island is accessible by regular boat service from Hiva Oa, but there is no airstrip. The 3½-hour boat trip costs 3000 CFP. The boat leaves on Thursday mornings at around 4 am and is supposed to return from Hiva Oa at 3 pm the following day. Travel from Omoa to Hanavave Villages costs at least 500 CFP. A complete tour of the island by boat costs 10,000 CFP.

Boat Motorised outriggers are available in Omoa from either Xavier Gilmore or Edwin Tametona (☎ 92-80-54). A round trip between Omoa and Hanavave is 4000 CFP; tours of the island are 10,000 CFP.

Fuel for yachters is available from Maria Siegel (☎ 92-80-10), Ivanna Tametona, Oumati Rohi, or Teri Vaki. A 750 ml bottle generally costs between 3000 and 5000 CFP.

Truck Roger Kamia (☎ 92-80-07) also offers truck tours of the island for 7000 CFP or more.

Horse Horses are available in Omoa Village for 500 CFP per hour or 5500 CFP for the day. For more information contact Roberto Maraetaata.

UA POU
Ua Pou is 110 sq km in area and has 1900 residents. It has a jagged, scarp-like relief and six main valleys. Mt Oave (1232 metres) is the highest point in the Marquesas. There are seven organised places to stay and the administrative area near the airport, Hakahau, has quite a few shops, a clinic, hospital and post office. Every other settlement (Hakatao, Hohoi, Haakuti, Hakamaii) is lucky to have one shop, except for Hakahetau and Hakamui, which have four. The islanders fashion stone and wood carvings and weave hats and mats for a small income. The best way to spend time on Ua Pou, says the intrepid David Harcombe, author of Lonely Planet's *Solomon Islands – a travel survival kit*, is 'horseback riding along the track that circles the island'. Up and over the bluffs from the docks at Hakahau is a beautiful little secluded beach – but watch out for the no-nos (gnats). The small beach at Hohoi is purported to have 'flowering stones'. The islet Motu Ua off the southern coast is another sanctuary for thousands of nesting birds.

Air Tahiti can be reached at 92-53-41.

Organised Tours
Christian Kervella (☎ 92-51-25, fax 92-53-89), BP 8, Hakahau, operates *Excursions Guides*, offering motorised tours and treks. He has a long list of possibilities, including an interesting-looking eight-day trek for US$840, everything included. His other tours start at US$20 per person and range upward.

Places to Stay
Hakahau *Chez Marguerite Dordillon* (☎ 92-53-15), 300 metres from the dock and 10 km from the airport, consists of a two-bedroom home with a double in one room and two singles in the other. There is a large living room and communal bath. Rates are 2000 CFP. Contact Marguerite at BP 17, Ua Pou.

Chez Rosalie Tata (☎ 92-53-11) is just a few blocks from the waterfront. Rosalie has one room with twin beds in a large family home, which the visitor shares. She also has a restaurant in her home. Rates are around US$15. Meals range from US$5 for breakfast to US$15 for lunch or dinner.

Chez Samuel & Jeanne-Marie (☎ 92-53-16), BP 19, Ua Pou, is one km from the dock, eight km from the airport and consists of two buildings; each has two bedrooms, all with a double bed, kitchen, and individual bath. Rates with meals are around 6000 CFP, depending on which room is rented. If staying just one night, add 500 CFP.

Pension Vaikaka (☎ 92-53-37, ask for Tina or Vero) is two km from the dock, 13 km from the airport, and offers absolutely no frills, with its two single mattresses with private bath in a traditional-style bungalow. Rates with meals are approximately 5500 CFP; deals are given for stays of four days or more and for groups. Contact Valja Klima, BP 16, Ua Pou.

Chez Dora* (☎ 92-53-69) is one km from the dock and has a house with two rooms, one with a double bed, the other with two single beds. There are private baths and an equipped kitchen. Rooms cost 2000/3000 CFP for singles/doubles. Contact Dora Teikiehuupoko, Hakahau.

Chez Guy Hikutini (☎ 92-53-08), BP 7, Hakahau, Ua Pou, offers a house with three rooms, each with a double bed. There are two bathrooms and an equipped kitchen. Rates are 1500/2000 CFP for singles/doubles, with special rates for extended stays.

Hohoi *Pension Puanea* (☎ 92-51-32) is in the mountains, 13 km from the docks and eight km from the airport. It comprises a wooden house with two rooms, each with a double mattress. There are also two single mattresses outside on a mezzanine. Bathrooms are 'Polynesian style' and outside, as are the showers. There is also an equipped kitchen. The terrace offers a view of both the village and the ocean. Rates for the first three nights with meals are 3000/5000 CFP per night for singles/doubles, dropping by 500/1000 CFP per night after that.

Places to Eat

In Hakahau there are a few inexpensive eateries – *Chez Rosalie Tata*, *Snack Vehine*, *Snack Havaiki* and *Chez Adrienne*. Prices range from US$5 to US$8 for breakfast and US$20 to US$25 for lunch or dinner. Chez Adrienne also offers takeaway plates in the 800 CFP range.

Getting Around

Car There is now no shortage of transport possibilities in Ua Pou. Road conditions necessitate a local driver and prices (which include driver and fuel) start no lower than US$20 per person, US$100 for the vehicle, for the shortest trip offered. A few of the many offering their (usually) 4WDs are: Edouard Bruneau (☎ 92-53-51); Ferdinand Bruneau and Gerard Hapipi (☎ 92-53-22, leave message); Joseph Tamarii (☎ 92-52-14); and Frederic and Julien Tissot (☎ 92-53-54).

Boat Boats (with drivers) are also available, some even offering interisland transport to Nuku Hiva or Ua Huka. Rudly Klima (☎ 92-53-37/86) offers fishing trips or interisland transport aboard his 8½-metre boat. Rates to Nuku Hiva start at US$350 for the one-hour crossing; Ua Huka takes 2½ hours and costs US$400. A short fishing expedition starts at US$350. Alain Alho (☎ 92-52-80, evenings)

Airport
Hakahetau Hakahau Motu Mokoe
Punahu Point
Haakuti Hakamui
Mt Oave
(1232 m)
Hakamaii
Hohoi
Hakatao

Motu Takahe
Motu Ua

Ua Pou

0   5   10 km

is in Hakatao Village and offers interisland transport at similar prices. Hakatao's community boat can also be hired for tours of the island for US$150 or interisland jaunts at cheaper prices than those above. Contact Etienne Kohumoetini (☎ 92-53-17/24). Other boat operators are Felix Taata (☎ 92-53-39, evenings) and Ruka Kaiha (☎ 92-53-30, leave a message).

Horse Horses are available for rent from Albert and Atere Kohumoetini (☎ 92-52-28) or Francis Aka. Tours are also possible. Rates start at 500 CFP per hour.

The Australs
&
The Gambiers

The Australs & The Gambiers

These archipelagos are the outermost and least visited islands in French Polynesia. Lying near the Tropic of Capricorn, they are also the most temperate.

The Austral Islands

The Austral Islands lie about 600 km south of Tahiti and consist of five high islands (Tubuai, Rimatara, Rurutu, Raivavae and Rapa) and two atolls (Hull and Bass). The islands are of volcanic origin and are not very high (100 to 200 metres), except for Rapa, the highest point of which is 1460 metres. Rapa, the farthest south, is sometimes called Rapa Iti (Little Rapa) to differentiate it from Rapa Nui, the Polynesian name for Easter Island. Tubuai (accessible by air) is the administrative centre of the Australs and offers accommodation with local families. Rurutu (also accessible by air) has the only modern hotel in the entire region. A number of new pensions and small lodgings have opened up in Tubuai as well as the far flung islands of Rapa, Rimatara and Raivavae, where heretofore no public accommodation existed.

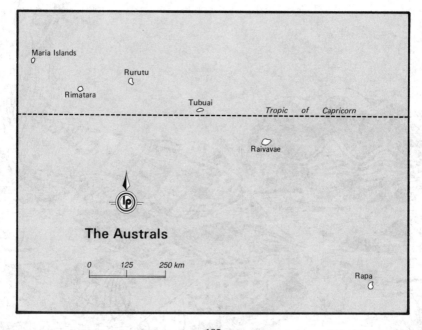

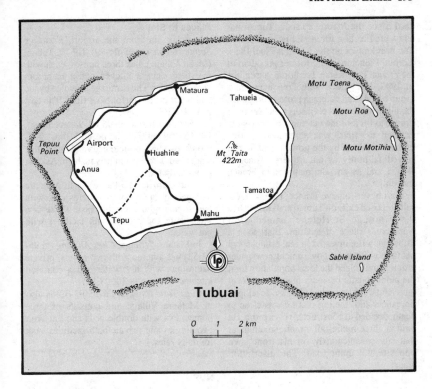

Tubuai

0   1   2 km

GETTING THERE & AWAY

An air service operates on Mondays and Fridays to Tubuai and Rurutu from Papeete, Raiatea and Moorea. The flight time is a little under two hours. There is no air service to Rapa, however. The fare is 19,450 CFP one-way to Tubuai and 17,350 CFP one-way to Rurutu.

The Australs are served by the 60-metre *Tuhaa Pae II* (☎ 42-93-67), BP 1890, Motu Uta, Papeete. The itinerary is Rimatara/Rurutu/Tubuai/Raivavae and also Rapa (occasionally), and Maria (once or twice a year). The round-trip voyage, which takes 15 days, costs 22,750 CFP. Food is an extra 2300 CFP per day for 'pension complete.' One-way passage from Papeete to Tubuai costs 2800/3920/4900 CFP for deck/bunk/cabin.

TUBUAI

Discovered by Cook in 1777, Tubuai is the largest of the Austral Islands and lies 670 km south of Papeete, with a population of about 1400. The climate is temperate and it has a windswept, desolate beauty. The white-sand beaches, fishing and horse riding provide the main diversions.

History

In 1789 Tubuai was the first settlement of the HMS *Bounty*'s mutinous crew, who called their outpost Fort George. After six months of considerable bloodshed between the natives and the mutineers, the Englishmen decided to leave and eventually settled on Pitcairn Island. All that remains of Fort George today is a rectangular ditch where the walls of the stockade used to be.

Illari Since the *Bounty* episode, Tubuai has had a predilection for attracting expatriates. The best known on the island is Noel Illari, a proud Frenchman and former president of the French Polynesian Territorial Assembly. In 1947, Illari sided with Pouvanaa and a group of Tahitian veterans protesting against the hiring of several civil servants sent from France to fill jobs the veterans felt they were entitled to. Illari was sentenced to five months in prison by the government he had served faithfully as an artillery officer in WW I and as an administrator in French Indochina.

Illari never forgave France. He became a self-imposed exile on Tubuai and established the Ermitage St Helene, named after Napoleon's place of asylum. Illari took a Tubuaian wife, invested in real estate, spent his time writing antigovernment newspaper articles, and helped the local population fight the monopolistic business practices of local merchants. In the early 1970s he developed lip cancer and, feeling that he was close to death, decided to construct his own tomb. He built a three-metre-tall granite monument that sits conspicuously on his front lawn opposite the main road. The inscription reads:

In memory of Noel Illari
Born in Rennese, France
11 September, 1897
died faithful to his God
to family and to his ideals
to his grateful country
after long years of moral suffering
within isolation and solitude at this place
Passersby, think and pray for him.

Next to the tomb is a sign that says:

Interdite aux Chiens et aux Gaullists
(Dogs and Gaullists forbidden)

Illari never succumbed to cancer but died just recently, years after the tomb was constructed. His widow rents out the best accommodation on the island.

Places to Stay
About six km from the airport, *Ermitage Sainte Helene* (☎ 95-04-79), BP 79, Tubuai (Mahu Village), has three houses, each with two bedrooms, a kitchen and a bathroom with hot water. The Ermitage is owned by the widow of the colourful Noel Illari. The cost is 3500 CFP.

Chez Terii Turina (☎ 95-04-98, evenings), BP 16, Tubuai, is a home with three bedrooms, two with double beds and one with a single bed, kitchen and private bath. Ask her about daily rates.

Chez Caro (☎ 95-03-78) is in Mataura Village and consists of two homes, each with two rooms with a double bed. There is a kitchenette and private bath facilities with hot water.

In Mataura Village, *Chez Ah Sing* (☎ 95-03-52) has a home with two rooms, private bathrooms with hot water and a common kitchen. The cost is 3000 CFP.

Chez Taro Tanepau (☎ 95-03-82) is also in Mataura Village and consists of three homes, two with double beds and one with two singles and private bath facilities. Ask for daily rates.

RURUTU
Rurutu is 572 km south of Papeete. It has a dry and temperate climate, especially in June, July and August. The population of this seldom-visited island is nearly 2000. The outstanding physical surroundings feature white-sand beaches which lie near the foot of mountains thick with vegetation.

Rurutu was discovered in 1769 by Captain Cook, and the navigator Eric de Bishop spent the last years of his life here. Archaeological finds on Rurutu suggest that the island was settled from the Society Islands in about 1100 AD. Though each island developed its own cultural distinctions, there was trade and contact between the Australs and the Society Islands, the Tuamotus and the Cooks. Today, much of the fine plaitwork available in Tahiti is done by natives of Rurutu living in Tahiti. Rurutu is renowned for its fine woven hats and mats.

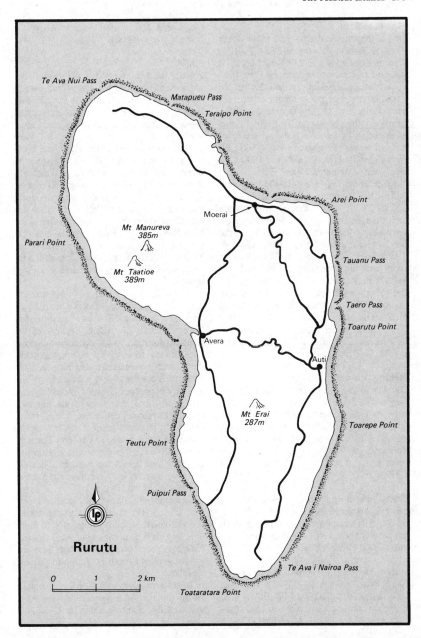

Te Ava Nui Pass

Matapueu Pass

Teraipo Point

Arei Point

Moerai

Mt Manureva
385m

Parari Point

Mt Taatioe
389m

Tauanu Pass

Taero Pass

Toarutu Point

Avera

Auti

Mt Erai
287m

Toarepe Point

Teutu Point

Puipui Pass

Rurutu

Te Ava i Nairoa Pass

0   1   2 km

Toataratara Point

Places to Stay

One of the more isolated hotels in the South Pacific is *Rurutu Village* (☎ 94-03-92), BP 6, Rurutu. Located near a white-sand beach, it has nine bungalows, constructed from fired coral blocks and bamboo. Amenities include a restaurant, bar, pool, tennis court, reef excursions and library (which comes in handy in this backwater setting). Rooms have one or two double beds, private toilet and hot water. The rates are 4500/5500 CFP for singles/doubles. Breakfast is 1000 CFP and lunch or dinner is 2500 CFP.

Chez Catherine (☎ 94-02-43) in Moerai Village has 10 rooms, five with double beds and five with two singles, all with private bathroom and hot water. The owners also have a bungalow in a separate location on the beach with one large room containing two double beds and two single beds, and another room with six cots. The unit also has two baths with hot water. There is a restaurant on the premises of the hotel. The rates are 10,000 CFP per person per day including meals. The price for the bungalow is 5000 CFP. The tariff for the room is 3000/5000 CFP for singles/doubles. 'Pension complete' is 6500 CFP per person.

Getting Around

Car M and Mme Iareta and Madeline Moeau (☎ 94-03-92) have a Nissan vehicle with capacity for seven passengers for round the island tours (for 12,000 CFP) and visits to points of interest (for 3500 CFP). Raymond Toomaru (☎ 94-02-43) has a 4WD land rover and will take you on a tour for 5000 CFP.

Boat Those needing ocean-going transport can call Haelemu Poetai (☎ 94-04-31, 94-03-58). His vessel accommodates up to 10 people and his services as a skipper will cost you 60,000 CFP per day.

Horse The horsy set will want to call Nicodem Atai (☎ 94-03-05), who has animals for rent at 10,000 CFP per day and, if you are interested, can take you on a horse-back tour of the island. M and Mme Iareta (see Car Rental, above) can also get you a horse if you want one.

RAPA

Perhaps the most isolated of all French Polynesia, Rapa lies 1074 km south-south-east of Tahiti. The island's terrain is rugged and barren, with grey cliffs of up to 300 metres towering over the sparsely covered landscape, which is home to about 500-plus people and plenty of goats. The island once had a volcano, which has since collapsed at its centre. There are six peaks, of which Mt Perehau is the tallest, reaching 650 metres above the island. The island has many deep caves and valleys, some of which open to the sea. These valleys comprise the 12 fjord-like bays that cleave deeply into the island's perimeter. During the days of the mail boats between Australia, New Zealand and Panama, one such bay served as a coaling station.

Boats visit Rapa infrequently and accommodation depends on whoever happens to open their home up. Thanks to government largess there is electricity. Because of its southerly location, in mid-winter the climate is positively freezing by Polynesian standards, with temperatures dropping to 5°C. The soil is comparatively poor on Rapa but a variety of produce is grown, including taro (the staple), peaches, passionfruit, figs and excellent coffee. Despite the home-grown coffee, the islanders seem to prefer Nescafé – they ship the beans to Papeete. There is abundant seafood in the waters and on the shoreline, and the Rapans eat a great deal of mussels, oysters, crab, shrimp, sea urchin and lobster, as well as goat.

Unfortunately, Rapa is difficult to reach (and to leave) because there is no airport and boats call on the island infrequently. In addition, Rapa is in a military zone, which means visitors require special permission from the government of French Polynesia to stay on the island.

To get permission to stay on Rapa, contact the Subdivision Administration des Îles Australes, BP 847, Papeete, Tahiti (☎ 42-20-20). Good luck.

History

Historically, Rapa has a strong Polynesian connection to Easter Island. 'Discovered' (but not claimed for Britain) in 1791 by the great explorer George Vancouver, Rapa is sometimes called Rapa Iti to distinguish it from Rapa Nui, otherwise known as Easter Island. The island has robust *pa*, fortifications constructed by its former Polynesian residents – dozens of terraces on steep cliffs supported by walls built with basalt blocks piled on top of each other. Carbon-14 dating indicates that there were approximately 2000 to 3000 inhabitants in the 18th century. Subsequent epidemics from the first ships quickly decimated the local population.

France established it as a protectorate in 1867 and annexed the island in 1881. Long negotiations with Britain were inconclusive in resolving the issue of ownership, though New Zealand hoped that France would cede Rapa to Britain so that it could become an entrepôt between New Zealand and Panama.

Places to Stay

The *Chez Lionel Watanabe* is the only show in town. This is a large home with a number of rooms and common bath facilities. There are vacancies all year except during school holidays and the Christmas holiday season. It would be advisable to write to M Watanabe c/o the Mairie (Town Hall), Rapa, well in advance re prices and to let him know of your plans. In fact, it's probably a good idea to write to M Watanabe and the government simultaneously. If you get a reply from either, you'll be lucky.

RIMATARA

With no airport, no sheltered harbour or even a dock, it's no wonder Rimatara is one of the most isolated spots in French Polynesia. Located 538 km south-west of Tahiti, it is far from the tourist track. Its eight sq km of land make it the smallest of the Australs. It's also the lowest – the highest point on the island is Mt Vahu, at only 83 metres. The narrow reef that hugs the island's rugged shore must be 'surfed' by whale boats from the *Tuhaa II*

when it calls on the island to bring supplies and visitors.

The main village is Amaru, which is composed of a few shops, a post office, a gendarmerie, a town hall, an infirmary and a school. Anapoto and Mutuara villages are connected by a few rutted dirt roads. Although the island has electricity, there are no rental autos, bicycles, boats, restaurants or even a lone bar. In fact, I am told that alcohol is not sold on the island. What the nearly 1000 inhabitants of Rimatara do for fun is anyone's guess.

Places to Stay

The *Chez Marie Taharia* is a home in the village of Mataura, near the sea, with three bedrooms, each with a double bed. Facilities include kitchen, living room and communal bath. Marie will rent you a room for 2000 CFP per person per day, or the whole house for 45,000 CFP for a month.

The *Mairie d'Amaru* has two rooms, each with a single bed, in the same building as the town hall in the village of Amaru. Facilities include kitchen, common bath and shops close by. The price is only 1000 CFP – very much a bargain, if you can get there.

RAIVAVAE

Like Rimatara, Raivavae can only be reached by boat. It is 632 km south-east of Tahiti, also very, very far from the tourist track. The island is roughly double the size of Rimatara (about 16 sq km in area) and has a 432-metre-high peak. There are five villages on Raivavae which are home to over 1200 inhabitants. The cool climate and fertile soil are perfect for growing cabbage, carrots and potatoes as well as more tropical crops such as coffee and oranges. Visitors who wish to drink alcohol should bring their own, because I have a strong suspicion that not too much is available here.

Places to Stay

The *Chez Annie Flores* is conveniently located near the boat landing for the *Tuhaa Pae II*, which is the only way (unless you have a yacht) that you will ever get to this island. The home has two bedrooms, each with a double bed, private bath and kitchenette. The price is 2000 CFP per person per day or you can rent the place for 25,000 CFP per month. It's easy to meet Mme Flores on the dock as the ship arrives because she has a stand selling fruit, fish and vegetables when the *Tuhaa Pae II* comes in.

The Gambier Islands

The Gambier Islands, comprising four high islands and a few atolls, was once an independent entity within French Polynesia. It had its own flag, and inhabitants were not required to serve in the military. This independent status no longer exists and none of the Gambier Islands are inhabited, except for Mangareva, which has a population of about 500. The population of the Gambiers once numbered about 5000 but most of the inhabitants have migrated to Tahiti.

An exciting plan for the Gambiers was once fomented by a young man of US and royal Tahitian blood, who inherited an uninhabited island near Mangareva and planned to settle there with his wife and child. He wanted to live a self-contained existence, free to do as he pleased, unencumbered by society's conventions, and had gone so far as to pack most of the family's belongings and contact a writer from *National Geographic* magazine to do a story. Unfortunately, his plans fell apart when he was arrested for growing several hundred marijuana plants in a taro patch on a Tahitian hillside. Several years later, his dream came true and he now lives happily with his family on his secluded island home.

GETTING THERE & AWAY
Air Tahiti visits Mangareva once a month from Tahiti. The flight time is four hours and 40 minutes, with a stop at Hao. Upon arrival in the Gambiers, a sea-shuttle is provided between Totegegie and Rikitea. The crossing time is 30 minutes.

The *Maire II* has a twice-monthly service to the Tuamotu and Gambier groups. It takes 12 days. The *Ruahutu* and the *Marava III* also go to the Gambiers (see the Getting Around chapter for more information).

MANGAREVA
Mangareva is 1650 km south-east of Tahiti and is surrounded by small mountainous islands. On one of these is the airport of Totegegie.

Of interest is the St Michel of Rikitea cathedral which, although in need of repair, is still in use and open to visitors. Across the path from the church is the 140-year-old rectory, occupied by the parish priest. A mile down the road is a tumble-down abbey surrounded by a well-tended vegetable garden. The garden is farmed by an industrious Mangarevan under the supervision of the priest, who sells the produce to islanders and to residents of the nearby nuclear testing site on Mururoa.

Also of interest are the ruins of a convent, a triumphal arch, watchtowers, prisons, a court and, dominating the village, the tomb of Gregorio Maputea, the last king of Mangareva, who died in 1868 after having requested status as a French Protectorate for Mangareva.

Mangareva's main industry is jewellery-making, which involves cutting and grinding items out of mother-of-pearl. Aesthetically, the island is very pleasing, with its rolling brown hills reminiscent of California's coastal mountains. It is the home of French Polynesia's former vice president and venerated politico Francis Sanford, and also the home of the President of French Polynesia, Gaston Flosse. Because of its proximity to the nuclear testing site, permission to travel to Mangareva must be secured from the government.

History
The Mangarevans preserve a tradition that a chief, 'Tupa' once came to Mangareva with a fleet of rafts from a 'vast and populous land'. Thor Heyerdahl used this as evidence that Peruvians (perhaps Incas or an earlier

people) came to Polynesia and brought the sweet potato, a native plant of South America, with them. The Mangarevan legend holds that Tupa cleared the coral reef that surround the island through a passage still called Teava-o-Tupa.

There is also a legend that Tupa Inca, the second emperor of the Inca world (ruling between 1471 and 1493) heard that seaborne traders had arrived from westward islands.

He sailed with a large fleet of balsa rafts to the Pacific, returning a year later with black people and gold.

Until the last century the lagoon routinely sheltered large rafts, which carried trade and commerce to faraway islands. Heyerdahl postulated that Mangareva was the destination of the Spanish explorer Sarmiento, who sailed with Mendana in 1567. However, a premature course correction caused them to

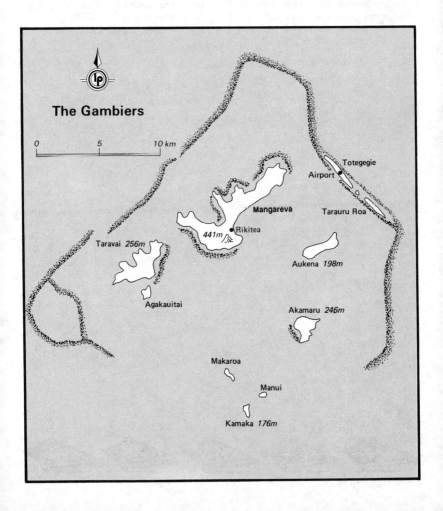

The Gambiers

0   5   10 km

Totegegie
Airport

Mangareva

Tarauru Roa

Taravai 256m

441m Rikitea

Aukena 198m

Agakauitai

Akamaru 246m

Makaroa

Manui

Kamaka 176m

discover the Solomons instead! Sarmiento had heard the story of the Inca journey and perhaps intended to do the same.

The coming of the missionaries to the Gambier Islands was anticipated in a vision by the prophet Taopere. In 1883, the Picpus fathers of France settled on the chief island, Mangareva, and by 1886 the entire archipelago had been converted to Catholicism. Under the tyrannical leadership of Father Laval, a Belgian priest, the converts on Mangareva built the largest cathedral in French Polynesia (St Michel of Rikitea), using fired limestone and mother-of-pearl for its interior. The strange saga of this fanatical missionary inspired one of Michener's stories in *Return to Paradise*.

Places to Stay

The *Chez Francois Labbeyi* in Rikitea is near the wharf. For reservations write to Francois Labbeyi, Mangareva, French Polynesia. There is one house and two bungalows. The rate is approximately 3000 CFP.

Glossary

Aito – Ironwood.
Archipelago – A group or chain of islands.
Ari'i – High chiefs, the nobility of pre-European Tahitian society.
Arioi – Travelling minstrels and entertainers of pre-European time, making up a religious society.
Atoll – A low-lying island built up from successive deposits of coral. The classic atoll is ring-shaped, enclosing a shallow lagoon.
Atua – God.

Bark cloth – See 'tapa'.
Barrier reef – An offshore reef sheltering a coast or an island from the open sea but separated from the land by a lagoon or expanse of sea. See 'fringing reef'.
Boule – A Polynesian (introduced by the French) version of bocce, or bowls.
Breadfruit – The staple food of the South Pacific, sought after by the *Bounty* expedition to transplant in the West Indies.

Copra – Dried coconut meat.
Coral – Members of the animal group known as *coelenterates* which also include jellyfish and anemones. Corals live together in colonies and produce a fibrous or calcified skeleton. As they die new colonies form upon the skeletons of the old, eventually building up a reef. Coral requires clear, warm water of an ideal depth in order to flourish.
Cyclone – A powerful tropical storm which rotates around a central low pressure 'eye'. In the Caribbean a cyclone is known as a hurricane; in the Pacific it is known as a typhoon.

Embayed – A coastline created by land subsidence when flooded valleys become bays.
Emergence – Geological activity which raises a land mass above the ocean surface to become an island.

Fare – House.
Fare Tupa'pau – 'Ghost house', where dead bodies were laid in pre-European Tahitian funeral ceremonies.
Fringing reef – A reef found around the shore of an island or along a coast which does not contain a lagoon – see 'Barrier reef'.

High island – An island, either volcanic in origin or the result of an upheaval from the ocean floor.

Kaina – A Polynesian person.
Kava – Beverage derived from the root of the pepper plant *Piper methysticum*.

Lagoon – An area of water enclosed by a reef.
Lee – Downwind side; to be in the lee of something is to be sheltered by it.
Leeward – The side of an island sheltered from the prevailing winds. See 'windward'.
Le truck – Local form of public transport; hybrid bus or jitney.

Makatea – 'Middle island', atoll islands raised up by some geological disturbance.
Mana – Sacred essence, prestige, power.
Manahune – The common people of pre-European Tahitian society.
Manava – Soul of a god.
Marae – Ancient Polynesian open temple.
Maru'ura – Feathered girdle, highest symbol of real and spiritual power.
Melanesian – People of the far west of the Pacific characterised by their dark skins. They include the people of Papua New Guinea, the Solomons, Vanuatu, New Caledonia and Fiji.
Micronesian – People of the north-west Pacific, believed to be of Malay-Polynesian origin. They include the people of Guam, the Marianas, the Federated States of Micronesia, the Marshalls, the northern Palau Islands and the islands of the Gilbert-Phoenix-Northern Line Islands region.
Monoi – Perfumed, processed coconut oil.
Motu – A coral islet.

Noa – Non-sacred.

Ora – Life.
'Oro – God of war and son of Ta'aroa; red feathers are his special symbol.
Oromatua – Ghosts.

Pahi – Traditional fighting canoe with raised platform above the twin hull on which the warriors would stand.
Pareu – Sarong-like wrap-around skirt.
Pirogue – Traditional outrigger canoe.
Pohe – Death.
Polynesian – People who colonised the central and southern Pacific islands – including Hawaii, Tahiti, the Cook Islands and New Zealand – through great sea voyages.

Ra'atira – The 'middle class' of pre-European Tahitian society.
Ro'o – Important pre-European Tahitian god.

Seamount – A volcanic mountain that rises above the surface of the sea.
Seaward – Side of an island facing the open sea, in contrast to a side facing a sheltered lagoon.
Sennit – Woven coconut fibre string.

Ta'aroa – Important pre-European Tahitian god.

Tahu'a – Craftsman priest.
Tamanu – Ebony-like wood.
Tamure – Modern, hip-shaking version of a traditional dance.
Tane – Important pre-European Tahitian god; also a word for 'man'.
Tapa – Bark-cloth, the everyday clothing in pre-European Tahiti. Made by beating the inner bark of mulberry or breadfruit trees.
Tabu, tapu – Taboo; the English word is derived from this Tahitian word.
Taro – Staple root vegetable.
Tatau – Traditional tattoos, from which the English word is derived. Both males and females were tattooed, particularly on the buttocks. Joseph Banks was one of the members of Cook's party who came back with a tattoo.
Tiki, Ti'i – Human-like wood or stone icon, generally representing family ancestors. Particularly found on traditional canoes.
Tiputa – Bark-cloth poncho.
Tiurai – Bastille Day.
To'o – Symbols of Tahitian gods.
Tu – Important pre-European Tahitian god.
Tupa'pau – Ghost or spirit; may be benevolent or malevolent.

Vahine – Woman.

Windward – The side of an island facing the prevailing winds – see 'Leeward'.

Index

PLANET TALK
Lonely Planet's FREE quarterly newsletter

We love hearing from you and think you'd like to hear from us.

When...*is the right time to see reindeer in Finland?*
Where...*can you hear the best palm-wine music in Ghana?*
How...*do you get from Asunción to Areguá by steam train?*
What...*is the best way to see India?*

For the answer to these and many other questions read PLANET TALK.

Every issue is packed with up-to-date travel news and advice including:

- *a letter from Lonely Planet founders Tony and Maureen Wheeler*
- *travel diary from a Lonely Planet author - find out what it's really like out on the road*
- *feature article on an important and topical travel issue*
- *a selection of recent letters from our readers*
- *the latest travel news from all over the world*
- *details on Lonely Planet's new and forthcoming releases*

To join our mailing list contact any Lonely Planet office (address below).

LONELY PLANET PUBLICATIONS
Australia: PO Box 617, Hawthorn 3122, Victoria (tel: 03-819 1877)
USA: Embarcadero West, 155 Filbert St, Suite 251, Oakland, CA 94607 (tel: 510-893 8555)
TOLL FREE: (800) 275-8555
UK: 10 Barley Mow Passage, Chiswick, London W4 4PH (tel: 0181-742 3161)
France: 71 bis rue du Cardinal Lemoine – 75005 Paris (tel: 1-46 34 00 58)

Also available: Lonely Planet T-shirts. 100% heavyweight cotton (S, M, L, XL)

Lonely Planet Guidebooks

Lonely Planet guidebooks cover every accessible part of Asia as well as Australia, the Pacific, South America, Africa, the Middle East, Europe and parts of North America. There are five series: *travel survival kits*, covering a country for a range of budgets; *shoestring guides* with compact information for low-budget travel in a major region; *walking guides*; *city guides* and *phrasebooks*.

Australia & the Pacific

Australia
Australian phrasebook
Bushwalking in Australia
Islands of Australia's Great Barrier Reef
Outback Australia
Fiji
Fijian phrasebook
Melbourne city guide
Micronesia
New Caledonia
New South Wales
New Zealand
Tramping in New Zealand
Papua New Guinea
Bushwalking in Papua New Guinea
Papua New Guinea phrasebook
Rarotonga & the Cook Islands
Samoa
Solomon Islands
Sydney city guide
Tahiti & French Polynesia
Tonga
Vanuatu
Victoria

South-East Asia

Bali & Lombok
Bangkok city guide
Cambodia
Indonesia
Indonesia phrasebook
Laos
Malaysia, Singapore & Brunei
Myanmar (Burma)
Burmese phrasebook
Philippines
Pilipino phrasebook
Singapore city guide
South-East Asia on a shoestring
Thailand
Thai phrasebook
Vietnam
Vietnamese phrasebook

North-East Asia

China
Beijing city guide
Cantonese phrasebook
Mandarin Chinese phrasebook
Hong Kong, Macau & Canton
Japan
Japanese phrasebook
Korea
Korean phrasebook
Mongolia
North-East Asia on a shoestring
Seoul city guide
Taiwan
Tibet
Tibet phrasebook
Tokyo city guide

Middle East

Arab Gulf States
Egypt & the Sudan
Arabic (Egyptian) phrasebook
Iran
Israel
Jordan & Syria
Middle East
Turkey
Turkish phrasebook
Trekking in Turkey
Yemen

Indian Ocean

Madagascar & Comoros
Maldives & Islands of the East Indian Ocean
Mauritius, Réunion & Seychelles

Mail Order

Lonely Planet guidebooks are distributed worldwide. They are also available by mail order from Lonely Planet, so if you have difficulty finding a title please write to us. US and Canadian residents should write to Embarcadero West, 155 Filbert St, Suite 251, Oakland CA 94607, USA ; European residents should write to 10 Barley Mow Passage, Chiswick, London W4 4PH; and residents of other countries to PO Box 617, Hawthorn, Victoria 3122, Australia.

Indian Subcontinent
Bangladesh
India
Hindi/Urdu phrasebook
Trekking in the Indian Himalaya
Karakoram Highway
Kashmir, Ladakh & Zanskar
Nepal
Trekking in the Nepal Himalaya
Nepali phrasebook
Pakistan
Sri Lanka
Sri Lanka phrasebook

Africa
Africa on a shoestring
Central Africa
East Africa
Trekking in East Africa
Kenya
Swahili phrasebook
Morocco, Algeria & Tunisia
Arabic (Moroccan) phrasebook
South Africa, Lesotho & Swaziland
Zimbabwe, Botswana & Namibia
West Africa

Central America & the Caribbean
Baja California
Central America on a shoestring
Costa Rica
Eastern Caribbean
Guatemala, Belize & Yucatán: La Ruta Maya
Mexico

Europe
Baltic States & Kaliningrad
Central Europe on a shoestring
Central Europe phrasebook
Dublin city guide
Eastern Europe on a shoestring
Eastern Europe phrasebook
Finland
France
Greece
Hungary
Iceland, Greenland & the Faroe Islands
Ireland
Italy
Mediterranean Europe on a shoestring
Mediterranean Europe phrasebook
Poland
Scandinavian & Baltic Europe on a shoestring
Scandinavian Europe phrasebook
Switzerland
Trekking in Spain
Trekking in Greece
USSR
Russian phrasebook
Western Europe on a shoestring
Western Europe phrasebook

North America
Alaska
Canada
Hawaii

South America
Argentina, Uruguay & Paraguay
Bolivia
Brazil
Brazilian phrasebook
Chile & Easter Island
Colombia
Ecuador & the Galápagos Islands
Latin American Spanish phrasebook
Peru
Quechua phrasebook
South America on a shoestring
Trekking in the Patagonian Andes
Venezuela

The Lonely Planet Story

Lonely Planet published its first book in 1973 in response to the numerous 'How did you do it?' questions Maureen and Tony Wheeler were asked after driving, bussing, hitching, sailing and railing their way from England to Australia.

Written at a kitchen table and hand collated, trimmed and stapled, *Across Asia on the Cheap* became an instant local bestseller, inspiring thoughts of another book.

Eighteen months in South-East Asia resulted in their second guide, *South-East Asia on a shoestring*, which they put together in a backstreet Chinese hotel in Singapore in 1975. The 'yellow bible' as it quickly became known to backpackers around the world, soon became *the* guide to the region. It has sold well over half a million copies and is now in its 8th edition, still retaining its familiar yellow cover.

Today there are over 140 Lonely Planet titles in print – books that have that same adventurous approach to travel as those early guides; books that 'assume you know how to get your luggage off the carousel' as one reviewer put it.

Although Lonely Planet initially specialised in guides to Asia, they now cover most regions of the world, including the Pacific, South America, Africa, the Middle East and Europe. The list of *walking guides* and *phrasebooks* (for 'unusual' languages such as Quechua, Swahili, Nepali and Egyptian Arabic) is also growing rapidly.

The emphasis continues to be on travel for independent travellers. Tony and Maureen still travel for several months of each year and play an active part in the writing, updating and quality control of Lonely Planet's guides.

They have been joined by over 50 authors, 110 staff – mainly editors, cartographers & designers – at our office in Melbourne, Australia, at our US office in Oakland, California and at our European office in Paris; another five at our office in London handle sales for Britain, Europe and Africa. Travellers themselves also make a valuable contribution to the guides through the feedback we receive in thousands of letters each year.

The people at Lonely Planet strongly believe that travellers can make a positive contribution to the countries they visit, both through their appreciation of the countries' culture, wildlife and natural features, and through the money they spend. In addition, the company makes a direct contribution to the countries and regions it covers. Since 1986 a percentage of the income from each book has been donated to ventures such as famine relief in Africa; aid projects in India; agricultural projects in Central America; Greenpeace's efforts to halt French nuclear testing in the Pacific and Amnesty International. In 1994 over $100,000 was donated to such causes.

Lonely Planet's basic travel philosophy is summed up in Tony Wheeler's comment, 'Don't worry about whether your trip will work out. Just go!'.